√ C+H
$5.95

W9-ASK-271

NEW YORK CITY, 1863

...ter Burning No. 677

POLICE
HEADQUARTERS

Mulberry Street

Broadway

FIVE POINTS
in this Approximate Area

THE SECOND REBELLION

OTHER BOOKS BY JAMES McCAGUE

FICTION

The Fortune Road

To Be a Hero

Fiddle Hill

Great Gold Mountain

The Big Ivy

NONFICTION

Moguls and Iron Men

The

Second Rebellion:

*The Story of the New York City
Draft Riots of 1863*

JAMES McCAGUE

THE DIAL PRESS, INC.   NEW YORK

1968

WINGATE COLLEGE LIBRARY
WINGATE, N. C.

Copyright © 1968 by James McCague

All rights reserved. No part of this book may be reproduced in any form or by any means without the prior written permission of the Publisher, excepting brief quotes used in connection with reviews written specifically for inclusion in a magazine or newspaper.

Library of Congress Catalog Card Number: 68-18636
Design by La Liberté
Printed in the United States of America
First printing, 1968

This one is for you, Mack:
for the friendship and counsel
that helped make the book

42824

ACKNOWLEDGMENTS

MORE THAN A HUNDRED YEARS AGO, things went on in New York City which in retrospect bear a startling resemblance to many of the events and conditions of our own time. The parallel need not be stressed: the city's ordeal in 1863 was to a great extent overshadowed by the clash of armies in the War Between the States, and has been all but forgotten since. But it may be good to remember that the nation's troubles were not fatal then, and will not be today.

In the considerable amount of digging necessary to reconstruct those violent times I am indebted primarily to the dedicated people of two fine institutions.

Special thanks are due to Dr. James J. Heslin, director of the New-York Historical Society; to Mr. Arthur Breton and Mr. Robert Woerner of the Society's library staff; and to Mr. Wilson Duprey of the excellent map and print collection there. My thanks to Dr. Heslin, in addition, for permission to quote extensively from the manuscript of Charles Chapin in the Society's possession.

Dr. Roy P. Basler, director of the Department of Research of the Library of Congress, Washington, D.C., was unfailingly cordial and knowledgeable, as was Mr. George Sloan of the Library's reference staff. Both of these gentlemen helped immeasurably to lighten the often difficult task of research.

My thanks are due also to Mrs. Betty Service of the Sarasota Public Library for many courtesies and much assistance along the way.

Finally, to the several good friends who listened to those evening readings as the book took shape and whose interest and encouragement were unstinting: my warm appreciation.

JAMES McCAGUE

Sarasota, Florida
November, 1967

CONTENTS

PROLOGUE: KENNEDY   xi

I. THE POWDER KEG

   1. July 4, 1863   3
   2. Empire City: The Opulent Society   13
   3. Empire City: The Disaffected   20
   4. The Violent Men   28
   5. Coppers, Clubs, and City Hall   36
   6. "They Will Amount to Nothing"   44
   7. "Poor Jones!"   49

II. EXPLOSION: THE FIRST DAY

   8. "No Draft!"   59
   9. "You Must Organize!"   67
  10. ". . . Take No Prisoners"   76
  11. Generals Fall Out   87
  12. "We'll Hang Old Greeley . . ."   93

III. THE SECOND DAY

  13. Alarms and Suspicions   103
  14. Riot into Rebellion   108
  15. "My Friends . . ."   116
  16. Barricades and Brooks Brothers   124

IV. THE THIRD DAY, AND THE FOURTH

      17. "Give Them Grape and Plenty of It"   133
      18. "The Mob Ain't Commenced Yet"   143
      19. Mr. Chapin's Vigilantes   153
      20. The Last Battle   158
      21. Victors and Vanquished   165

EPILOGUE: AFTERMATH   173

NOTES   191
BIBLIOGRAPHY   203
INDEX   207

PROLOGUE: KENNEDY

THE TIME WAS WELL PAST TEN-THIRTY ON MONDAY, JULY 13—perhaps closer to noon. The draft-enrollment office already had been sacked and set on fire. When he reached the corner of Lexington Avenue and Forty-sixth Street, John A. Kennedy saw the black smoke of burning boil up above the intervening rooftops. Milling knots of people blocked the adjacent streets. Leaving his carriage, he set out for Third Avenue on foot. He was in civilian clothes and carried a natty bamboo cane, unlikely garb for the superintendent of police of the New York Metropolitan Police District. Nevertheless, he had gone barely half a block when he was recognized. The cry went up:

"It's Kennedy! Get him! Kill him!"

A band of toughs rushed at him, led by a man in a ragged army jacket. Kennedy was knocked down but struggled up and slashed his assailant across the face with his cane. The cane was torn out of his hand; he was knocked down again. John Kennedy was sixty years old but still an active and powerful man. Again he scrambled to his feet and fought back. But they seized him, beat and kicked him, finally hustled him to the edge of a steep embankment left by a street-repair crew, and pushed him over. He got up and staggered across a vacant lot toward Forty-seventh Street with the mob streaming in pursuit. Some of them had knives, bludgeons, iron bars. There were women among them, howling like harpies. Kennedy was caught, savagely mauled again, and flung into a mudhole in the middle of the lot.

"D—n the Yankee Perlice son of a —— (not lady); down with him; duck him; drown him," the *Tribune* would quote their cries next day.

Once more Kennedy staggered up, bleeding now, dazed and badly hurt. Still the mob raged after him. At Lexington Avenue they caught him again, just as he crumpled into the arms of a prominent resident of the neighborhood named John Eagen, who had been attracted by the commotion. Eagen managed to convince the mob that their victim was dead. Not till then would they leave him. He looked dead, indeed, and he very nearly was. Eagen stopped a passing teamster with a wagon. They loaded the limp body into the wagon bed, concealed it under some old sacks, and headed for 300 Mulberry Street.

In their wake the terror grew.

I | The Powder Keg

Chapter 1 | July 4, 1863

ONCE AGAIN THE CITY PAUSED TO CELEBRATE the national day of independence. Whether it was a matter for celebration, though, might be debatable.

"From one point of view," conceded Horace Greeley in an editorial on page four of his New York *Tribune*, "this is doubtless the darkest Fourth of July which has dawned on us since the commencement of our National existence. From another, we sincerely believe that it is the brightest . . ." And Mr. Greeley, a Republican and a stalwart Abolitionist, went on to make his point: The nation was at last "free of the shame of Human Slavery."

Grant that the sentiment was praiseworthy. Horace Greeley, an honest editor and a shrewd one in spite of his well-known eccentricities, still must have realized that he was straining very hard indeed for a word of cheer, for a New York journalist in this difficult year of 1863. It was true enough that President Lincoln's Emancipation Proclamation, designed to buttress the Union cause with moral righteousness before the world, had been in effect—theoretical effect—since January 1. As yet it had freed no black masses in the Confederate States. And it would not, without armed conquest to put teeth into it. But Union arms did not appear to be getting on with the job very speedily. In this third year of a brutal and unpopular war, the Army of the Potomac had just recently been placed in charge of its sixth commanding officer. He was an obscure general named George G. Meade. Meade had replaced Fighting Joe Hooker, who had replaced Ambrose Burnside, who had replaced John Pope, who had replaced the

3

soldiers' idol, George B. McClellan. . . . And McClellan, of course, had replaced the Army's first commander, unlucky Irvin Mc-Dowell, who had led it out to First Bull Run in a long-ago time of high and gallant hopes that now seemed as unreal as a dream. The changes wrote their own tale of bitter frustration and growing discouragement. It was no longer easy to believe in victory, or even in the rightness of the cause.

The Proclamation had sent no groundswell of popular enthusiasm rolling across the North, certainly. The thousands who had climbed into army regimentals to go forth and die for the Union, if necessary, had not joined up to fight for any bunch of niggers. They were saying so, often with a noisy vehemence that sounded close to mutiny, and the folks back home agreed. An Abolitionist minority aside, the "shame of Human Slavery" simply did not arouse men to any great pitch of crusading indignation. The Slavery Question was a pesky irritant; it beclouded a war that was cloudy and complicated enough without it. From the start, a good many influential people in New York, as elsewhere in the Union, had been convinced that the cotton states' right to secede was altogether legal and valid. The longer hostilities ran on, the more unpleasant they became, the more such people spoke out to denounce their national government for denying that right. In New York City some names above reproach were lending themselves to the cause of peace at any price—men such as Samuel F. B. Morse, distinguished inventor of the telegraph, and the eminent attorney Samuel J. Tilden. There were, besides, all those less honest men eager to make private or political capital out of every Union reverse. Throughout the waning months of 1862 and the early ones of 1863, New Yorkers' condemnations of the Lincoln Administration and their demands for an end to the war had grown so strident that the city frequently seemed—and had been called—a center of Copperhead conspiracy.

Small wonder. At times the Administration appeared bent on its own downfall. Now there was the Enrollment and Conscription Act, rammed through Congress in March. Free Americans were going to be drafted into the army willy-nilly if Abe Lincoln had his way. There was some doubt that he would. To call the draft controversial was to be rather too mealymouthed. Nobody could really claim to know the public mood this Fourth of July in

1863. But no one could deny, either, that it simmered in a murky mixture of doubt, disgust, impatience, and brewing resentment.

The big news story of the day—it was a Saturday—added little save confusion.

The *Tribune's* headline at the top of column one, page one, was hardly encouraging:

THE REBEL INVASION

Somewhat more optimistically, the welter of subheads that followed conveyed a sense of big events and high drama on the move. LONGSTREET TAKEN PRISONER, said one. And the dispatch beneath, filed the day before at Hanover, Pennsylvania, stated flatly: "The most terrible fight of the war has taken place. Our men never stood up so heroically. To-day was the most awful of all. The loss on both sides has been tremendous. . . ." The story continued with a long, involved account of military maneuverings, clashes, and carnage, tending, hopefully, to sketch the dim outlines of a Union victory. Obviously the correspondent was being cautious; he was not sure, and no doubt readers would recall reports of other victories that had turned out later to be no better than stalemates, if that.

In other arenas, certainly, the action seemed a trifle sluggish. From the Mississippi River, where Ulysses S. Grant maintained stubborn siege lines around Vicksburg, telegraphic information via Cairo, Illinois, said simply: "A gentleman at the front reports everything in status quo." From Memphis: "Everything is quiet in this section." From Philadelphia the news was better, if badly exaggerated: "Rumors from Fortress Monroe by the Old Point boat have given rise to the serious impression that Richmond has been closely invested by Gen. Dix, and is probably captured." A brief item out of Portland, Maine, told of the Confederate blockade runner *General Banks* bottled up in Halifax harbor, Nova Scotia, despite repeated attempts to slip past the Federal gunboat watching her. That was doubly reassuring; no more than a month earlier the Confederate armed cruiser *Tacony* had "terrorized" the New England coast, stirred up a flurry of panic in New York, and brought on some indignant questions regarding the whereabouts of the U.S. Navy. Now, at least, the Navy was on the job.

There were some jarring notes among the civilians, to be sure. Over at the Brooklyn Navy Yard, ship joiners were out on strike. They were getting two dollars to two-fifty a day and wanted three dollars, the same as ship's carpenters. (Nevertheless, reported the *Tribune*, the new gunboat *Maumee* had been launched on schedule.) And a reprint of General Order No. 5 from the district of Indiana and Michigan, Military Department of the Ohio, issued at Indianapolis on July 3, declared in part: "The peace of Indiana has lately been disturbed by violence, murder and other acts contrary to law, and having their origin in certain secret political societies, clubs or leagues. . . ." All citizens were enjoined by the brigadier general commanding the district to "discontinue and peaceably break up such organizations."

The order put words to something everybody knew already, or thought he did. For a fact, more states than Indiana crawled with secret societies of various radical hues. Copperheads, Secessionist agents, or simple crackpots were busy everywhere in the embattled Union this summer.

Still, *Tribune* readers turning to page two were comforted immediately by the feeling that things in general were proceeding normally. "The stock market opened very strong this morning," it was noted, "and most of the leading favorites were higher." As usual there were several columns of recruiting notices for a host of volunteer regiments. A typical one announced: "100 Men Wanted—the 17th Regiment, New York State Volunteers, is now re-organizing for three years service. This popular regiment has seen active service in battle under McClellan, Pope, Burnside, and Hooker. . . ." A bounty of two hundred and fifty dollars was offered to each man re-enlisting, one hundred seventy-five to each new recruit. The three-year enlistment period was significant. Like the odious Enrollment and Conscription Act, it was a sign that the military was facing up at last to the harsh fact of a war that was going to take time and manpower, and plenty of both. But there was no lack of other volunteer units, still recruiting on the old thirty-day basis.

Several pages of advertisements conveyed a reassuring business-as-usual note. For New Yorkers bothered by physical ailments this summer, the makers of Martin's Life Cordial touted their nostrum as "The Great American Remedy for Cholera,

Cholera Morbus, Cholera Infantum, Dysentery, Diarrhea, Summer Complaint, Pain and Cramps in the Stomach, Sour Stomach, and Heartburn." The well-dressed gentleman's attention was solicited in behalf of shirt collars of steel, white-enameled, and "free of all complaints having to do with wilting, creasing, etc." A publisher held out the promise of escape from the horrors of war with Mrs. Lillie Devereaux Umsted's new novel, *Rockford, or, Sunshine and Storm.* The work was summarized as "a story alternating between the quiet life of a country seat and the gayety and evil of a fashionable circle in New York."

Civic problems went on, however, war or no war. In a short and somewhat irritable paragraph on the editorial page, Mr. Greeley's paper informed its readers that the superintendents of the poor for King's County had recently awarded one Charles Kelsey a contract for coal to heat the county's poorhouses at fifteen dollars per ton, "apparently regardless of the burden they impose upon the taxpayers." And speaking of the poor, a pathetic little notice on page five pleaded for the public's attendance at the children's service of the Five Points House of Industry on Sunday. "The children," it was explained, "are gathering their pennies for a lot in Greenwood Cemetery to bury the little orphans in." The Five Points was a notorious slum in the Sixth Ward; within a little more than a week, respectable New York would be reminded of it and its poor somewhat more pointedly.

Never mind. It was the Fourth of July and people were seeking diversion. Phineas T. Barnum's famous museum on Broadway at Ann Street advertised continuous shows every hour, featuring the world-renowned midget General Tom Thumb "and his Beautiful Little Wife"—adults twenty-five cents, children fifteen. The management of Laura Keene's Theater had scheduled three performances of the comedy *Wives of Paris*, with an all-star cast. Each performance was to be preceded by a band concert and fireworks display and "followed by a tight-rope act by ROSITA AND ALEXANDER, who will make Ascensions from Stage to Gallery, and across the street during the day."

The traditional parade down Broadway was sadly lacking in magnificence this year, however. No fewer than twelve regiments of the New York State National Guard normally stationed in the city, totaling upwards of eight thousand men, had been hustled off to Pennsylvania in response to President Lincoln's urgent call for help in stemming the rebel invasion. As a result, only a few cavalry units were on hand to parade. New Yorkers reacted by staying away in large numbers.

Political oratory, that other Fourth of July tradition, promised considerably more excitement. Governor Horatio Seymour was down from Albany to address a mass meeting of the New York Democratic Union Association at two o'clock at the Academy of Music.

This, a spacious and imposing hall on Fourteenth Street, was a favorite city showplace widely used for society's grand balls and similar gala functions. And the governor, of course, was a prime attraction. Reporting the affair on Monday (newspapers did not publish Sunday editions), the *Tribune* would admit that "The assemblage was large, nearly one half of whom were ladies." Among the political elite present in the audience or on the rostrum were William Marcy Tweed, state senator and rapidly rising Tammany chieftain; District Attorney A. Oakey Hall; and a clutch of lesser bigwigs in the city's dominant Democratic organization. No one there had come to listen to the usual Independence Day platitudes, however. And no one was disappointed. The purpose of the meeting and the temper of its audience were apparent almost immediately.

Appropriately enough, the program began with a reading of the *Declaration of Independence*. "The preamble was received with silence," noted the *Tribune* reporter on the scene, "but the clause asserting the right of revolution as well as every clause in the indictment against the King of Great Britain which could by forced construction be imagined to find a parallel in the acts of the present Administration, were received with applause."

The governor was then introduced.

Horatio Seymour was a man in his fifty-third year, an able speaker, and no stranger to New York politics. A Utica attorney and a longtime conservative Democrat, he had served competently if not brilliantly in a previous term as governor from 1852 to 1854. Throughout the growing tensions of 1860 and 1861 he had remained prominent by his vigorous advocacy of compromise to avoid secession by the cotton states, though he had refused to seek the nomination for another term. Yielding to party pressure, however, he had campaigned in the March election of 1863 on a platform urging conciliation and an end to the war and had squeaked through to a narrow victory. The state had, in fact, elected a Republican legislature. But Seymour, piling up a landslide vote in three of New York City's most populous wards, had ridden into office by a total margin of some twenty thousand. The fact was self-evident: the city was a strong citadel of antiwar sentiment. And ever since the election, Horatio Seymour had made himself even more the hero of New York's working classes by his unremitting attacks on the Enrollment and Conscription Act. Not only had he denounced it as unconstitutional and urged the President to postpone enforcement of the Act until the courts could pass on the question, he actually had prevented the drafting of any New York men, up to the present, by challenging the state's quotas as unfair.

On this Fourth of July there was—or there seemed to be—a very real hope that the despised draft might be shunted aside altogether. No wonder, then, that the governor was given a noisy and prolonged ovation. And his opening words made it clear that he still was speaking as a partisan politician fighting the good fight: "I appeal to you, my Republican friends, if you yourselves, in your serious moments, believe that this [national unity] is to be produced by seizing our persons, by infringing upon our rights, by insulting our homes and by depriving us of those cherished privileges for which our fathers fought and to which we have always sworn allegiance. . . ."

The Academy rocked to a burst of cheers and clapping. But for most of the remainder of a fairly brief speech, what Seymour had to say was scarcely rabble-rousing. Lately, in other public appearances around the state, he had censured the draft and the Administration in terms far more inflammatory. He had lifted listeners' hackles by declaring, for example, that "One out of about two-and-a-half of our citizens is destined to be brought over into Messrs. Lincoln and Company's charnel house." There was nothing like that this afternoon. Seymour did not even mention conscription in so many words. But he struck fire from his audience one more time, near the close of his address, when he declared portentously: "Remember this: that the bloody, treasonable and revolutionary doctrine of public necessity can be proclaimed by a mob as well as a government!"

Afterward that *would* be remembered, as almost too prophetic to be coincidence. It was a strange thing for an elected official to be saying, anyway, and it is not on record that Horatio Seymour ever explained what he meant. But a good many people in the Academy of Music that afternoon probably were sure they understood. No doubt excited whispers buzzed about the hall under the uproar of applause. For it was widely rumored that New York City had an armed uprising in store unless the draft was called off. There were other rumors too, all sorts of them; the city was alive with rumors. Men were being enlisted and drilled in secret, their object—rebellion. Any number of gangs and clubs made up of city toughs were levying special assessments on all members, the funds to be spent buying their leaders out of the draft if worse came to worst. Just the night before the Fourth, a fiery manifesto had been surreptitiously handed about town—any number of people had seen copies—inciting the populace to revolution: FREEMEN, AWAKE . . .

The governor took his seat again. A succession of other speakers strode to the rostrum: former Governor Thomas H. Seymour of Connecticut, a brother of Horatio; the Honorable George H. Pendleton of Ohio, just returned from Washington, where he had appeared as an advocate of that foremost Copperhead hero of them all, Clement L. Vallandigham, also of Ohio; and a Richard O. Gorham, Esq. or Governor Parker of New Jersey was to have spoken also but had begged off, pleading the press of urgent duties in connection with the dispatching of his state's militia to the battlefield in Pennsylvania. The announcement drew some jeers.

As reprinted in the press later, none of the speeches was particularly noteworthy. Mostly they were a rehash of the antiwar, anti-Administration Democrats' recurrent themes in defense of secession and states' rights and against the draft. It was old but it was what this audience had come to hear, and there was plenty of applause as the points were made and remade. Gorham, the final speaker, went a good bit further than any of his colleagues when he asserted that the first thing to be done was to arm New York State "to the teeth" under the command of Governor Seymour. There was loud enthusiasm at that, and when it quieted down Gorham shouted defiantly that they could then "dispense with Provost Marshals." This, an obvious reference to the draft (which was to be administered by U.S. provost marshals), set off the applause all over again. Whereat, wrote the *Tribune* man, Mr. Gorham proceeded to "argue at some length the power of New York, were the Union dissolved, to exist and prosper as a separate sovereignty."

Radical as that sounded, it was not really a new thought either. Back in January of 1861 Mayor Fernando Wood, convinced that "disunion has become a fixed and certain fact," had proposed in a letter to the Common Council that New York withdraw from the Union and go it alone as a free city, "with the whole and united support of the Southern States." And he had added: ". . . with but a nominal duty on imports, her local government could be supported without taxation upon her people. Thus we could live free from taxes, and have cheap goods nearly duty free. . . ." What was more, the Common Council had been very favorably disposed toward the mayor's Utopian paradise. But the firing on Fort Sumter had put the quietus on such talk, at least openly. With a war actually going on, it had come a bit too close to outright treason.

Now, here it was, out in the open again. And on that note the meeting ended.

Treason? Horace Greeley's *Tribune*, solid and sober and pro-Administration, would report the facts and quote the several speakers without comment on the following Monday, July 6. In the ugly climate of this summer of 1863 such meetings had become commonplace, after all. The crowd, babbling its approval, filed out into Fourteenth Street and slowly broke up to go its separate ways—not conspirators, just citizens. Nothing had happened, really, but a blowing off of steam in the good old American fashion.

That evening there were fireworks. The city fathers outdid themselves here, possibly trying to make up for the disappointing skimpiness of the afternoon's parade. There were seventeen separate displays scattered in various neighborhoods about the city, each with its brass band on hand to help do the honors. Central Park was the scene of the finest effort of them all, its *pièce de résistance* a giant pyrotechnic representation of the battle between the *Monitor* and the *Merrimac*, with "a waterline two hundred feet long . . . Fortress Monroe in the distance, light-houses, vessels

of war, steam frigates, etc., etc." Some three hundred thousand
people were there to watch, according to the *Tribune*. Afterward
many of them said it was the best show ever put on in New York
City.

That evening, too, Tammany Hall held *its* Independence Day
powwow in the Wigwam, at Nassau and Frankfort streets.
Tammany in those days already ruled the city, was rapidly growing toward supremacy as a Democratic power throughout the
state, and yielded place to no one as an opponent of Abe Lincoln
and the Republican party. Yet in his feature address the organization's grand sachem, the Honorable Henry C. Murphy, declared
emphatically that, "While we firmly remonstrate against the invasion of our rights, we will sustain the President in the impending
struggle by all the aid in our power to bestow, and our patriotic
prayers for his success against the enemies of the Union."

That was more like it.

The *Tribune* quoted Mr. Murphy without comment also in its
Monday morning edition. Over the weekend, too, the shape of
events in Pennsylvania had begun to emerge somewhat more
clearly. The three-day battle that would be named for the town of
Gettysburg was indeed a victory. It had ended Robert E. Lee's
invasion of the North, and with it the Confederacy's last real hope
of winning the war. But it was going to take some while yet
before anyone, North or South, would grasp that latter truth.

Down in Washington, the speeches of "the two Seymours" on
Saturday were reprinted in Monday evening's newspapers. Reading them, Gideon Welles, Abraham Lincoln's Secretary of the
Navy, jotted sourly in his diary: "A couple of partisan patriots,
neither of whom is elated by Meade's success, and whose regrets
are over Rebel reverses."

Chapter 2 | Empire City:
The Opulent Society

NEW YORK HAD ACHIEVED ITS UNIQUE EMINENCE in the eyes of the Republic a long time before the 1860's. There was more to it than mere size. In a sense the city stood as a model for all America's mightiest drives and dreams. In another sense it was a bewildering blend of the nation's best and worst.

Some claimed, proudly, that it was George Washington who first had called New York "the Empire City." Whether or not he actually was the first to put its future into words, the big seaport town at the mouth of the Hudson River had begun seriously to build a commercial empire with the opening of the Erie Canal in 1825. By the 1850's the title was literally true. The gold rush to California had lined the city's slips and piers with flash clippers bound to and from Panama, Cape Horn, and Eldorado. The boom in railroad building was making it the center of an iron web that reached out to all the trade sources in the hinterlands. Long before the decade ended, New York had become a veritable Mecca of wealth and vested interest, its nabobs the arbiters of the national taste in fashion, of the arts, and of popular opinion of every shade and sort.

For years the city had grown at a fantastic pace. It still was growing. The census of 1860 showed more than eight hundred thousand people living and working there, all of them crowded into the narrow south end of Manhattan Island. Across the East River, Brooklyn still was a separate city, not a borough, though to all intents and purposes it had become part of the metropolis. To

13

WINGATE COLLEGE LIBRARY
WINGATE, N. C.

the north, Yorkville, Manhattanville, and Harlem still were
sprawling suburbs. But uptown was reaching out for them in
giant grabs, swallowing up the onetime fields and pastures of the
countryside as it went. Long since, the residential districts south
of Bleecker Street had been taken over by shops, factory lofts,
and office buildings. The streets around City Hall Park, once
lined with gracious homes, now were crowded with the establishments of commerce too.

The central areas of the city proper were terribly congested.
New York's unending battle against snarled traffic had been raging for a good ten years at least. It was waged with only marginal
success. By the early 1860's the colorful stages or omnibuses, each
with seats for thirty passengers and room for as many standees in
addition, were being replaced with modern horse cars on most of
the main thoroughfares. But cars did not noticeably relieve the
crush. The wide, straight avenue of Broadway was perpetually
crowded, pavement and sidewalks alike. In the morning, vehicles
bound downtown filled it from curb to curb with a river of rumbling wheels and trampling hooves; in the evening the direction
was reversed but the flood was undiminished. City authorities
had no real plan for the direction of traffic. A pedestrian trying to
cross from one sidewalk to the other faced a hazardous passage
that often took a half-hour or more. Recognizing the problem, a
few progressive merchants had petitioned for the building of ele-
vated foot bridges across Broadway for their customers' protection. Conditions on Third Avenue, Fifth, and other main arteries
were slightly better, though still crowded.

As late as 1859 a man named Amos Eno had been derided as a
fool for building his fine new Fifth Avenue Hotel far uptown on
Madison Square. An inn so distant from the heart of things, said
the doubters, would never pay its way. Instead, the Fifth Avenue
was now *the* hotel in town—a six-story, white-marble showplace
famed for its separate bathroom in every suite—a startling inno-
vation—its steam elevator described in the hotel's literature as "a
perpendicular railway intersecting each story," and its sumptuous
public rooms on the street floor, favorite rendezvous of the elite.
The Fifth Avenue, in fact, had made Madison Square fashionable,
as society's upper echelons retreated northward before the ex-
ploding population. Here, and in the avenues nearby, stood the

rococo mansions of the very rich. They vied with one another in the magnificence of their ballrooms, banquet halls, and art galleries. Their owners seemed to feel a compulsive urge toward ostentation and extravagance. The spectacular Wall Street plunger, spender, and sportsman Leonard Jerome ordered black-walnut paneling, plate-glass mirrors, and costly carpeting for even the stables where he housed his blooded horses and lacquered runabouts.

On a plane just below the upper tendom, New York's brownstone era was in full flower. Early in the 1850's, novelist James Fenimore Cooper had admired the new style of building: ". . . noble edifices of five and six stories," he wrote his wife, "with a good deal of ornamental pretension." In the 1860's solid blocks of such buildings stood along Lexington Avenue and most of the streets in the Twenties, inhabited by the impregnably well-to-do.

War had brought no austerity to the city. Quite the contrary; anything that money could buy was available in New York, in lavish measure. The old families of wealth and background—the Astors, Rhinelanders, Schermerhorns, Gracies, Joneses—still ruled society. But ever since the influx of "vulgar wealth from California," a rising class of the newly rich fought savagely for leadership in a feverish competition of parties, banquets, grand balls, and various gilded rites. If anything, the excitement that went along with war spurred extravagances to newer, more exalted scales. The more elaborate functions were often justified as charitable—to benefit the wounded soldier boys in army hospitals. But French chefs and the latest modes from Paris were in demand as never before. It was estimated by the social plenipotentiaries who made a profession of such matters that the wardrobe required by the belle bent on a successful season would include forty-five new gowns, seven capes or cloaks of various styles, and forty-eight lace-trimmed chemises of cambric or Irish linen, together with furs, muffs, and similar appurtenances, not to mention jeweled fans, combs, assorted ornaments, gold and silver hairnets, and so on—all this to the tune of twenty thousand dollars at a rock-bottom minimum. Lorenzo Delmonico's, on Fifth Avenue at Fourteenth Street, was the city's premier restaurant. A distinguished British nobleman, sated after having been wined and dined there by a succession of society's top hosts, was heard to murmur that the canvasback duck and not the eagle ought to be known as America's national bird.

Gambling was one of the city's besetting sins. As early as 1851 a report to a New York association for the suppression of that vice had noted that there were six thousand establishments devoted to faro, raffles, lotteries, and policy. Two hundred of them, the report stated, were "first class," which meant that they were frequented by men of the highest social standing.

"Park Row, Barclay and Vesey streets constitute the Wall street of these despicable characters," declared the New York *Herald* in one of several indignant articles on the subject. And it added: "Many of these common gamblers, compared with whom the skulking pickpocket is respectable, mingled with the leaders of fashion in this city. They saunter along Broadway in the morning, drive out on the avenue in the afternoon, lounge at the opera in the evening, and cheat in Park Row and Barclay street till five o'clock in the morning. They are the most distingue at the springs and watering places. . . ."

Other commentators described the staffs of liveried servants, the full-length mirrors, fine paintings, gilt and rosewood furniture, and the delectable cuisine featured by the more exclusive gambling palaces.

Crusading journalists like the *Herald*'s James Gordon Bennett frequently railed against the antics of the idle rich, to be sure. The newspaper cliché that great wealth was usually ill-gotten, wrung from the misery of the downtrodden masses, was widely current. But if New York owned to a god, which many of the reformers doubted, surely his name was Money. Read today, the indignation has a curiously hollow, theatrical ring to it. The poor had no true spokesmen, in the press or anywhere else, and how they felt about things no one really knew. The strange fact was that even with the Union fighting for its life, it seemed to occur to hardly anyone that the gaudy didoes of the upper classes were inappropriate or unpatriotic.

In a way, in fact, the war was responsible for them. The sharp operator in the know, the financial favorite son, and the adventurer armed with nerve and shrewdness—they all were finding money easier to come by than it ever had been before. Railroads, shipping, and military commodities of every kind were piling up

fortunes for unscrupulous entrepreneurs at a frenzied clip. Profit-
eering was almost universal and shamelessly overt. Gold speculation was very nearly a sure thing. Every Union defeat debased
the Federal currency and drove gold prices higher. And many of
the biggest speculators kept their agents at the various military
headquarters in the field, and thus operated with advance knowledge of each campaign and battle that impended. It was, as
someone remarked with a good deal of wry truth, a rich man's
war and a poor man's fight.

It had taken the Enrollment and Conscription Act to bring
that home to the poor man, though.

There was something deeply disturbing about a national military draft at best. It was not unheard of for states to raise their
army quotas by various forms of compulsion, true. But a state
government in the 1860's exerted a neighborly, close-to-home sort
of authority. Or at least it seemed so to most people. Washington
was different—distant and unfeeling, somehow alien. And for the
average citizen, this new Act was the first effort the Federal government had ever made to reach out its long arm and lay its
heavy hand directly on his—*his!*—shoulder. Such a thing threatened to upset the good old precepts of states' rights in the North
almost as rudely as Union armies were seeking to upset them in
the South. In it were the implications of grave change, toward a
new, demanding attitude by government and away from the old,
easygoing ways. No doubt men sensed this rather than understood it. What they did understand, all too clearly, was that the
Act was an infernally irksome piece of legislative arrogance. The
very circumstances of its birth smacked of bastardy. Hatched as a
confidential project of the War Department under fanatical
Edwin M. Stanton, it had been rammed through a complaisant
Congress on the pretext of wartime urgency and handed to the
public as a *fait accompli.*

For all that, it was not as bad as such a law might have been.
States and districts were to be given credit on their quotas for all
residents previously enlisted as volunteers, and exemption was
provided for underage youths, the lame, the halt, and the sole
supports of widowed mothers, among others. Most of the Act's
sweeping stupidities were not calculated to distress any great
areas of public opinion. Thus, Gideon Welles might complain

bitterly because the Army had the right to draft enlisted seamen right off the decks of U.S. naval men-of-war, but he would find little sympathy outside of the Navy. What stamped the Act as iniquitous and brought down anathema on the heads of Edwin Stanton and Abe Lincoln was the provision excusing any man who could put up three hundred dollars to pay a substitute if his name was drawn.

Startled, perhaps, by the chorus of outrage that broke over that, the War Department denied any intent to favor the rich. The provision was defended as an incentive to spur voluntary enlistments, nothing more. Few people saw it that way, though. In practice, rich men had three hundred dollars and poor men did not. The draft was class discrimination on the face of it.

Resentment had swept the Union during the spring of 1863. It first had churned into violence among the tough, hard-worked, and underprivileged coal miners in Pennsylvania's anthracite fields. There were disorderly protest meetings, beatings, and murders of officials by night-roaming gangs. The objectors were organized and determined, and the violence spilled over into states farther west. A vast amount of panicky confusion and fuzzy thinking went on through all this. Men did not have to be Confederate sympathizers to feel strongly about a law they thought unjust, of course. And there were other factors than the draft involved. In fact, there was a whole host of seething discontents abroad in the land—fears, doubts, half-formed grudges against no-one-quite-knew-what. Plain folk were restless and uneasy. They sensed that they were caught in the great drift of changing times, in a nation shifting inexorably from a pioneer, agrarian economy to something bigger and incomparably more complicated. History was happening, and it was not easily grasped from the worm's-eye view. But the draft was an obvious, tangible provocation. It was obvious, too, as a made-to-order rallying cry for every Secessionist-lining politician who chose to use it, and all of them did. So, inevitably, objectors became by definition suspect Copperheads. Troops marched into the troubled areas and the violence grew.

Out in southern Illinois things went on which made a young cavalry officer by the name of James Fox wonder what this war meant, after all, and where it might be headed. Fox was unimpor-

tant—just one of many ordinary men deeply troubled, that summer, by the spectacle of a Union that seemed more concerned
with punishing its own people than in fighting the Confederacy.
Later he would write ruefully: ". . . such searching [of] smoke-
houses, garrets, barns and cellars, such hanging men up to trees
for the purpose of extorting secrets, such breaking up and dispersing courts and grand juries . . . I never before heard of at any
time, in Illinois or any other state."

Southern Illinois was a long way from New York, as such
goings-on were a long way from mass meetings at the Academy of
Music. Yet, if the turmoils that racked the Union that summer
sprang from poor men's resentments, then New York might have
paused to wonder too. For New York was a city of extremes. If
nowhere else in America did the rich thrive so blatantly, no other
city's poor were so numerous, either—or lived so wretchedly.

Chapter 3 | Empire City: The Disaffected

BROADWAY WAS THE BOUNDARY LINE. But a casual observer would not have guessed it. The great street looked like high spirits and vigorous prosperity. It teemed with well-dressed promenaders, hurrying crowds, and splendid carriages. It was a street of fashionable ice-cream saloons and expensive shops that resembled white-marble palaces. P. T. Barnum's hall of marvels was a magnet for all visiting America. Long before the 1860's, though, knowing New Yorkers were calling Broadway's West Side "the dollar side," its East "the shilling side." It was an apt distinction.

Only a few steps east of lower Broadway, beyond Anthony (the present Worth) Street, lay a region of slums that extended to the East River. Curling like a fat slug around the southern tip of the island, it had encroached steadily northward along the river until its straggling shantytowns ultimately reached past Forty-second Street.

The heart of this crowded, seamy stretch was the Sixth Ward. They called it the Bloody Ould Sixth, with good reason. And the heart of the Bloody Ould Sixth was the blighted area known as the Five Points. It was formed by the intersection of five streets, of which Anthony was one. The others were originally named Cross, Little Water, Orange, and Mulberry. They met in a triangular plaza about an acre in extent, with a tiny park at the center of it bearing the euphemistic title Paradise Square. (Today, altered past all recognition, it forms part of Columbus Park.) In colonial days the whole area lay at the bottom of a large pond, or lake, named the Collect. Beginning in 1808, however, the Collect was drained and filled in, a project noteworthy as the first big public work in the city's history. But much of the filled land was left low and marshy, and consequently the first buildings put up there were by the early 1820's settling and sagging into dilapidation. Discouraged also by foul odors and malarial agues rising from the old swamplands, those early residents who could afford it began to join the migration uptown. Thus the Five Points was left to the very poor. Mostly these were Irish, with a heavy sprinkling of free Negroes. By the early 1840's the area had sunk into utter squalor.

A distinguished visitor, the English novelist Charles Dickens, was conducted through the Five Points about that time during an extended tour of America. It was far worse, he wrote, than Whitechapel, the Seven Dials, or any of the notorious London slums he had described so vividly in *Oliver Twist*. Noting pigs rooting in streets knee-deep in mud, families holed up in dens "where dogs would howl to lie . . . ruined houses open to the street . . . hideous tenements which take their names from robbery and murder," he concluded that ". . . all that is loathsome, drooping and decayed is here."

Dickens, no admirer of America, saw very little that pleased him on the tour. But there is plenty of evidence that he did not exaggerate about the Five Points. The place held a morbid fascination for native writers too. "Gates of Hell," "Jacob's Ladder," and "Brickbat Mansion" were typical tenement names—as if the inhabitants took a perverse pride in their own misery. One noxious dead-end alley bore the name Cow Bay, because the site had been a favorite watering place for cattle on the shore of the old Collect. In a book titled *Hot Corn*, published in 1854, an anonymous American described scenes even worse than Mr. Dickens had observed.

"If you would see Cow Bay," he wrote, "saturate your handkerchief with camphor, so that you can endure the horrid stench. Grope your way through the long, narrow passage—turn to the right, up the dark and dangerous stairs; be careful where you place your foot . . . for it is more than shoe-mouth deep of steaming filth . . . take care and not upset that seething pot of butcher's offal soup that is cooking upon a little furnace at the head of the stairs—open that door—go in—Look: here is a Negro and his wife sitting upon the floor . . . eating their supper off the bottom of a pail. Another Negro and his wife occupy another corner; a third sits in the window, monopolizing all the air astir. In another corner, what do we see? A Negro and a stout, hearty, rather good-looking white woman. Not sleeping together? No, not exactly that —there is no bed in the room—no chair—no table—no nothing— but rags, and dirt, and vermin, and degraded, rum degraded human beings."

It was the normal thing for several families to share tenement rooms that rented at anywhere from two to ten dollars a month, indication enough of the depths of their poverty. It was normal, too, for mothers and daughters to practice their trade as whores, undisturbed by the family routine that went on around them. Otherwise, business enterprise in the Five Points confined itself largely to greengrocers and pawnshops. The pawnbrokers were almost all fences who dealt in stolen goods; the greengrocer shops were shabby dives where far more cheap liquor was sold than vegetables. Many of them had back rooms where the most vicious of the criminal elements congregated. Drunkenness and sex were the only solaces for the all-pervading misery. Children roamed the streets, ragged and barefoot summer and winter, begging, stealing, and scavenging.

Beneath many of the tenements, too, were dank cellars and dark, twisting tunnels where the poorest of the poor lived, often without seeing the light of the sun for days on end. Often they died and were buried there. In one such den, it was told, a little girl stabbed to death for a penny she had begged lay unnoticed for nearly a week before her mother finally scraped a shallow grave in the dirt floor and disposed of the corpse.

Negroes were no worse off, amid such conditions, than their white neighbors. And it appears that there was little if any attempt at segregation by either side. The immigrant Irish were social outcasts of the same stripe.

It was a phenomenon of the times, for the great waves of immigration pouring across the Atlantic had come almost wholly from Ireland throughout the early years of the century. Being refugees from British oppression in the home isle, the overwhelming mass of these Irish families were penniless, illiterate, and unskilled, with an ingrained grudge against authority—undesirables by practically any yardstick. In the late 1840's the dismal potato famines in Ireland had swelled the influx to gigantic proportions; all through the 1850's and 1860's it still continued. Not surprisingly, such floods of the underprivileged were resented most actively in crowded ports of entry like Boston and New York, where they landed in the greatest numbers. Citizens who thought of themselves as native Americans despised the poor Paddy; his rough, alien ways; his papist religion; and his uncouth, barbaric brogue with a bitter prejudice that is difficult to comprehend today. Everywhere he was herded into slums and shantytowns, derided and shunned, barred from all but the most menial and degrading jobs.

Not all of New York's foreign-born population was Irish, of course. There was a very large German colony, too, and a good smattering of Italians, a few Chinese, and others. As a class, however, the Germans were quiet, hard-working, and unobtrusive, while none of the other nationalities was numerous enough to be troublesome. By the time of the War Between the States, on the other hand, census figures showed almost a quarter of the city's residents to be Irish or of Irish descent. And virtually all of them were squeezed into the East Side slums.

Somewhat north of the Five Points, and running diagonally up from Chatham Square to Astor Place, was the famous Bowery. Among out-of-towners visiting New York it probably rivaled Broadway as the best-known thoroughfare on the island, with an honorable history that went all the way back to the colonial era. There was a tradition that George Washington had stopped at the popular Bull's Head Tavern there for a refreshing tankard of Bowery ale on the triumphal day of the British evacuation in 1783. In the early years of the new century some of the finest theaters in America had drawn audiences of the city's elite to the Bowery, and its concert saloons and genteel beer gardens had attracted a high class of family trade. By the 1860's those times were long past. Changing conditions—the tidal influx of immigration and the blights of poverty and congestion—had ruined the Bowery too.

It still was a street devoted to entertainment, though the quality had slipped a long way downhill. "Actresses too corrupt and dissolute to play elsewhere appear on the boards at the Bowery," wrote a contemporary critic. "Broad farces, indecent comedies, plays of highwaymen and murderers are received with shouts by the reeking crowds which fill the low theaters. . . . There is not a dance hall, a free-and-easy, a concert saloon, or a vile drinking place that presents such a view of the depravity and degradation of New York as the gallery of a Bowery theater. . . ."

This was a rather large statement to make, perhaps, for those same concert saloons and dance halls likewise had become hang-outs for hoodlums, pimps, and prostitutes and the down-and-out in general. Nevertheless, the Bowery clung to the pretense, at least, of a sort of shabby respectability that set it somewhat apart from the worst of New York's slums. That was especially true of its upper reaches, probably due to the high concentration of poor but law-abiding German families who shared the tenement areas east of Astor Place with the dominant Irish. But the pretense grew progressively thinner as the Bowery ran south. And it vanished altogether in the jungle of waterfront shambles spreading south and east from Chatham Square and the Five Points to the East River.

Here, centered around Cherry, Water, and Roosevelt streets, was New York's old Fourth Ward. It differed from the Sixth only as a political subdivision and by virtue of the bustling commercial activity always present on a seaport waterfront. One side of South Street, overlooking the river, was lined with deepwater slips and piers; during busy periods it frequently appeared to be roofed over by the slanting bowsprits and dense rigging of ships from every quarter of the globe. Directly opposite, across the cobbled street, stood warehouses, ship chandlers' shops, and the busy offices of shipping firms. But just one short block away was Water Street, given over to smoky drinking dens, bordellos, and sailors' resorts standing almost cheek by jowl—more than forty of them in a single half-mile stretch. Among the most notorious was Kit Burns' Sportsmen's Hall, with an amphitheater on the ground floor in which dog fights, rat fights, and dog-and-rat fights were featured. As an added attraction there was Kit's son-in-law, Jack the Rat. For ten cents Jack would bite the head off a live mouse; for a quarter he would perform the same operation on a rat. In One-Armed Charley Monell's Hole-in-the-Wall, another cele-brated dive, a giant female bouncer named Gallus Mag specialized in subduing obstreperous patrons by dragging them to the door with an ear clenched between her teeth. If a victim objected too strenuously, she bit the ear off, and was reputed to keep a large jar of such trophies pickled in spirits behind the bar. Bawdy houses occupied the upper stories of most of these establishments, the girls usually garbed in the lowcut bodices, short skirts, black stockings, and scarlet boots with bells around the tops which became virtually *de rigueur* for the city's fancier class of harlots.

Many of these places were headquarters for gangs of river pirates who preyed on waterfront commerce. Brawls and killings were common occurrences in nearly all of them. And many of the proprietors of the district's cheap hotels were not above robbing —and, if necessary, murdering—guests in their beds. On Cherry Street, a block beyond Water, some famous crimps—Tommy Haddon, Dan Kerrigan, and Mrs. Bridget Tighe were among the most renowned—made a profitable business of supplying shang-haied seamen to outbound ship masters. Police usually patrolled Fourth Ward streets in squads of a half-dozen or more. But they seldom ventured inside the worst of the dives even in pursuit of a wanted criminal. It was safer, if less effective, to wait in the street till he came out.

Everywhere in the ward there was squalor and misery equal to the worst the Five Points could show. In the 1860's, and for a great many years afterward, in fact, the Fourth claimed the distinction of possessing the worst single tenement house in all New York. This was a ramshackle old pile at Numbers 36 and 38 Cherry Street, called Gotham Court. Its inmates knew it more familiarly as Sweeney's Shambles. From its cellars convenient holes cut into a large sewer below afforded refuge for gangs of petty thieves and caches for their loot, while the hordes of rats and the gases of corruption that issued from the sewer made the Court itself a plague spot of disease. The Arch Block was another disreputable old rookery, best known for a three-hundred-and-fifty-pound Negro bawd called Sue the Turtle who lived there. Popular hearsay had it that she had been named by a slumming newspaper reporter. He likened her to "a huge black turtle standing on its hind legs."

Sensation-seekers paid a good deal of attention to such characters and to such flamboyant fleshpots as Sportsmen's Hall and

One-Armed Charley's. But among them and around them the vast, submerged masses of the city's poor eked out their bare subsistence, largely ignored by the more fortunate. When they could find work they were New York's toilers, its cheap labor, the doers of its hard and dirty jobs. When they could not, they had little recourse but to turn to crime. Inevitably, a great many of them became habitual criminals. In 1862 the scanty records still extant show police arrests totaling somewhat more than eighty thousand men and women—very close to one in ten of the city's population. The fact was noted. New Yorkers were not precisely complacent about it. All through the 1850's and 1860's, in fact, the city did not lack reformers. The vice, crime, misery, and general sin rampant in its slums were emphatically deplored by journalists on the printed page, by ministers thundering from pulpits, and by a legion of ardent do-gooders speaking before the conclaves of various uplift societies. Running through all the indignation, though, there seemed to be a strong preoccupation with the spectacular and the grotesque—with the Kit Burnses, Jack the Rats, Gallus Mags, and Sue the Turtles. Very little was said about practical measures to alleviate the plain, grinding poverty out of which most of the evils sprang. Public morality of the time expressed itself in a strangely smug and self-righteous attitude toward the poor. There was a widely prevalent assumption that their misery and misfortune stemmed in some vague way from *ungodliness*, that if they could only be led to see the light of salvation their wretched condition would somehow be improved. As a result, actual relief measures were few.

A pair of sincere humanitarians, the Reverend Lewis M. Pease and his wife, had opened the Five Points House of Industry in 1856. It was the sole welfare agency in the district; in the whole city, for that matter. The Peases managed by dint of great effort to keep an orphanage going and to provide some work for the neediest cases. Much of it was sewing for New York's garment manufacturers, who had loads of cheap cloth carted over from their lofts around lower Broadway. But the Peases were ahead of their time, unfortunately, and the good they did was limited by scanty resources. Other Protestant missions active in the Five Points area from time to time were all too prone to dispense their meager charity with large doses of hymn-singing and soul-saving.

And since the majority of Five Points souls were Irish Catholic, they reaped considerably more resentment than gratitude.

Some notable revival meetings were held in the Fourth Ward. Many of them invaded the actual premises of the worst dens on Water Street, whose proprietors piously declared themselves happy to be helping in the Lord's work. And the ministers who presided claimed some dramatic conversions among the habitués. In the emotional heat stoked up by the hellfire-and-brimstone evangelism of the era, it was possible. But conditions in the ward did not noticeably improve. Eventually newspapermen who looked into the revivals denounced several of the clergymen as humbugs. The upshot: sin went its evil way unchecked.

Yet the plight of the poor did draw some help of a more substantial kind. Quite early in the century the sachems of Tammany Hall, struggling toward political domination of the city, had begun to see the implications in so massive a block of potential votes. They were realists and self-seekers, not philan-thropists. Nevertheless, theirs was the only practical hand-up that thousands of destitute and bewildered slum folk ever knew, and the results were far-reaching. Federal statutes on the naturaliza-tion of foreigners had always been liberal. Tammany was instru-mental in the drafting and passing of laws encouraging state courts to still greater leniency in applying them. By the middle 1830's the immigrant vote—which is to say, the Irish vote—had become a power in the city. Tammany controlled it. But Tam-many was also controlled by it. The Irishman's native talent for politics and his clannish instincts, flourishing in reaction to the lowly status forced on him by his American superiors, made him a first-rate organization man.

His unruly inclination toward violence in the settling of grievances was something else again. But it too found a natural outlet in the seamy, steamy climate of the times. The first politi-cally oriented gangs appeared in the dead ends and back alleys of New York.

Chapter 4 | The Violent Men

THE CITY HAD A BACKGROUND OF PERIODIC TUMULTS that had begun more than a century earlier.

A slave insurrection had had to be quelled by armed force in 1712. In 1741 a worse one, known as the Slave Plot, had seen desperate Negroes try to burn and sack New York. It was put down bloodily, a score or more of its leaders hanged or broken on the wheel. (The place of execution, as it happened, was an island in the old Collect.) The Doctors' Riot of 1788 was a different kind of outbreak—public indignation erupting over the robbing of graves by medical students seeking cadavers. A bitter cold spell coupled with a business slump during the winter of 1807–08 had resulted in riots by mobs of unemployed demanding work or bread. It was this first display of temper by the city's poor that had led to the filling in of the Collect as a make-work project. There were bread riots again in 1837—warehouses looted, stocks of grain destroyed, the militia finally called out, all on account of anger over the high price of flour. Perhaps it was worth noting that poor New Yorkers could be an impatient lot.

Most of these disturbances were spontaneous. Organized lawlessness, as such, had little part in them. The city's first gangs were comparatively inconspicuous.

Toughs who hung about the back rooms of Paradise Square greengrocer shops began to band together, apparently, sometime in the middle 1820's. As the neighborhood went steadily downhill, its dog-eat-dog atmosphere encouraged gangsterism, and before long the whole Five Points area was dominated by various hoodlum aggregations. A few, like the Kerryonians, professed to be essentially social, brought together by sentimental loyalties to old home counties in Ireland. More often the rosters were made up of pickpockets, footpads, and similar petty criminals operating under the aegis of one or another of the district's dealers in stolen goods. But it was gang nature to war among themselves. Sometimes richer pickings were the prize. As often, it was simply the natural truculence that was never far beneath the surface in the Five Points. Presently the toughest of the original gangs began to develop along quasi-military lines. Thugs were recruited for their prowess with fists, knives, bludgeons, or that celebrated gangsters' weapon the slung-shot. Basically this was nothing more than a large handful of lead shot tied in a bag of leather or stout cloth at the end of a short length of strong cord; it had the advantages of being cheap, easily made, and fearfully effective. Whirled rapidly through the air by a skilled and muscular thug, then brought crashing down on a victim's head, the slung-shot could be a terrible weapon indeed—frequently a lethal one.

Most gangs enforced a rough sort of discipline on their members. An esprit de corps grew up. In many cases there was even a semblance of uniforms. Thus—to name two who achieved an early notoriety—the Shirt Tails always wore their shirts outside their trousers, while the Plug Uglies customarily went into battle wearing big plug hats stuffed with feathers, wool, or other shock-absorbent material as helmets against enemy slung-shots and flying brickbats.

For a while the Roach Guards, named for the owner of a popular Paradise Square hangout, ruled the roost as the largest gang in the district. But internal dissension arose among them. At the height of a particularly bitter falling out, so the legend goes, some troublemaker tossed the carcass of a rabbit into the meeting room. Taking the cue, the dissident clique walked out, formed a new gang, and called themselves the Dead Rabbits. Possibly the story is apocryphal. But in the low slang of the day "rabbit" meant "tough guy," and *dead rabbit* signified the very toughest of the tough. In any case, the new gang soon left no doubt that it lived up to its name. In the home territory the Dead Rabbits battled the rump Roach Guards, the Chichesters, the Plug Uglies, and others to a standstill. A strong sense of neighborhood loyalty bound them all together against outsiders, however. When they

ventured on major forays outside of the Five Points, the ranks
closed; the bully boys all rallied 'round, and the Dead Rabbits
were the acknowledged leaders.

Early in the game, various local politicians began to appreci-
ate the gangs' value as bodyguards, messengers, ward heelers,
multiple voters, and intimidators of the opposition on election
days. In return—the classic arrangement—gang members could
count on official tolerance of their run-ins with the law. Given the
conditions prevailing in the Bloody Ould Sixth, the system could
scarcely have failed to work. But it was Captain Isaiah Rynders
who came along to make big business of it.

The captain's past, including the validity of whatever claim he
had to the rank, was cloudy. It was said that his youth had been
spent as a riverboat gambler and gun-and-knife fighter on the
Mississippi. Obviously, he was tough. It turned out that he was
also shrewd, with a knack for political rough-and-tumble and a
keen eye for the main chance. He appears to have arrived in New
York in 1834 or 1835. The Sixth Ward first began to notice him as
the owner of one of the sleazy greengrocer shops in Paradise
Square. Soon he had acquired a total of six, along with the gang
sponsorships that usually went with them. By 1843 he had made
his Empire Club, a fancy gaming resort at 25 Park Row, the
Tammany command post for all the Sixth—and himself the un-
disputed king of the Five Points.

As Tammany prospered, so did Captain Rynders. He owned
or exacted tribute from scores of bawdy houses, saloons, gambling halls, and crooked pawnshops all over New York. Gang
toughs, political hacks, and hangers-on jumped at his orders.
(One of them was a nimble opportunist by the name of Edward
Z. Judson, who later went west, took to calling himself Ned Buntline, and won fame and fortune as the literary discoverer of
Buffalo Bill Cody and the author of innumerable blood-and-
thunder thrillers.) A U.S. marshal's appointment came Rynders'
way. With it came respectability, or its outward appearance. And
his Dead Rabbits—they were his by this time, lock, stock, and
barrel—waxed in numbers and in arrogance.

There were other gangs about the city. Every poor neighborhood seemed to spawn its own. Even the stolid German settle-
ments on the middle East Side had a few, though they never

became more than minor nuisances. The Fourth Ward was infested with some extremely vicious ones—the Buckoos, Slaughter Housers, Daybreak Boys, Hookers, Swamp Angels, and Patsey Conroys, among many others. But Fourth Ward gangsters did not lend themselves readily to political uses. Most of them were a harder breed of cutthroat, committed to river piracy, warehouse robbery, and the strongarming of seamen in dockside alleys, as against the tamer pursuits of ward heeling and vote stealing. Even the crookedest of politicians, too, were wary about fronting for ruffians so far beyond the pale. So the waterfront gentry went their own way, shunning other gangs and fighting their bloodiest battles against their mortal enemies, the police.

On the Bowery it was different. There the Dead Rabbits found their bitterest rivals.

The Bowery Boys—often spelled Bowery B'hoys, for most of them were militant sons of Erin—claimed somewhat more honorable origins than the Five Points bruisers. Few of them were criminals, except incidentally. Many even held honest jobs, usually as butchers, laborers, or bouncers in the Bowery's gin mills and dance halls. Almost to a man they were volunteer firemen, members of the various brigades on which New York had relied for its fire protection since the earliest times. These outfits took enormous pride in themselves and in their brassbound engines and pumpers. They gave them fond names like *Shad Belly*, *Yellow Gal*, *Big Six*, *Black Joke*, and so on; kept them groomed to a glittering sheen; and would drop everything to haul them through the streets on a mad run at the first peal of a fire bell, day or night. Too, every company took a ferocious pride in being first on the scene of a big conflagration. It was not unusual for a building to burn to the ground while burly volunteers battled for possession of the available fire plugs. And it was not unusual, either, for nearby buildings to be broken open and looted in the course of the fire fighting. Businessmen and insurance companies complained but accepted it as part of the cost of the system.

Membership in one of these volunteer fire brigades carried great prestige with it. William Marcy Tweed—not yet *Boss* Tweed, though he already was well on his way in the early 1860's —had started as a fireman on the Bowery. So had other high Tammany chieftains. And out of this stemmed much of the

Bowery Boys' eminence in city politics. But the Boy, or B'hoy, yielded place to no one as a stomp-and-gouge bully in his own right.

Compared to the Five Points gangster, he was a bit of an aristocrat, and looked the part. He was a strict conformist. On his chin was a goatish beard much like the one worn by the cartoonists' stock character Uncle Sam. He kept his hair cropped in back, but long, luxuriant, and liberally doused with Macassar oil in front. In his leisure hours he swaggered about the Bowery in a long frock coat, neckerchief, plug hat, and loose trousers usually tucked into the tops of heavy, hobnailed boots. He was never without a large and businesslike knife, or a pistol if he happened to own one. The contemporary public was much taken with the Bowery Boy. Popular songs and penny-dreadfuls were written about him. Guidebooks to the city sights nearly always mentioned him with a kind of perverse pride, even while they warned visitors that, "Respectable people avoid the Bowery as far as possible at night. . . . Those who do not wish to fall into trouble should keep out of the way. . . ."

The Bowery Boy, in fact, came close to becoming an American folk hero in his own lifetime. Not until the rousing Prohibition era of the 1920's would the gangster again be glamorized with such a raffishly romantic aura.

When Dead Rabbits and Bowery Boys mixed in their free-for-alls, they did it openly. Place and time were frequently agreed to in advance, though the surprise raid was a favorite tactic also. The panoply was not unlike a caricature of medieval knights arrayed for the tourney. The Dead Rabbits liked to strip to their undershirts for fighting. Their standard, a dead rabbit impaled upon a pole, was frequently borne in front. Bowery Boys advanced behind such well-known heroes of the prize ring as Tom Hyer, Bill the Butcher Poole, and Yankee Sullivan (who later capped his career by going west and getting himself hanged by a San Francisco Vigilance committee). But there was little chivalry about the actual hostilities. Both sides fought in earnest and for keeps. Cobblestones and brickbats flew. Those affluent enough to have pistols or muskets used them. For close work, clubs, knives, slung-shots, brass knuckles, and iron bars came into play. When all else failed, they fought with fists, feet, and teeth. The kick in the groin, the thumb in the eye, ears and noses bitten off, were expected and accepted as part of the fun. Maimings were common. There often were fatalities, and innocent bystanders sometimes fell. But political protection was strong. Though police usually tried to arrest the ringleaders and break up the melees, charges seldom followed, punishment almost never.

The times dripped with mawkish sentiment and strange, turgid emotions. When Bill the Butcher Poole was murdered by a onetime henchman in the course of an internecine Tammany feud in 1855, his last words were quoted breathlessly in the New York press: "Goodbye, boys; I die a True American." More than five thousand admirers marched in the funeral procession, along with several brass bands blaring dirges. Spectators jammed Broadway from Bleecker Street to the Battery, where the chief mourners boarded a cortege of ferryboats for Brooklyn and Greenwood Cemetery. Not many legitimate heroes ever departed the city more impressively.

In part, no doubt, this public preoccupation with men of violence grew out of the strains and anxieties that tore the Union as civil war approached. It was a long-drawn ordeal of unrest, anger, and bewilderment that had started decades back.

Almost from its inception the Abolitionist movement gathered ardent supporters in New York. Yet the city as a whole was a strong pro-slavery center. It could not have been otherwise. Banking and other business houses had important investments in the cotton states. Throughout the East Side tenement districts the very thought of an army of freed slaves swarming into the city was a nightmare. The feeling had no racial bias in it, at first. It was a matter of simple economic survival. Already underprivileged and underpaid, often out of work altogether, New York's laboring classes saw the free Negro as a potentially ruinous competitor, that was all. But it was an attitude that could easily turn to something uglier. And it very soon did. The first overt resentment was directed at white Abolitionists, however. Some of their homes were stoned during random disorders in 1833. In June of 1834 an attack on a prominent leader named Tappan mushroomed into a series of full-fledged riots that went on for two days and nights and left a dozen buildings in ruins. Significantly, Negro families in Paradise Square caught the brunt of it. But it ended in an orgy of indiscriminate brutality to colored and whites alike. Afterward the police claimed to have proof that Five Points gangs had been involved.

In the meantime, a touchy situation was made no better by the rise of the Native American, or Know-Nothing, party, with its doctrines of anti-Catholicism and America for Americans. New York's huge population of foreign-born made it fertile ground for this sort of demagoguery, of course. And Tammany Hall, where the Irish already were strong, was especially vulnerable. To muddy the waters still more, Tammany was split from within by a fractious minority calling itself the Equal Rights party. Even the gangs felt the pull of conflicting loyalties. On the Bowery, heavily Irish and German though it was, the American Guards sprang up as a belligerent Know-Nothing contingent. An Irish saloonkeeper promptly raised the O'Connell Guards in rebuttal. In the spring elections of 1834, savage fighting raged for three days around the polling places. Tammany candidates finally beat out their Whig and Native American opponents, but it was a near thing. Very likely this election marked the gangs' first decisive participation in city politics, for it appears that all three parties had hoodlum forces at work.

Tammany patched up its inner breaches for the time being and stayed in power. But the general unrest remained. Abolitionist appeals to the public conscience grew more and more insistent. The Native Americans, though they won few national elections anywhere, continued to make noise and win converts. From Washington came rumbles of widening disunion all through the remainder of the 1830's and the 1840's. None of this was peculiar to New York. But in New York the confusion threw some odd bedfellows together. According to their own tenets, certainly, Native Americans had no logical place in their party for immigrant Irishmen. In the storm of jingo prejudice they whipped up, nevertheless, the age-old Irish hatred of the English was easily aroused. The city had no English population to amount to anything. But Isaiah Rynders, a rabid anglophobe, chose for reasons of his own to jump the Tammany fence and go off on a Know-Nothing rampage. His defection was brief, but while it lasted it was a hellbender.

In May of 1849 a mob of his Five Points bullies drove the

popular English actor William C. Macready from the stage of the Astor Place Opera House and stopped the performance there. Prominent New Yorkers reacted indignantly. A special delegation called on Macready at his hotel, urged him to try again, and promised no more untoward incidents would occur. Rynders, meanwhile, had inflammatory handbills distributed about the city, denouncing "British oppression" and calling on all true Americans to act. Three days later Macready did attempt to appear again. A mob more than ten thousand strong stoned the Opera House, set it on fire, and fought the police so savagely that a National Guard regiment was at length called out to restore order. They did, but the casualties totaled twenty-three dead and nearly thirty injured. As for William Macready, he was so shaken that he fled aboard a train for New Rochelle in disguise and soon returned to England. The mob, still bent on mischief, returned to attack the Opera House again some days later. This time it was dispersed without bloodshed, but only because artillery was wheeled up and placed in position to sweep both Broadway and the Bowery. For more than a week afterward a mob milled sullenly about the New York Hotel in the belief that the actor still was hiding there.

In their own way the incidents, known as the Astor Place Riots, were an ominous milestone. For the first time the power of the New York underworld had been used, not simply as a tool of corrupt politics—that was already commonplace—but by a demagogue for his own prejudicial ends. What was more, the gambit had been successful. Isaiah Rynders could boast that his mob had had its way in spite of New York's very biggest bigwigs, in spite of the National Guard too. For the Opera House had been shut down, the despised Englishman driven from the city.

Worse was to come.

Chapter 5 | Coppers, Clubs, and City Hall

FOR THE TWENTY-ODD YEARS OF ITS EXISTENCE, New York's Municipal Police force had had an undistinguished history. Not even so simple a thing as putting its patrolmen into uniform had gone off well. The first attempt, early in the 1840's, had aroused outrage on the Bowery. Policemen dressed like British bobbies were an affront to Irish pride, the B'hoys had declared. And such a succession of street brawls followed that the authorities presently gave in. Thereafter patrolmen went about their duties with no other identification than a star-shaped copper badge. Hence the origin of the derisive term "copper," later shortened to "cop."

A few years later the familiar blue frock coat with brass buttons—topped off at first by a plug hat—was accepted on New York streets. It was a somewhat hollow victory. Throughout the 1840's the alliance between organized crime and a venal City Hall flourished steadily.

By the 1850's graft in the selling of city contracts, licenses, and political favors of all sorts became so flagrant that the New York City Common Council was popularly called the Forty Thieves, after an early Five Points gang. When the gang itself happened to break up about that time, cynical citizens said that it was due to shame at the comparison. With police appointments in the Council's hands, it was inevitable that the force too was soon shot through with corruption. The man aspiring to a job as patrolman was usually expected to pay as much as one hundred dollars to some influential officeholder, plus another forty dollars to the captain of the police district involved—who had himself invested two hundred dollars or more for *his* preferment. Applicants were poor men as a rule. The fact that they were willing to put out such sums indicates the potential for graft which must have existed right down the line.

It was no wonder that organized crime prospered. The criminal overlords paid handsomely for its immunity. The wonder is that the police force was able to attract any honest men at all. Yet somehow it was—not only honest men, but a remarkable number with courage and resolution as well.

The rank-and-file New York policeman of the time is something of a shadowy figure, not easily visualized. We know little about his background or his character. Few of the early departmental records have survived. The policeman on the beat was not, like a Bowery Boy, "picturesque." Hence he was not widely sentimentalized in the penny press of the day. Undoubtedly he was recruited from the laboring class. He was very likely to be Irish— or a high proportion of his mates were—simply because the urban laboring classes of the time *were* preponderantly Irish. At an educated guess, he may have differed from his natural enemies among the Dead Rabbits and Bowery Boys only in his attitude toward law and order. On the record he was a formidable head-cracker and knockdown fighter whenever the occasion required, as it frequently did. He could hardly have existed in his difficult milieu without a fairly free and easy moral outlook. Yet if by and large he was not above pocketing his small share of graft or stretching a point for some local Tammany satrap, he seldom was backward about tackling his duty when good men led him, either.

In the Fourth Ward such men fought a long and often discouraging battle to hold the vicious waterfront gangs in check. And up in the Eighteenth a tough police captain named George Washington Walling won one of the force's few real victories of the period.

The Eighteenth Ward was a sprawling shantytown area about midway up the East Side. It was the particular bailiwick of a close-knit band of holdup men who called themselves the Honeymoon Gang, and for some years they had operated almost unhindered by the police. When he took over in 1853, Walling found the district living under a reign of terror. Burly Honeymooners, taking their stations each evening at all the busiest street corners, would knock down and rob every passerby who looked prosperous enough to be worth the trouble. Arresting the thugs was pointless. Charges were promptly quashed, and they returned to the same old stands. Walling switched to a more basic approach. Naming six of his biggest, brawniest men to a roving strongarm squad, he put them into plain clothes and armed them with stout locustwood clubs. No arrests, he ordered—simply beat every Honeymooner senseless on sight. He had noticed, he said later, that even the toughest of the bully boys with his slung-shot or his brass knuckles was strangely averse to standing up to a club wielded by a policeman who meant business. It was a discovery destined to have a strong influence on police tactics in the future. For Walling's method worked. Within two weeks, it was said, the Honeymoon Gang had fled south to the Five Points, where political protection was more potent.

The lesson was not forgotten, but for a long while it was not heeded, either. Conditions went from bad to worse as the 1850's rolled along. Politically, the old Whig party faded in a lingering death. But the struggle between Tammany Hall and the Native Americans hardened into something very close to all-out war. Election days saw rioting, polls smashed up, ballot boxes stolen or stuffed on a scale no one ever had dared before. This kind of thing went on even in the better residential precincts, and the gangs took an increasingly bold part in it. The climax came in 1856.

Mayor Fernando Wood sought a second term that year. His first had boomed graft and chicanery at City Hall to an all-time high. By means of it he had made his control of Tammany iron-clad. And he was personally popular—a tall, dashing, handsome man; dapper in dress and hail-fellow in manner; a habitué of all the most glittering saloons and gambling resorts. He was, besides, a calculating and audacious politician. The Dead Rabbits and their lesser satellites of Paradise Square were solidly behind him, Captain Isaiah Rynders having returned to the fold after his Know-Nothing excursion. Many of the Fourth Ward's gangs, men who seldom went in for political favor, had rallied to the Wood banner. Against this array the Native American candidate, Isaac O. Barker, mustered not only the violent support of the Bowery Boys and their hangers-on but also—strange bedfellows again— the endorsement of reform elements appalled at the mayor's brazen looting of the public till.

On the eve of election day Wood furloughed the bulk of the Municipal Police force. Strict orders were issued for every idle patrolman to vote early (the right way, presumably) and then stay away from the polls. Every man on the force had already contributed to the Wood campaign fund, by no means all of them willingly.

Dead Rabbits and Bowery Boys thus skirmished almost without interference while honest folk voted as best they could. When the results were announced, Fernando Wood was mayor again by a plurality of nearly ten thousand. The total number of ballots cast showed such an amazing increase over the last previous election, however, that it seemed certain a great many of them must be bogus. Or so the Native Americans claimed. They cried fraud. There was no recount.

But repercussions of the affair carried all the way to Albany, where the new Republican party had won control of the State Legislature. Once before, in 1853, the Legislature had cast a critical eye at the goings-on in New York City. That time they had amended the city's charter, taking the power of appointments to the Municipal Police force away from the Common Council and placing it in the supposedly cleaner hands of a board including the mayor, the city recorder, and a city judge. There had been no improvement. All the amendment did was channel the graft collections from one set of pockets to another. And it was obvious that under Fernando Wood's regime the police force had sunk into virtual impotence.

Now, as one of a series of acts passed in the spring of 1857, the Legislature abolished the New York Municipal Police altogether. In its place a Metropolitan Police District was created, comprising Manhattan, Staten Island, Brooklyn, and a number of smaller communities on the mainland north of the city proper. Moreover, the governor was empowered to appoint a new board of five police commissioners; they in turn would have a free hand in naming a superintendent of police. The commissioners appointed by Governor King, a Republican, were all men who had campaigned actively for reform in New York City. Hopefully, the new police force was to be free of Tammany's control at last. But finding a new superintendent proved difficult. Several nominees declined the honor. And it may have been significant that the man who finally accepted, Frederick A. Talmage, had been city recorder at

the time of the Astor Place Riots eight years before. The Board of
Commissioners then formally ordered Mayor Wood to disband
the Municipal Police.

He replied by charging that the amending act was unconstitutional, and therefore the Board had no legal standing. That threw
the whole matter into the courts. In the meantime, Wood issued
an order calling on all members of the Municipal Police force to
stand fast. Fifteen captains and some hundreds of the rank and
file elected to do so. The rest of the force, Captain George Walling among them, were sworn in as members of the Metropolitan
Police. For some weeks, then, New Yorkers were treated to the
bewildering spectacle of both forces busily recruiting to bring
themselves up to full strength, while rival patrolmen walked the
city's beats in a sort of armed truce. On June 16 the truce blew
sky-high.

In its burst of reforming zeal, the State Legislature had
stripped the mayor of other appointive rights besides those con-
cerning the police force. Among them was the office of city
street commissioner, a rich plum for the graft-minded. The governor's appointee was one Daniel Conover. But Fernando Wood
had put his own man, Charles Devlin, in the job—at a price of
fifty thousand dollars, his enemies charged—and refused to back
down there also. When Conover arrived to take office, he was
thrown bodily out of City Hall. Whereupon he had a pair of
warrants sworn out for the mayor's arrest. One charged incitement to riot; the other, physical violence to Conover's person.
Wood retaliated by stationing three hundred Municipal patrolmen in City Hall and defied anyone to serve the warrants. Captain Walling volunteered to try. In a courageous effort to forestall
the violence that now loomed, he entered City Hall singlehanded,
was allowed to reach Wood's office, and actually seized him "as I
would any person subject to arrest." But that was as far as he got.
After a brief scuffle, Walling too was thrown out into the street.
Stubbornly he tried to go back in. He still was trying when fifty
Metropolitan policemen came marching briskly up Chambers
Street with the obvious intention of reinforcing him. Municipals
boiled out into the street to meet them, and a spirited, club-
swinging, head-cracking melee raged for half an hour. The Metropolitans, badly outnumbered, finally broke and fled in disorder.

Eventually the Board of Commissioners had to call for a National Guard regiment. At that point Fernando Wood gracefully permitted himself to be arrested and was immediately released on bail by an obliging judge. There is no record that he ever stood trial on either of Conover's charges.

Clashes between Metropolitans and Municipals went on all summer. And as might have been expected, law enforcement suffered. Indignant newspaper pieces told of citizens held up in broad daylight, even on such busy streets as Broadway, while policemen fought each other for the privilege of going to the rescue. Possibly there was a good deal of exaggeration to such tales. It was a fact, all the same, that arrests grew rare. And rarer still was the thug not immediately turned loose by a magistrate who sided with one or the other of the contending police forces. For a while New York must have teetered close to anarchy.

Riots worse than any that had gone before broke out on the Fourth of July, 1857. The Dead Rabbits touched off their holiday festivities with a raid in force on the Bowery Boys' headquarters. The Boys rallied for revenge. The Municipals, long schooled to a hands-off policy in such affairs of honor, declined to intervene. The Metropolitans, to their credit, did try to restore order. They tried, in some cases, with individual heroism that approached the foolhardy. But they still were undermanned and ill-organized. And in the pinch, Dead Rabbits and Bowery Boys were perfectly willing to unite against the common foe, rout the coppers, and then resume their private warring. Nothing like that ever had happened before, and it held dire implications for the future. Desperate, the Board of Commissioners appealed to Captain Isaiah Rynders. But now—another bad sign—not even Rynders was listened to. Trying vainly to talk peace to a contingent of his Five Pointers, he was caught in a sudden Bowery Boy onslaught and severely manhandled. The fighting went on. It lasted three days, all told, and then—once more—National Guard units had to be turned out. Intermittent skirmishes continued for almost a week before order finally was restored. And all the while, of course, the city's criminal element reveled in a field day of robbery and plunder.

Somewhat tongue-in-cheek, the New York *Times* printed an odd, self-righteous little sidelight on the trouble:

We are requested by the Dead Rabbits to state that the
Dead Rabbit club members are not thieves, that they did not
participate in the riot with the Bowery Boys, and that the
fight in Mulberry street was between the Roach Guards of
Mulberry street and the Atlantic Guards of the Bowery. The
Dead Rabbits are sensitive on points of honor, we are assured,
and wouldn't allow a thief to live on their beat, much less to
be a member of their club.

No doubt New Yorkers felt reassured.

Early in the fall the courts handed down a final verdict. The
legal status of the Metropolitan Board of Commissioners was
affirmed. Then at last Mayor Wood surrendered and the Municipals were disbanded. Still, Metropolitan recruitment was slow.
The disgraceful events of the summer had left the public with
little faith in the new setup and an unfortunate contempt for
police in general. At the same time, more than a decade of corruption and loose law enforcement had brought criminals of
every stripe flocking into New York. Some contemporary authorities estimated that about thirty thousand toughs were affiliated
in varying degrees with the city's gangs. And other thousands,
undoubtedly, had been attracted by the prospect of easy pickings
and were not subject even to the gangs' sketchy discipline. The
financial panic of 1857 broke later that fall. It too kept the slums
seething in unemployment and discontent. Several months passed
before the commissioners were able to get on with any real reor-
ganization of the police force. Even so, it would have been un-
realistic to expect a complete housecleaning. The Metropolitans
would be an improvement, but they would not be a model police
force. New York faced a long, uphill road to effective law and
order, and time was shorter than anyone knew.

Tammany's grip on the city scarcely had been shaken. With
no real program to offer, the Native Americans faded from contention at the polls as the threat of actual civil war loomed closer.
Fernando Wood was re-elected mayor again in 1859. Not until
1861 was he ousted at last. And then it was political throat-
cutting that accomplished it, not an aroused electorate rising up
in wrath. William Marcy Tweed had bided his time while he
built up his own solid faction at Tammany Hall, and this was the
year he chose to pull the props from under Wood. In the split that

resulted, Republican George Opdyke slipped into the mayor's office. It was little more than an interim defeat, however. Opdyke, a banker and importer, was an honest, affable businessman, not a strong political leader. And Tammany, Tweed's now, retained firm control of the Common Council.

Fernando Wood was undismayed. His tenure had been a long, shameless expedition into financial piracy, and he was wealthy with the spoils. Retiring to Wood Lawn, his estate far out on Broadway in the Seventies, he presently ran for the U.S. House of Representatives. He still had his following in New York. He was elected, and would remain an undistinguished fixture in the House for nearly twenty years to come. As mayor he had made it clear that his sympathies lay with the seceding cotton states, and they had not changed. He was already deeply involved in Copperhead machination, if not outright conspiracy; his brother Benjamin, publisher of the pro-Secessionist New York *Daily News*, made an able and active lieutenant. A pretty pair, the two of them, but they had to lie low for the time being.

War had come. New York exploded in patriotic frenzies. Ladies of fashion threw themselves happily into lint-scraping, the knitting of socks, and other home-front activities for the hero soldier boys. New York crowds cheered themselves hoarse for local regiments marching off to the battlefields.

That phase passed. Down in Washington the Lincoln Administration floundered through the war's first year in a manner to inspire no one's confidence. By September of 1862 that indefatigable diarist Mr. Gideon Welles was brooding over news of disaffection in the Union's largest city:

> H. H. Elliot, Chairman of the Prize Commission in New York, writes me that the public mind there is highly excited and on the eve of revolution. There is undoubtedly a bad state of things in New York, and he is surrounded by that class of Democratic partisans whose sympathies and associations were with the Rebels, and who are now party opponents of the Administration. . . .

In September, 1862, the ultimate provocation of a national military conscription act had not been mentioned seriously. But now it was July of 1863 and the draft was the law of the land, though it had still to be enforced.

Chapter 6 | "They Will Amount to Nothing"

THE WEEK FOLLOWING THE FOURTH OF JULY was relatively quiet in New York. The newspapers, at least, reflected a surface calm only faintly stirred by the restlessness underneath.

Dispatches from Pennsylvania continued to occupy much space on the front pages. Daily they filled in the details of what was now, beyond all doubt, *THE GREAT VICTORY* at Gettysburg. Lee, the invincible, was beaten: *THE REBEL ARMY TOTALLY DEFEATED*. Its remnants were flying for their lives toward the Potomac River. But within a day or two the lengthy paragraphs of stirring battlefield description began to give way to the implacable lists of Union casualties. And as days passed the grim roster of New York's dead grew, close-packed column after column, tempering the city's jubilation. As the days passed, too, there began to be hints of irksome delay in reaping the fruits of victory. It seemed that early enthusiasm had been guilty of some exaggerations. No more was said of the South's General Longstreet in captivity. George Meade seemed, little by little, to fall into the same fits and jerks of hesitation that had afflicted all his predecessors. Lee, it appeared, might yet get his army across the Potomac to safety in the Maryland hills. It was unthinkable, surely; but still . . . Still, it was a good week for the Union. There was victory in the west also: Vicksburg fell. The *Tribune* hailed that news with a smugly vindictive headline in its Tuesday evening edition: *THE PIRATE CONFEDERACY CAVING IN*.

In view of the good news, perhaps it was no coincidence that Horace Greeley's paper chose that same Tuesday edition as the place to bring a less palatable matter into the open:

PRO-REBEL ATTEMPTS AT REVOLUTION

That the more determined sympathizers in this vicinity
with the Slaveholders' Rebellion have for months conspired
and plotted to bring about a revolution in the North which
should place the whole tier of Free States bordering on the
Slave region in alliance with and practical subordination to
the Rebel Confederacy, is just as certain as that we are involved in Civil War. Had Meade been defeated at Gettysburg—as the Copperheads had no doubt he would be—they
would have been ready to raise the flag of rebellion and pro-
claim McClellan the head of a Provisional Government. Here
follows one of their manifestoes which was extensively circulated through our city on the night before the 4th. . . .

There followed the full text of a long, inflammatory handbill
calling itself a DECLARATION AND PROTEST OF LIBERTY AGAINST
USURPATION AND TYRANNY. It proceeded to make thirteen points;
in substance they said nothing that had not been said by Governor Seymour and his fellow speakers at the Academy of Music on
Saturday and by a great many other dissidents before them. But
they said it in terms of pure, unbridled hate. Two of the points
were a fair sample of them all. Number five declared in part that
the Federal government ". . . has become a filthy hybrid; a monster smeared with the bloody sacrifice of its own children; a de-
testable compound of crimes and vices; a despotism which cannot
fitly be described in decorous language. . . ." And number seven
said flatly: "Should the Confederate army capture Washington
and exterminate the herd of thieves, Pharisees, and cutthroats
which pasture there, defiling the temple of our liberty, we should
regard it as a special interposition of Divine Providence in behalf
of justice, judgement, and mercy." In conclusion, Abraham Lincoln and his Administration were "arraigned" for a whole lexicon
of "tyrannies, bloodshed, widespread defraudings, robberies, pan-
derings, desolations, wastes, and cruelties they have perpetrated."
The document was signed "Spirit of '76."

McClellan's name was not mentioned anywhere in it. Apparently he was Horace Greeley's own idea. But it was quite true
that General George B. McClellan was about the closest approach to a Union idol the war had produced thus far. His dis-
missal from command of the Army of the Potomac had done little

to boost Abe Lincoln's popularity with the man in the street. And since then there was a widely held impression that Little Mac considered it high time the war was ended and the Confederacy permitted to go its own way. But incitement to rebellion . . . ?

The *Tribune* did not appear unduly nervous about it. The manifesto and Greeley's prefacing editorial were buried on an inside page. The inference was clear: since Meade had *not* been defeated at Gettysburg, the Copperhead plotters would seem to have missed their chance, were worthy of nothing but a loyal citizen's contempt—but would still bear watching.

Especially, the *Tribune* might have added (but did not), see-ing that this was the week the draft was scheduled to begin.

The War Department had asked no help from the local au-thorities. The big job of listing New York City's eligible men was in the hands of Federal enrollment officers and clerks, though the provost marshal in charge, Colonel Robert Nugent of the Sixty-ninth Regiment, was a city resident. He was also an Irishman and a Catholic, which might or might not help to make conscription somewhat less offensive to its prospective victims. Enrollment had in fact been going on for some time. On Thursday, July 9, the *Tribune* reported under the innocuous heading:

LOCAL MILITARY MATTERS

The enrollment of all able-bodied men in the first nine Congressional districts of this state, in accordance with the act calling out the national forces, is nearly completed, the number of names taken amounting in the aggregate to about 300,000. The enrollment in the Sixth District was completed a week ago, and preparations are now being made to transcribe the names from the rolls to slips of paper, so that everything may be in readiness for the draft when ordered by the Presi-dent. . . .

At some length the item then assured readers of the extreme care which was being taken to ensure accuracy in the work. Able-bodied New Yorkers probably could not have cared less, but could take whatever comfort there was in the fact that their gov-ernment proposed to clap them into the Army with the utmost fairness and efficiency. In closing, the *Tribune* added the not very encouraging information that between sixty and seventy thou-sand men "of the first class" would be "the first to go."

There really was not much else that a pro-Administration paper could say on the subject. Nothing about this war was popular with anyone. Just the day before, Horace Greeley had felt it necessary to clarify his own position on that score. In an oblique reference to earlier reports of mediation offers by Napoleon III of France, he had editorialized somewhat querulously: "We have never been able to see why our Government should repel the friendly interposition of other Governments for the restoration of Peace to our distracted country. . . ." Mr. Greeley granted that past difficulties with some of those governments was undoubtedly an excellent reason for caution. But it was no reason, he insisted, "for abruptly repelling their good offices." That was bad enough; in going stubbornly ahead with its conscription law, the Administration was making things still more embarrassing for its friends. As one of them—one of New York's very few—the *Tribune* could not gracefully take an opposition stand. But the draft was a prickly piece of news. Best report the simple facts and let it go at that.

Other New York papers were bound by no such restraint. Their comments rose to a choleric crescendo as the week passed.

"The manner in which the draft is being conducted in New York is such an outrage upon all decency and fairness as has no parallel and can find no apologists," huffed Benjamin Wood's *Daily News*. "The evident aim of those who have the Conscription Act in hand, in this State, is to lessen the number of Democratic votes at the next election. . . ."

The *Journal of Commerce*, too, accused those in power in Washington of using the draft for their own ends. And it added a slap at the Abolitionists: "Some men say, 'now that the war has commenced, it must not be stopped till slaveholding is abolished.' *Such men are neither more nor less than murderers.*"

A long, intemperate article in the New York *World* compared the odious Act with the British Navy's press gangs of previous centuries, kidnapping poor Englishmen and sending them to their deaths at sea. The only difference, fumed the *World*, was that the draft was "incomparably worse."

Even the *Tribune* conceded that "Since the commencement of the work a number of persons have been arrested for obstructing the officers, and are now under bail to answer." The case of a young man named Henry Biesel was cited. Upon his release Mr.

Biesel had immediately turned about, charged the arresting deputy marshal with assault and battery, and had *him* taken into custody. The *Tribune* forbore to draw the obvious conclusion: the incident was a cogent example of official New York's sympathetic attitude toward objectors.

Overall, though, the city's reaction had been mild, on the whole. A few enrollment officers canvassing laboring-class neighborhoods had been threatened and reviled. Provost Marshal Joel B. Ehrhardt of the Ninth District had been attacked by a group of dissenters at Broadway and Liberty Street, had held them off at pistol point for some hours, and though finally rescued by police, had been compelled to withdraw without completing his rolls. Such instances notwithstanding, the hardbitten populations of the Five Points, the Bowery, and the Fourth Ward seemed to be accepting the whole business meekly enough. There were plenty of rumors, threats, hints of dire things in the wind. But the *Tribune*, for one, saw nothing in them. "Many stories have been circulated," an editorial noted, "to the effect that bands, gangs and companies have been organized here and there with the intention of resisting the draft, and that the members are armed and drilled, hold secret meetings and so forth; but from all that we can learn, no such organizations exist, and even if they did they will amount to nothing."

The writer reported all quiet in Brooklyn, too. But he admitted—overlooking the apparent contradiction—that there was a great deal of excitement abroad in the streets. "The draft appears to be the general subject of conversation all over the city."

That was the final word on Saturday morning, July 11, the day set for the actual drawing of names to begin. The Ninth District office was the only one of several in the city that was ready. But there, at Number 677 Third Avenue, near Forty-sixth Street, operations got under way as planned.

Chapter 7 | "Poor Jones!"

THE DOORS OPENED PROMPTLY AT NINE O'CLOCK. A large, impatient crowd had been waiting in the street, and more than a hundred men and women immediately pushed their way inside. There were some mutterings and sullen faces among them, but the mood seemed on the whole amazingly good-natured, considering all the early fuss that had been raised about conscription. The only uniforms in evidence were those of a small detail—only two or three troopers, apparently—from the Invalid Corps. This, made up of veterans unfit for combat service because of wounds or other infirmities, was the unit normally assigned to light garrison duty in civilian areas. Thus, whether by design or not, any appearance of military coercion in the proceedings to follow had been held to a minimum.

A contemporary drawing of the scene shows a large, high-ceiled, rather bleak room, barren of all decoration save for a pair of crossed American flags fastened to the gas fixture overhead. The hollow lottery drum to be used in the drawings was mounted in plain sight, on a dais in the center of the room. Directly in front of this was a long table at which the enrollment clerks, eight or ten of them, sat with their sheaves of papers. No railing or other barrier separated them from the crowd; its front ranks pressed right in upon them, and the rest of it filled every corner of the room in a tight-packed, jostling mass.

The procedure was brisk and businesslike. There were no important personages on hand. No speeches solemnized the occasion, and no invocation was given. Taking his stand upon the dais, Captain Charles E. Jenkins, U.S. provost marshal for the Ninth

Congressional District, "in a clear voice read his orders from the President of the United States and his instructions from Provost Marshal General Fry." He then announced that the drawing would begin with the Twenty-second Ward; that he had appointed Charles H. Carpenter, one of the enrollment clerks, to do the drawing; and that another clerk, George W. Southwick, would turn the drum. A little self-consciously, perhaps, Carpenter removed his jacket and rolled up his right shirt sleeve. "At a quarter before ten o'clock," wrote the *Tribune* reporter present, "everything being in readiness, the wheel was turned several times, when the lid was unlocked, and Mr. Carpenter, who had in the meantime been blindfolded, introduced his bare arm into the box and brought forth one of the little rolls. Captain Jenkins opened the ballot and read aloud the name of

"WILLIAM JONES, 46th street near 10th Avenue."

The crowd had waited through the preliminaries in tense impatience. Now it rustled, stirred, and unexpectedly reacted with amusement. The name was shouted out into Third Avenue. Snickers, guffaws, rough jeers, ran among the packed hundreds gathered there:

"Well, how are you, Jones!"

"Good for Jones!"

"Poor Jones!"

The draft had pounced on its first fall guy; the lightning had struck the other fellow, and all the momentarily reprieved seemed to find it irresistibly funny. William Jones was present. It was said that he took it all in good spirit, though apparently no one thought of recording any remarks he may have made.

The drawing went on. The crowd did not wander away. Instead, it grew, if anything, throughout the day. Here and there men grumbled, swore, and exchanged abusive opinions of the Abolitionists, Mr. Lincoln, and the well-heeled rich. Now and then a woman shrieked that she'd never let them take her man. But there was no disorder. The names of the unlucky were announced matter-of-factly, impersonally, as if by rote. Some of them helped to keep the humor from going sour. A half-dozen of the district's enrollment officials heard their own names called, to the crowd's vast and vocal satisfaction. A neighborhood politician, a city councilman named Joyce, was drawn. There was a sardonic round of cheers for Joyce. "Mother Cull" drew some laughter and crude wit. But it turned out that "Mother" was the actual name of a man living on West Forty-sixth Street. By six o'clock that evening 1,236 names had come out of the drum—a considerable day's work. Captain Jenkins announced that only 264 more would fill the district's quota; the drawing would be resumed on Monday morning. The spectators filed out, the doors of Number 677 were closed, and the crowd on Third Avenue slowly dispersed.

Elsewhere in the city the draft's first day passed with only one small hint of trouble. Into Central Police Headquarters at 300 Mulberry Street came a tip warning of a plot by the Knights of the Golden Circle to seize the U.S. Arsenal at Seventh Avenue and Thirty-fifth Street.

The circumstances surrounding this tip are vague, and probably were at the time. Then as now, such tips, frequently anonymous, were a routine part of police work. In any case, the Knights of the Golden Circle were much too real to be ignored. Largest of the many quasi-military secret societies which had sprung up out of the national turmoil, they were like practically all of the others—Democrat-oriented and rabidly pro-Secessionist, professing a militant patriotism dedicated to "restoring the Union as it was." The organization was known to have a large and active membership, perhaps as many as three hundred thousand altogether. And though its main strength was centered in the states of the old Northwest—today's Midwest—New York's own Fernando Wood was generally believed to be its leader, with such eminent Copperheads as his brother Benjamin and the Ohioans Clement L. Vallandigham and George Pendleton as top associates. There was a great deal of mumbo jumbo about the whole business. Members were sworn in with solemn oaths of faith and secrecy, and customarily identified one another by means of a complicated sequence of passwords and responses based on the letters in the name of John C. Calhoun, South Carolina's late, great champion of the slave states. In the superheated emotional atmosphere of a nation locked in civil war, this sort of rigmarole was impressive. It tended to invest the Knights with a somewhat exaggerated aura of ominous threat. Undoubtedly a high percentage of the membership was harmless—either crackpots, sincere peace men, or the type of habitual joiner always attracted by secret ritual and the trappings of mystery. But undoubtedly, also, the order had its hard core of bitter and desperate partisans who might be capable of real treason if sufficiently aroused. The Knights were by their nature active objectors to the Enrollment and Conscription Act, of course. And so, on the face of it, any harebrained rumor of a plot to interfere with the draft by violence was likely to name them as prime movers. Still, considering some of the things that already had happened around the Union that spring and summer, such a plot was not by any means farfetched.

Just in case, Superintendent of Police John A. Kennedy dispatched a Sergeant Van Orden with fifteen patrolmen to the arsenal. They found a good-sized crowd loitering about the vicinity, but no real signs of a disturbance in the making. The sergeant marched his men into the building and stationed them at their guard posts without incident, and after a while the crowd began to drift away. If there had in fact been any mischief plotted, the plotters would seem to have been singularly lacking in resolution.

So much for the tip, and so much for all the other rumors that had drifted about New York City for the past week or more. It appeared that the *Tribune* had been right: the angry talk and the dire predictions amounted to nothing.

Long afterward, however, a man by the name of Charles Loring Chapin would remark on the poor judgment that had led authorities to choose a Saturday on which to begin the draft drawings. "The opportunity was thus given," he would point out, "for the list of . . . names drawn to be conned over and commented upon during Sunday by men who enlivened their discussion by the plentiful use of bad whiskey."

This was hindsight, to be sure. At the time, Mr. Chapin undoubtedly had no more intimation of what was to come than any other average, respectable New Yorker. But when it did come, it happened that his job would give him a uniquely intimate observation post. Charles Chapin was an operator with the Metropolitan Police Department's telegraph bureau. This, located in the basement of the big stone headquarters building on Mulberry Street, was the nerve center of the department's communications system—five main telegraph lines that branched off to cover the city, providing instant contact with each of the thirty-two local

N. Y. Historical Society

"AN HONEST AFFABLE BUSINESSMAN, NOT A STRONG POLITI-CAL LEADER..." George Opdyke, Republican mayor of New York City. *(p. 43)*

*"RIOTERS, PERFECTLY
FRENZIED WITH
LIQUOR, ROAMED
ABOUT IN EVERY
DIRECTION..."* The artist
for the *New York Illustrated
News* may very well have
sketched this scene from life.
(p. 75)

N. Y. Historical Society

SACKING OF THE BROWNSTONE HOUSES IN LEXINGTON AVENUE BY THE RIOTERS ON MONDAY, JULY 13

N. Y. Historical Society

"*...ARMED THEM WITH STOUT LOCUST WOOD CLUBS.*" Police Captain George W. Walling, the gangsters' nemesis. *(p. 38)*

Prints Division, N. Y. Public Library

"*AS RELENTLESS AS DEATH IN THE PERFORMANCE OF THE DUTIES HE NOW ASSUMED.*" Metropolitan Police Commissioner Thomas C. Acton. *(p. 77)*

N. Y. Historical Society

"*LONG YEARS OF CORRUPT POLITICS AND PANDERING TO THE MOBS...*" Fernando Wood, ex-mayor of New York and reputed leader of the Knights of the Golden Circle. *(p. 166)*

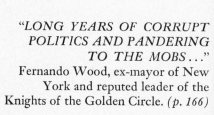

precinct stations in the Metropolitan District. The system was a relatively new one, possibly the most modern in the nation at the time. The force which manned it, though small, was well organized and efficient. It consisted of a superintendent, James Crowley; his deputy, Eldred Polhamus; four telegraph operators; and two linemen. And in the week ahead they would all earn their pay many times over. Chapin himself was, at thirty-five, already a man of considerable attainments in his field. A member of an old New York family—his father was politically active and a former editor of the *Sun*—he was a lifelong friend of Samuel F. B. Morse and had been one of Morse's first telegraph operators at the age of sixteen, in fact. Before he was twenty he had been among those chosen to go to Europe to build the first telegraph system in Germany. Later he had been called to St. Petersburg to give a personal demonstration of telegraph operation before Czar Nicholas I of Russia. In the United States he was credited, among other things, with having introduced telegraphy into American railroad operation, as a divisional superintendent on the New York and Erie in 1852. Backed by such credentials, it appears that Chapin enjoyed the friendship and confidence of high police officials at Mulberry Street to a degree unusual in a civilian employee.

In 1890, a man getting well along in years, he would look back on the week that followed the beginning of the draft and jot down some of his recollections, not always accurately as to detail, but with honesty, shrewd insight, and some acerbic comments on things as he saw them. Apparently his account was written purely as a record for his family, with no thought of its publication. It fills two thick notebooks. Later they were presented by his granddaughter to the New-York Historical Society, where they are today.

On Sunday, July 12, 1863, however, Mr. Chapin's journal still was a matter for the distant future. The day itself was scarcely noteworthy. It was a hot one, sultry and still. Governor Horatio Seymour was in town again, this time for a brief inspection tour of the New York harbor defenses enroute to a seashore holiday at Long Branch, New Jersey. The governor expressed himself as dissatisfied with what he saw. Neither the guns in the harbor fortifications nor the warships based at the Brooklyn Navy Yard, he asserted, were adequate to repel a possible foray by any of the notorious Confederate commerce raiders then at sea. The point was a touchy one for New Yorkers, already extremely conscious of their exposed position in the nation's premier seaport. The governor may have meant his remarks as additional barbs for the much criticized Republican Administration. On the other hand, they could hardly be challenged as the pro-Southern sentiments he had been accused of harboring. But not even the partisan Democratic press chose to make very much of them, and the tour passed without any official fanfare.

Mayor George Opdyke—who disliked Seymour personally in addition to their obvious political differences—spent a quiet day at his home, Number 79 Fifth Avenue, and attended the theater with friends that evening. His family was away at the seashore.

Throngs of ordinary citizens trooped into Central Park in search of coolness and fresh air. Many of them climbed to the top of the reservoir there, apparently hoping that the higher altitude might be blessed with a breeze. But there was none. In the city's meaner districts the poor sought relief from their steamy tenement cells in the streets. And wherever they congregated, the draft seemed to be the major topic of conversation, as the *Tribune* had noted on Friday. Strangely, however, only one editor bothered to try for a specific sampling of the public temper now that conscription was a reality. That was James Gordon Bennett of the *Herald*, who assigned a reporter to make a swing through the Twenty-second Ward and write what he saw and heard. The *Herald* had hurried a special edition onto the streets with a complete list of the names drawn on Saturday, and everyone seemed to have a copy. Saloons in New York, as in most American cities, did not close on Sundays, and like Mr. Chapin, the reporter was impressed mainly by the heavy drinking that went on. The mood had turned surly again; yesterday's levity was gone. The journalist quoted one barroom conversation, led off by a man who predicted black eyes and bloody noses "if Lincoln attempts to enforce the draft in New York."

Said a fellow drinker, jabbing straight at the sore spot: "Aye, indeed, bad luck to him. Does he think that poor men are to give up their lives and let rich men pay three hundred dollars in order to stay home?"

Another, having downed his third bourbon, opined that, "If we had them in Cork the devil a bit of them would cross our path with their 'lattetats.' " And a fourth bravo, fortified with "four brandies and three gin cocktails," cried truculently, "Let them come on, and I will resist the whole draft myself!"

But his story in Monday's paper would make the reporter's own opinion clear. He saw all this as nothing but low comedy, and would write it up that way. Perhaps he failed to visit the old frame barn on Broadway near West Fifty-eighth Street that housed the "Black Joke," pride and joy of Volunteer Fire Company Number 33. Or it may be that he did drop by and was not greatly impressed by anything he heard there, either. By chance, though, a neighborhood tough and small-time political hanger-on, Pete Masterson by name, was one of those called up in Saturday's drawing. And Masterson happened to be the Black Jokes' captain. On an idle Sunday afternoon in summer the engine house was a natural gathering place for the burly fire boys and their admiring satellites, and afterward there were those who professed to recall some ominous threats made there. But this was all hearsay. Later a few writers would mention it, vaguely and without any documentation. Even the name of Masterson is doubtful; some said that one Thomas Cassidy was the Black Jokes' drafted captain.

Tough talk was cheap that Sunday. Few read anything sinister into it.

So the day passed. By evening some uglier things were happening. The police, denying any expectation of unusual trouble, seem nevertheless to have been very alert to the possibilities, and headquarters was well informed. The first report of any consequence was telegraphed in by Thomas Dusenbury, one of sixteen plain-clothes detectives on the force. A certain John Andrews, he said, was making inflammatory antidraft, anti-Negro speeches to crowds along Allen Street in the Tenth Ward. Andrews was not unknown to the police. A down-at-heel lawyer from Virginia, he had been in the city since 1859. Police regarded him as "an habitual associate of thieves and prostitutes," though he did not, apparently, have a criminal record himself. Dusenbury seemed to think the man's activities suspicious enough to be followed up, for he concluded his report by saying that he would stick with Andrews. And Sergeant John Young, chief of detectives at headquarters, thought it sufficiently important to be called to Kennedy's personal attention. The superintendent refused to be alarmed. He took no action, and Dusenbury evidently lost his man sometime later, for nothing more was heard of Andrews that night. It was a pity. His further activities might have told much.

Other reports came in. Around the Five Points several Negroes were attacked and badly beaten in the streets. In a Baxter Street dive known to be a favorite haunt of Five Points gangsters, Detective John McCord heard an unidentified man boasting that next day would see a Negro hanging from every lamppost in New York. Throughout the early hours of the night, too, an unusual number of fires were reported around the foot of Carmine Street in lower Manhattan. Significantly, the area was a Negro slum, and some of the reports mentioned a gang, or gangs, of drunken white men seen prowling about the vicinity. Still it appears that Kennedy issued no special orders. From his own point of view, no doubt, he had valid reasons. Drunken brawls were everyday occurrences in the Five Points, certainly, and fire was a constant danger in all slum districts. Too, some disorder probably had been expected as a natural aftermath of the draft's first day. There was little to indicate that the police could not handle it in the normal, routine way. Monday would be a new day, a working day, with men too busy at their jobs to stir up mischief. . . .

The city finally slept. Or most of it did. There were some, possibly a great many, who did not go to bed at all that Sunday night. Sleep must have been difficult in the stifling heat. But there can be no doubt, either, that something else was at work during the dark hours after midnight. Perhaps most of it was plain discontent—a sullen ferment of resentments bottled up too long and now goaded toward the bursting point. And somehow, sometime along toward Monday's dawn, some mysterious catalyst set the rampage off.

II Explosion: The First Day

Chapter 8 | "No Draft!"

By nine o'clock, Charles Chapin would recall later, "indications of the coming storm began to show themselves."

In fact, the indications were apparent somewhat earlier than that. The police, if not precisely taken by surprise, were a little slow to get the word. The day had dawned hot and overcast, with a promise of greater sultriness to come. The sun was scarcely above New York's rooftops when the advance guard of an exodus from the lower East Side moved slowly across Broadway and gathered along Eighth and Ninth avenues on the middle West Side. This in itself was unusual, for slum toughs seldom wandered far outside their own stamping grounds unless bound on gang forays or election-day assignments. By six o'clock the movement was well defined. Milling groups along both streets began to clot together into two great, loose mobs. Their manner was angry, the evidence of some common purpose unmistakable. A great many of the men were armed, mostly with sticks, iron bars, bludgeons, and brickbats—the usual crude weapons of poor men looking for trouble. Here and there speakers began to harangue anyone who would listen, and around them crowds quickly thickened and grew. Unfortunately for the record, eyewitnesses were few at this early hour. Reporters for the city's many newspapers were not yet on the streets and would not be for some time. No one was able to say with any certainty that these roughly dressed, angry men were Dead Rabbits, or Bowery Boys, or members of any other of New York's organized gangs. And no one was able, later, to name any of the rabble-rousers or repeat what they were saying. At 300 Mulberry Street the night force went off duty at six o'clock and the day men came on. In the midst of the routine of changing shifts, the first reports reaching there were apparently scanty and struck no one as especially alarming. But it soon became plain enough—it could almost be taken for granted, anyway—that this was a demonstration against the draft.

What several observers did notice was the very large number of women among the groups. Many were armed like their menfolk, and most were even shriller and more savage as the noise and fury steadily mounted. Still, for a while, the loose crowds and clumps of people showed little disposition to act.

Then, as they grew in numbers they began a slow drift northward along Eighth and Ninth avenues, the women trailing behind like camp followers. Smaller groups began to split off from the main bodies, darting into side streets to invade shops, factories, and construction sites—where the working day began early in the 1860's—and urge the workmen there to join the march. A majority of them did. Some claimed later that they had little choice, would have been beaten up had they hung back. And this was true. But mob hysteria was growing; it was a contagious thing, and many undoubtedly were caught up in it and carried away. The draft was, after all, a legitimate target for a poor man's resentment, and Sunday's long, drunken brooding had no doubt left hangovers. As yet, too, it was a comparatively orderly demonstration. A few foremen and proprietors were manhandled when they objected to the disruption of their work forces. A great many more were threatened, warned that their premises would be wrecked or burned down if they tried to interfere. The mob still was something of a headless monster, its purpose not quite hardened. But it was feeling its strength.

It was almost eight o'clock now. Away from the line of march, people all over town were shaking off the Monday-morning doldrums and going about their business, unaware that this day would be in any way unusual. In the fancier residential districts uptown, well-to-do New Yorkers were sitting down to breakfast and the morning paper of their choice. On Mulberry Street police officials still saw no reason for alarm. Around seven A.M., according to the New York *Times* next day, Superintendent Kennedy was informed that the entire crew of a street contractor in the Nineteenth Ward had failed to appear for work. The *Times* would infer that this was headquarters' first inkling that something was amiss. The circumstance was unusual, obviously. It might even presage a strike or some similar trouble. But at the time it could hardly have been construed as a warning of what was to come.

The mob's two straggling columns, meanwhile, finally streamed together in a large vacant lot just east of Central Park. No one, then or afterward, ever documented the precise line of march which brought them there. For that matter, no one ever was able to explain why they had congregated on the city's West Side to begin with, why they headed north at all, or why they crossed the park from west to east. It could scarcely have happened by chance, for the location was an unlikely one for such a rendezvous. The area was then, as it still is, an upper-class residential district, though considerably less built up than it is today. It was far north in the New York of 1863—a long way from the normal territory of these slum dwellers, and on a very roundabout route indeed toward the logical targets of the mob's wrath. These could only be the draft office on Third Avenue a block or so south of Forty-seventh Street or the one scheduled to open that morning on lower Broadway. Nevertheless, there the mob was. And again for a while agitators proceeded to harangue its masses. Still there were no reputable witnesses present to identify these agitators or to report their words. To the very end, with only a few exceptions, the leaders of this mob would remain shadowy, faceless men. But their job could not have been difficult. Shortly after eight o'clock the mob was on the move again. It poured south down Fifth and Sixth avenues in two hurrying, close-packed columns, flourishing weapons in the air and bellowing defiance of Abe Lincoln, provost marshals, and the Federal government in general. Somewhere along the line it had acquired placards, either prepared beforehand or improvised as anger mounted. NO DRAFT!, they read, the big, crudely daubed letters tossing above the flood. If they had not known exactly what they meant to do before, these people had made their minds up now.

They might have been stopped earlier. They were very nearly unstoppable now. Far south on Mulberry Street reports continued to clatter off the telegraph sounders. It became apparent that something more serious than a mere demonstration of protest was under way. About eight-thirty Superintendent Kennedy made his first countermove. Captain G. T. Porter of the Nineteenth police precinct was ordered to the Third Avenue enrollment office with sixty patrolmen from the precinct station, on East Fifty-ninth Street near Third. Captain F. C. Speight was dispatched with a force of sixty-nine from the Twenty-ninth precinct house, on East Twenty-ninth Street near Fourth Avenue, to guard the Broadway office.

About that same time, the heads of the mob's twin columns swept out of Fifth and Sixth avenues into Forty-seventh Street. Turning east, they merged into one. "These bodies were so large," wrote Charles Chapin later, "that they filled the broad streets from curb to curb in a compact mass and occupied twenty-five minutes in passing at any single point."

He added that, "It was a strangely weaponed, ragged, coatless army as it heaved tumultuously toward Third Avenue."

Certainly, the mob had grown to formidable size by this time. Some others who saw the mass of marchers rolling down Forty-seventh Street estimated it later as anywhere from five to fifteen thousand strong. And at nine o'clock Kennedy realized that he had an emergency to deal with. Out over the police telegraph system went the message: "To all stations in New York and Brooklyn: Call in your reserve platoons and hold them at the stationhouse subject to further orders."

Thus far the marchers had not behaved badly, for a mob. While they had gone on dragging workers from their jobs along the route and enlisting them, willy-nilly, there still had been little pillaging or destruction. But now, as the large mass of the mob tramped down Forty-seventh Street, smaller masses began to spill over onto the Harlem and New Haven Railroad right-of-way which ran nearby. There they proceeded to tear down the telegraph poles and cut the wires. Several men burst into a hardware store on Forty-seventh and seized axes and hatchets to help in the work. Whether this was part of some prearranged plan or an impulse followed on the spur of the moment, it appears to have been the first deliberate effort made to cut the city off from outside aid. (A bit later in the morning witnesses were to report seeing a gang of burly Irish women armed with crowbars methodically tearing up the tracks of the Fourth Avenue street railway.)

The mob itself, growing every minute, streamed on down Forty-seventh and swung south into Third Avenue. It was within sight now of its objective.

Captain Porter and his sixty patrolmen had arrived at Number 677 some time before. They found about two hundred men and women already collected in the street—a rougher-looking crowd than Saturday's. There were clubs and knives in evidence and some drinking going on, bottles passing from hand to hand, the air noisy with surly imprecations. In the forefront, some witnesses declared, were Pete Masterson—or Tom Cassidy—and his boys of the Black Joke Volunteer Fire Company, all decked out in their black shirts and leather firemen's hats. They jeered at the police detail, swaggered truculently, but kept their distance as Porter lined his patrolmen up across the front of the building with drawn nightsticks. When the main mob's vanguard came sweeping down from Forty-seventh Street, it too hesitated, plainly taken aback by the show of police force. But the vast mass of the mob behind could not be stopped. It pushed on in its shouting thousands until eventually it clogged Third Avenue for several blocks both north and south of the enrollment office. Third was a busy avenue at that hour of the morning, but horse cars and carriages bound downtown were stalled, their horses unhitched and driven off. Many of the cars themselves were heaved off the rails and overturned. Drivers and passengers were dragged into the street. Those who looked like laboring men were recruited, the reluctant ones with curses and blows if necessary. Well-dressed citizens were sometimes threatened and reviled but allowed to go their ways. The NO DRAFT! placards were paraded back and forth to the accompaniment of wild cheering. Still there was no concerted rush on the enrollment office. Faced with the file of big bluecoats and locustwood clubs, the mob's nerve appeared to falter. Inside the office, after some delay, the drawing of names began.

James Crowley, superintendent of the police telegraph bureau, was among the thousands of New Yorkers on their way to work that morning. He had taken the Third Avenue street railway as usual, and it happened that his was one of the cars stalled in the congested street. Here, too, gangs had started to chop down telegraph poles and rip down wires; it was the first thing Crowley saw as he left the car. And he knew—whether or not anyone in the mob did—that this Third Avenue telegraph line was an important part of the police system. For the moment the telegrapher in him overcame discretion. Shouldering through the crush to the nearest gang of choppers, he ordered them to stop.

"He's one of them!" bawled a man. "Hang him!"

Others closed in. "Smash him!" they shouted. "Kill him!"

Crowley was seized and roughly manhandled, threatened again with hanging. But he kept his head, managed somehow to convince the crowd that he meant them no harm, and slipped away at last. In the confusion he got free of the swirling mob and ran the few blocks to the Nineteenth precinct police station. There he hurried off a telegram received at the Mulberry Street headquarters at nine-fifteen: "Laborers have suspended work and are gathering with crowbars and other weapons for grand demonstration at 677 Third Avenue. Trouble brewing. Telegraph lines cut. Rush large force."

Possibly this was the clearest, most concise summary of what was going on that headquarters had yet received. Apparently it was already too late, though the timing of the events which followed is somewhat puzzling. Some newspapers would say next day that the drawing of names did not get under way at Number 677 until ten-thirty. And still the mob seems to have milled about in disorder for some little time before it acted. Most witnesses recalled afterward that a pistol fired by some unknown man in the crowd was the spark that touched off the explosion. Others, recalling no shot, thought that the calling out of the morning's 264th and final name was the signal.

The office windows crashed in, shattered by a hail of bricks and cobblestones. The Black Jokes charged forward, were beaten back by police clubs, then shoved irresistibly on again by the weight of the howling throng behind. For a few furious minutes the police stood their ground. But it was hopeless—sixty men against thousands. As they were forced back, Captain Porter ordered them into the building for a final stand. Before they could bar the door, however, the mob was on them in a yelling, overwhelming mass that filled the office. Provost Marshal Jenkins and his people snatched up their enrollment lists and fled through a back door. Stubbornly sticking together, the policemen fought their way out behind them without losing a man. A rear alley led out into Second Avenue, and thus they made their escape. The rioters did not bother with pursuit. For a while they busied themselves with smashing the hated lottery drum and the office furniture and trying to break open the marshal's iron safe. When it resisted their best efforts, they presently drenched the wreckage with turpentine—several cans of which had been brought along for the purpose, apparently—and set it on fire.

After that a number of things began to happen at once, or so close together that it became next to impossible to sort them all out in any exact sequence. The mob still was growing by the minute. It was so huge already that only a fraction of it had been able to crowd into the enrollment office or even to get very close. The rest, wild with excitement as word was passed of the police rout, milled farther up and down Third Avenue and over into the streets east and west. Again, witnesses were struck by the savage behavior of the women. Wrote one: "Prominent among those who made the first attack, and who also urged on their relatives and acquaintances . . . to carry on the work of demolition, were quite a large number of women. These latter were also armed, principally with bricks and stones, which they used with much precision in sending them through the windows and aiming them at the heads of those who made any show of resistance. . . ."

The mob was ready for anything now, and there was a tumultuous, yelling rush to meet a detachment of fifty Invalid Corps troopers who just then came marching north up Third Avenue. Some of these troopers were leathery veterans and some were scarcely more than striplings, but they all had been blooded in battle and bore the wounds to prove it. And they were well armed, with bayonets affixed to muskets and sabers at their sides. But they came a trifle late. Superintendent John A. Kennedy had asked help of the military authorities in the city at about the same time he had sent Captain Porter's detail to Number 677. The troop commander, Lieutenant Abel Reade, himself limping on a foot maimed at Fredericksburg, had expected to reinforce the patrolmen. Instead he was just in time to meet the aroused mob head on. A shower of paving stones and brickbats knocked several of his men down. Shocked at so rude a reception, Reade halted his command, formed it in a double line blocking the street, and called on the mob to retire. It came on. He ordered his front rank to fire a volley of blank cartridges over the foremost rioters' heads. Then, as they still came on, he ordered his second rank to load with ball and aim low. That felled a half-dozen of the mob and brought the rush up short for a moment. But almost instantly a wave of men and women surged ahead again through the stinging powder smoke, cursing and screaming for revenge. Bewildered troopers felt the muskets wrenched out of their hands as they tried to reload. Hopelessly outnumbered, swarmed under, clubbed and stabbed with their own weapons—men in no condition, anyway, for this kind of hand-to-hand fighting—they broke and ran south down Third Avenue with the horde yelling at their heels. Most of them got away, though some were chased as far as Twentieth Street before the mob gave up. At least two were not so lucky.

One, doubling into Forty-first Street, found himself cut off and surrounded at the corner of First Avenue. A woman tried to run him through with his own bayonet. Another, not quite lost to pity yet, struck the blade aside and took it away from her. But the struggling victim was knocked down, beaten and kicked savagely, and at last left dead on the sidewalk. A second trooper tried to escape by scrambling up a rockpile near Forty-second Street. But a mass of toughs followed him, "grabbed him, and taking him to the top of the rocks stripped his uniform off him, and after beating him almost to a jelly, threw him over a precipice some twenty feet high on the hard rocks beneath. . . ."

These would be incidents briefly noted in the *Tribune* next day. Reporters from nearly every New York paper were gathering at the scene now. Their front-page accounts in Tuesday's early editions would pull the whole grim picture into a true perspective, of sorts. In these waning hours of Monday morning, however, no one yet understood the full magnitude or the bitter fury of this thing running loose in the city's streets.

Chapter 9 | "You Must Organize!"

AT CENTRAL POLICE HEADQUARTERS, as the minutes ticked away after nine o'clock, the situation must have appeared somewhat clearer. Reports had been telegraphed in from every precinct by that time, and most of them were on the encouraging side. Captain Speight and the sixty-nine patrolmen assigned to the Broadway enrollment office had encountered a large, noisy crowd there but had been able to disperse it without difficulty. The drawing of names was proceeding in a normal, orderly manner. Elsewhere around the big Metropolitan Police District there were some signs of unrest—mostly crowds gathering and loitering—but no open disorders. It seemed that Third Avenue was the only trouble spot. But there conditions were plainly not improving.

About this time, too, the telegraph lines to most of the precincts in the northern sections of Manhattan went dead, thus verifying the word from James Crowley. For the moment it was not too serious, since all stationhouses already had been ordered to stand by. But Superintendent Kennedy grew more and more concerned for the safety of Captain Porter's detail. Presently he ordered Captain Speight's detail to Number 677 Third Avenue also. Some time later he ordered other captains to send additional detachments from their precincts. Then, apparently dissatisfied with the scanty information coming in, he decided to go out and make a personal inspection. He set out alone and unarmed, driving his own light one-horse carriage. It was the act of a brave man, which John A. Kennedy unquestionably was, and perhaps of a rash one as well. At that point, though, there probably seemed ample reason to believe that the mob soon would be brought under control.

The better part of an hour passed; perhaps a little more. Headquarters routine went on, no doubt. No one recalled later how the time passed or bothered to put it down on paper if he did. Presently a wagon pulled up in the street outside. In it were two men, with something under a pile of old sacks in the rear. One of the men was John Eagen, resident of a neighborhood to the north around Lexington Avenue, who may or may not have been prominent enough to be known to some there at headquarters. It appears that there was a little difficulty about his admittance, at any rate. He had brought back John A. Kennedy, or what was left of him, but it took a while before the fact sank in. The mob had got Kennedy.

So badly battered was he, so covered with mud and clotted blood, that his closest associates failed to recognize him at first. According to Charles Chapin, "It was difficult to believe that this could possibly be the body of the Supt. of Police and it was refused admission. Only certain jewellry [sic] which he was known to wear established the fact." As soon as it did, Kennedy was hurried off to Bellevue Hospital. Examining surgeons there found his body bruised from head to foot and stabbed or slashed in a score of places. It would be touch and go whether he lived or died.

In the meantime, the Metropolitan District was without a superintendent of police. And now fresh reports were coming in, telling of new defeats for the police—the mob triumphant everywhere.

Captain Speight and his men, heading up Third Avenue toward the beleaguered enrollment office, never had reached there. At Forty-fourth Street the advance guard of the mob had met them in overwhelming numbers and turned them back after a brief, brutal skirmish. A second squad of police, and then a third, had managed only to rescue several downed patrolmen before retreating south on Third Avenue with half their men wounded. Some of the rioters had muskets now, probably taken from the routed Invalid Corps detachment. Worse than that, though, were their massive numbers—a flood of angry humanity that simply could not be handled. A fourth police detail had arrived in Third Avenue, led by a Sergeant McCredie; and shortly afterward a fifth, under Sergeant Wolfe. McCredie, an aggressive, able officer known throughout the force as Fighting Mac, took command of the combined squads. Though totaling only forty-four un-wounded men, they had counterattacked and driven the mob back as far as Forty-fifth Street. Then fresh masses roaring down the avenue and out of the streets on both sides had rolled over them, broken their ranks, and sent them stumbling south in an-other retreat. Not a man of the forty-four had come out of it without injuries. Sergeant McCredie, driven up the front steps of a Third Avenue residence, had been hammered so viciously that he was smashed bodily through the splintered panels of the door. Half-stunned, he had dragged himself up the stairs to a second-floor room, where a young German immigrant woman had just time to hide him on a bed between two feather mattresses. When she persuaded the mob that he had jumped from the window, they set fire to the house and left. The young woman, taking McCredie on her back, somehow made her way over to Lexington Avenue and put him in a hansom cab, which eventually got him to the nearest precinct station. But his injuries were serious; Fighting Mac was out of it.

Such small personal details would not be known till a great deal later, of course. But the main facts were becoming all too plain—full-fledged riot, and no immediate prospect of its being mastered. Other police detachments, flung into the fighting after the rout of McCredie's force, had been chewed up and forced back also. The mob was surging southward almost to Thirty-fifth Street now, starting to loot and destroy, leaving a trail of flaming buildings behind it. Long afterward Charles Chapin's memories remained vivid:

"The scene on 3rd Ave. at this time was appalling.

"It was now noon, but the hot July sun was obscured by heavy clouds which cast dark shadows over the city.

"From the Cooper Institute at 9th St. to 46th St. the avenue, house-tops, windows and steps were crowded with rioters, or spectators.

"As one glanced along the dense mass of men and women the eye rested upon huge columns of smoke rising from burning buildings—for the mob had now begun to plunder and burn—at the north, giving a wild and terrifying aspect to the scene.

"The number of people in the street at this time was roughly estimated to be 50,000. Here and there along the avenue could be seen street cars which had been overturned and thrown from the tracks. . . ."

Among the worst of the fires was the one at the Third Avenue enrollment office, now burning fiercely. The building was a tenement, its upper stories occupied by laboring-class families who should by any rule of reason have had the mob's sympathy. But there was little reason at work here anymore. The watching throng cheered with delight as the flames took hold and frightened tenants came tumbling out into the street. At first, efforts were even made to prevent their leaving the building, and a few men who tried to calm the mob were brutally beaten. One contingent was ordered, or took it upon itself, to hurry to the bell tower at Fifty-first Street and prevent the ringing of any alarm. Apparently this failed, for an engine company and a hose company soon came up. The mob cheered and parted to let them through, then closed in and blocked their every effort to get to work. Finally the crews could only stand helplessly by while the buildings at numbers 675 and 679 Third Avenue also blazed up. In the end most of the block was gutted.

"The rioters were composed of the employees of the several railroad companies; the employees of Brown's iron foundry in 61st St. [and] various factories and street contractors," wrote an eyewitness. But, he conceded, "many had been forced."

The *Tribune*'s reporter wrote that, "The vast crowd swayed to and fro, racing first in this direction, then in that, attacking indiscriminately every well-dressed man. The general cry was 'Down with the rich men!' "

Though the main body of the mob had swept on southward, several thousand still milled about in this section of Third Avenue, apparently at loose ends, their appetite for violence only whetted by the destruction of the enrollment office. And presently a man climbed onto the roof of a shanty at a construction site across from the burning buildings and addressed the crowd. Next day the *Tribune* would identify him as "Mr. Andrews of Virginia" —the first mention of the notorious John Andrews in connection with the actual rioting. But the *Tribune*'s man, who seems to have been the only journalist on hand at this particular spot, admitted in his story that he could hear very little of Andrews' speech. And he added that "any attempt to make a note might bring on . . . an assault from someone in the crowd." But it was obvious, he also added, that Andrews was making a violent attack on the Federal government and the draft and that the crowd listened to him with intense enthusiasm. Many of them, believing at first that he was Benjamin Wood of the New York *Daily News,* hurrahed lustily for Wood. Among some others ran a rumor that he was a reporter for the *Evening Standard.* This was received with less enthusiasm. There were cries of "Hang him! Hang him!" before the crowd realized its error.

Other witnesses, agreeing that the speaker was indeed John Andrews, later described him as about six feet tall, blond and good-looking, with a short beard, and well dressed in a blue coat and striped trousers. Several of them were able to hear somewhat more of what he said than the *Tribune* man.

"You have done nobly," they quoted him, "but I tell you what I want, and what you must do if you wish to be really successful. You must organize!"

"That's the talk," cried voices from the crowd. "You're the boy, my chicken!"

"You must organize and keep together and appoint leaders," Andrews went on, "and crush this damned Abolition draft into the dust."

There was "tremendous cheering" from the crowd.

"If you don't find anyone to lead you," Andrews shouted, "by Heaven! I will do it myself!"

This too drew a wild outburst. Apparently the harangue went on for some time in the same vein. Thereafter, for a while, Andrews dropped out of sight in the confusion. The mob, its fury rekindled, went stamping off on new adventures and allowed the firemen to move in and save what was left of the smoldering block.

Another newspaper reporter was recognized at the corner of Third Avenue and Forty-sixth Street. "Here's a damned Abolitionist," somebody yelled. "Let's hang him!" He was taken by the hair and dragged to a post supporting a store-front awning. But something else distracted the crowd for a moment and he broke away. As he ran down Third Avenue, a well-aimed brickbat struck him on the head; and while he lay stunned in the street, his pockets

were rifled, his watch and all his money stolen. Later he was
pursued and struck down again. But the men of a hook-and-
ladder company beat his tormentors off and helped him into the
firehouse at Fiftieth Street and Lexington Avenue. They barred
the door, and the crowd, after some aimless threats, finally went
off in search of other prey.

The great number of those who had listened to Andrews,
however, probably made up the same mob which soon afterward
stormed down on the Bull's Head Hotel on Forty-third Street
near Lexington. Two or three men who appeared to be leaders
sprang up the front stoop and beat down the door with axes. The
others swept in, plundered and wrecked the place, set it on fire,
and went on. More than once during these first hours of rioting it
was noticed that the mob seemed to be well supplied with cans or
bottles of turpentine. And this inevitably suggested to some observers that the burning was more than a mere destructive impulse. Too, there had been a branch office of the American Telegraph Company at the Bull's Head—the only apparent reason
why it was singled out for attack. The mob's earlier efforts to cut
the lines of communication in the city, and between the city and
the outside world, still continued. Even as flames crackled
through the Bull's Head, other rioters were ripping up the tracks
of the New Haven Railroad for several blocks above Forty-second
Street.

But while this kind of purposeful destruction did argue the
existence of a rough overall strategy by some leader or group of
leaders, various motley bands and gangs now began to pour out
of the Five Points, the Fourth Ward, and all the city's squalid
shantytowns. As always, the grapevine seemed to rival the telegraph itself for speed. These gangs were made up of men and
women—and children, as well—bent only on plunder and the
venting of poverty's ancient grievances in whatever mischief they
could find to do.

In most sections of Manhattan, in these early phases of the
disorder, they met little or no police resistance. Off-duty patrolmen still were being mustered at stationhouses. The heavy fighting that raged southward along Third Avenue required most of
the forces that could be thrown together immediately, and there
still was some confusion as to the nature of the mob outbreaks
and their main objectives, if any. Lone patrolmen caught out on

their beats were fair game for the rioters. One, chased by a crowd on Lexington Avenue, tried to take refuge in the basement of a fine, large mansion at Number 44. But the door was locked, and as he pounded on it in desperation, the lady of the house appeared at an upstairs window and screamed, "For God's sake don't open the door, the house will be destroyed." Her cry, commented the anonymous witness who told the story, "seemed to give the mob the idea to do it." Windows were smashed, the door battered down. The mob swarmed in. Furniture was tossed out into the street and either set on fire or carried off. A valuable library of books and paintings was wantonly torn to pieces, silverware and other valuables stolen, the house itself finally set alight. In the midst of it all the lady of the house with her children and servants fled to the precinct police station, where they were given shelter. The patrolman's fate was not recorded; he too is thought to have escaped in the mob's preoccupation with its loot.

As a gesture of conciliation, Provost-Marshal Nugent had ordered the Broadway enrollment office closed at eleven-fifteen, thus effectively putting the draft out of business in New York City. But the crowd dispersed by Captain Speight that morning, or another one, was back by early afternoon. Not all of its members were toughs, apparently. One man was heard to speak out boldly. "This is an unspeakable outrage," he is supposed to have cried. "As an American citizen, I am ashamed." He got a bloody head for his trouble. The office was broken open, its furniture and equipment smashed, and the building fired. By this time other gangs, perhaps split off from the victorious mob in Third Avenue, were roaming up and down Broadway unchecked. A whole block of buildings between Twenty-fourth and Twenty-fifth streets was burning fiercely. More and more stores, here and in other parts of the city too, were being attacked and plundered now. And, ominously, a great many of them were hardware or sporting-goods establishments, in which the looters were concentrating on guns and other weapons.

Early in the afternoon, also, another large crowd appeared at Mayor George Opdyke's home on Fifth Avenue. No one had thought to provide a police guard for it. But a neighbor, a Colonel B. F. Manierre, called out forty or fifty other residents of the area and organized a hasty defense force. Many of them owned firearms. Stationing themselves about the premises, they met the crowd with such a show of determination that it drew back after a brief, bloodless encounter. A few police detectives had contrived to attach themselves to the fringes of this group without exciting suspicion, and they recognized one of its leaders as a minor underworld character by the name of Peter Dolan. They seized him as the crowd withdrew—probably the first arrest of any rioter that day. Most of these would-be attackers, they reported later, were mere teenage boys. Balked at the mayor's house, a large group of them straggled aimlessly south down Fifth Avenue and presently joined a great throng massing in front of the Colored Orphan Asylum between Forty-third and Forty-fourth streets. From the very beginning, of course, much of the antidraft resentment had been tangled inextricably with latent racial hatreds. Now they were flaring up, naked and vicious. Mr. Chapin expressed the mob's warped logic about as well as anyone: "There would have been no draft but for the war—there would have been no war but for Slavery—the Slaves were black—*ergo*, all blacks were responsible. . . ."

The orphanage was a handsome brick building set in its own spacious grounds. It housed two hundred Negro children, none of them more than twelve years old, attended by a staff of fifty adults. Fortunately the superintendent, one William Davis, kept his head when the mob began to show signs of ugliness. Bolting the front door and barricading it with chairs and tables, he and his assistants hurriedly assembled the children and marched them out through a rear exit. By the time the mob had nerved itself to the point of attacking, they were across the grounds and aboard omnibuses on Madison Avenue, bound for the Twenty-second precinct police station. Bursting in belatedly, the rioters raced through the building venting their frustration on everything in sight. Furniture was hacked apart with axes, draperies torn down, even the few cheap toys left behind by the children carried off or smashed to bits. One frightened little colored girl, somehow overlooked in the exodus, had hidden under a bed. They found her and they killed her. And the rest of it went according to the now familiar pattern—fires set throughout the building, mobsters howling exultantly in the street outside, others fanning out to pillage shops and homes nearby. When two volunteer fire companies answered the alarm, the mob massed to drive them back.

Nevertheless, Chief Engineer John Decker and fifteen of his firemen fought their way through, connected up their hoses, and made their way into the burning orphanage. A brave try, but fruitless; the mob rallied, plunged in after them, and threw them into the street again. The orphanage burned to the ground, and three other buildings in the block along with it, while Decker was twice knocked off his feet and dragged to a lamppost amid furious cries of "Hang him! Hang him!" In the confusion and the heady flush of victory, they finally lost interest and let him go, but it was a near thing for several minutes.

"They had not yet begun to wantonly destroy life," commented Chapin wryly and not altogether accurately.

That would come. For the moment these roaming mobs were aimless, yet moved by resentful strivings after form and purpose. Already groups of rioters had begun to descend on railroad yards and depots in many localities, ordering the service stopped, the workmen enlisted in the cause. Horse barns of the omnibus companies and street-railway lines were visited too. Managers and foremen had no choice but to obey. It appears that much of this was less a matter of plan than of some vast, angry urge to bring all orderly life in the city to a standstill. Here and there even well-dressed passersby were seized and hustled along with the mobs. Clubs were brandished over their heads, wrote one witness, and they were "frequently kept encouraged by clouts on the sides of their heads."

Wrote another: "About 4 o'clock P.M., the rioters, perfectly frenzied with liquor, roamed about in every direction attacking people and burning every house in which they thought a policeman had taken refuge. . . ."

And still another: "Boys went through the streets, flourishing and firing off pistols, men brandished guns, and mad and hoarse with passion and bad spirits, cursed and swore and threatened every one disagreeing with them in their excesses. Some threatened to kill every 'Black-Republican-nigger-worshiping s__ of a b____,' and burn their houses."

Caught up in scenes like this, fleeing the streets to wait in dread and uncertainty behind barred doors—some feeling a great, slowly growing anger, too—respectable citizens could only wonder: where were the police?

Chapter 10 | " . . . Take No Prisoners"

JOHN KENNEDY LAY UNCONSCIOUS IN BELLEVUE, still nearer dead than alive, and the Metropolitan Board of Police Commissioners had fallen heir to his responsibilities. Already it was apparent that the gentlemen faced a sterner trial than any board had faced since the Metropolitan's painful birth in 1857. They were short-handed at that. Commissioner James Bowen, a recently appointed brigadier general of volunteers, had left for active duty with the Union army some weeks earlier. One of the two members remaining, John C. Bergen, was a Brooklyn resident. And since first reports indicated "great excitement" in Brooklyn—though no actual outbreaks as yet—it seemed logical for him to take charge there and on Staten Island. Commissioner Thomas C. Acton, the Board's president, was thus left in sole command of the police forces in Manhattan.

His associates knew him as a man of nervous temperament, quick in action but cool and firm—a rare combination, plainly. Charles Chapin declared flatly that, "The mantle of authority could not have fallen upon more fitting shoulders." That was written after the fact, but at the time it was no doubt encouraging to citizens like Chapin that the commissioner was a longtime Republican politician in New York, a vigorous backer of the Federal government's war policies, and a founder of the famed Union League. If the disorders threatening to tear the city apart did indeed spring from any militant Copperhead movement—a suspicion inevitable in view of the past week's crop of rumors—Thomas Acton was not the man to coddle it. He would be, in

76

Chapin's words, "as relentless as death in the performance of the duties he now assumed."

He would need to be, for his position was not without its weak spots. A broker by occupation, he had only slight experience in the practical details of police work. He faced some sticky political complications as well. Edward Morgan, the outgoing Republican governor of New York, had appointed the present Board of Commissioners to five-year terms in one of his last official acts before turning the office over to Horatio Seymour. And it was no secret at all that Seymour, determined to replace all three commissioners with Democrats of his own choosing, had been seeking diligently for some legal way to oust them. Superintendent Kennedy, himself a Democrat, had not been on the best of terms with the board, while the police force as a whole still was subject to Tammany pressure in many ways. In the first bewildered shock as news of the rioting broke, in fact, many New Yorkers felt serious doubts that rank-and-file policemen, most of them Irish Catholics, would fight very hard against Irish Catholic rioters. All this must have crossed Thomas Acton's mind as he pondered his opening moves.

Reconstructing those first tense hours, it seems more than probable that the matter of possible Copperhead conspiracy was very much on his mind too. At that point, certainly, the mob's behavior had strongly suggested some definite plan of action. The preliminary massing far north near Central Park; the cutting of telegraph lines during the march on the enrollment office; the concerted fury of the drive down Third Avenue afterward—all these appeared to argue a nervy and intelligent leadership with bigger goals than mere troublemaking. Almost from the moment he took charge, the commissioner's decisions indicate that he was aware of the possibilities. The very first one set his counter-strategy in motion. Police reserves already were mustering at New York's thirty-two precinct stations in response to Kennedy's previous order. Now, convinced that it would be a mistake to throw them into battle piecemeal, Acton ordered them all into 300 Mulberry Street as fast as they could get there.

When they did—*if* they did—he might have something more than a thousand men at his disposal, minus the few absent on sick leave or for other reasons and the small forces that would have to be left to guard the stationhouses. The total strength of the Metropolitan Police District at this time was roughly 2,400 men of all ranks, though only 1,620 were patrolmen. But of this total, a large percentage were assigned to Brooklyn and other communities and could not be withdrawn in any considerable numbers as long as threats existed in their home bailiwicks. Besides, most of the precinct stations north of Sixtieth Street were now out of touch with headquarters because of the severed telegraph lines, hence had not received Acton's order. When they would was an unknown factor. (As events turned out, it was later estimated that he never had more than about eight hundred men available at any one time.) In these first hours after taking command, with several large detachments already committed to the fighting in Third Avenue, he could count on only the headquarters force itself and those of nearby precincts in the south end of Manhattan—probably fewer than fifty men all told.

Acton immediately contacted Mayor Opdyke also, asking that military details be requested from the Federal garrisons of the harbor forts and from all militia units that could be mobilized. Opdyke did so. His Honor was a nervous man. Quite early in the morning a crowd had begun to assemble sullenly in City Hall Park. So far the police detail at the Hall had held it in check, but it was growing steadily, already demonstrating loudly under the mayor's own window. In addition, Opdyke had called an emergency meeting of the New York Common Council. But the Council was strongly Tammany-Democrat and well aware that any mob in New York City probably represented good Tammany votes. Only a half-dozen councilmen appeared—no quorum; the Council could do nothing. It was to be politics as usual, then, riot or no riot. Before long, the crowd still growing in size and truculence, Opdyke would deem it prudent to move his office to a suite at the St. Nicholas Hotel on Broadway at Spring Street.

So Acton waited. Concentrating his reserves at headquarters had been a hardnosed decision to make, for it meant virtually stripping large areas of the city of all protection. If his calculated risk misfired, it could lay him open to bitter censure. What his thoughts were during those first hours of confusion he never said. If he had his doubts, he kept them to himself.

He did not have to wait long. Every plain-clothes detective

then on duty had been sent out to mingle with the rioters and
pick up what information he could. The afternoon still was young
when their first reports began to forecast the mob's next big
objective.

The great, hard core of the riot—by all odds the toughest and
most determined of the rioters—was the vast mass of men and
women who fought their way south in Third Avenue after sacking
Number 677. Having beaten off the counterattacks led by Captain Speight, Sergeant McCredie, and others, these finally came
to a halt around Thirty-fifth Street. They seem to have spent some
time there, milling about in aimless violence. Large groups wandered away to plunder and destroy in the streets east and west.
But the mob was far from satisfied with its victory; it was only at
a temporary loss for some fresh direction. And presently it was
being exhorted again, this time for a drive on the New York State
Armory on Second Avenue at Twenty-first Street and on the
Union Steam Works a block to the north. This latter had been
converted into a factory for the manufacture of army carbines.
And it was obvious to anyone, of course, that both buildings held
large stocks of firearms and ammunition. It was common knowledge, too, that the armory occupied only the top three stories of a
warehouse owned by an importing firm in which Mayor Opdyke
was a partner, making it a natural target for the rioters' spite.
Above all, it seems apparent that the mob's leaders, perhaps surprised by the scope of their own success thus far, were only now
beginning to realize that if their bully boys were properly armed,
they might annihilate opposition completely and have the whole
of New York at their mercy. (Significantly, "To the armory!" was
one of the cries reported about this time by witnesses at the
burning enrollment office several blocks north.) The idea caught
on quickly, though it took a while to get the unwieldy mob moving again. Shortly after two o'clock a march on the armory began.

The detectives' first warnings had been relayed to Captain
John Cameron of the Eighteenth precinct a little earlier, and he
had a police detail on guard at both the armory and the Steam
Works. At two o'clock, further information pointing to the armory
as the more likely to be hit, thirty-two men of the Twenty-fifth
precinct were dispatched there under a sergeant named Burdick.
The Twenty-fifth was the headquarters precinct, its patrolmen

regarded as an elite corps selected for their size and burly phy-
siques and called the Broadway Squad. For this mission they
were armed with carbines in addition to pistols and the ubiquitous nightsticks. Still they were overmatched.

By two-thirty a crowd of some ten thousand was swarming in
Second Avenue before the armory. As before, many of them were
women armed with cobblestones and brickbats. But now there
was a noticeable scattering of guns in the crowd. An hour or more
passed in desultory firing and showers of missiles hurled at every
policeman who showed himself at a window, while the mob
worked itself up to fighting pitch. About four o'clock it was ready.
A big man with a sledgehammer led the charge on the main
entrance. He was shot dead as he smashed his hammer through
the door panels. So was another man, identified as a prominent
gang leader from the Five Points, who jostled him aside and dove
through ahead of him. But the masses coming on behind trampled over both bodies, battered the wrecked door off its hinges,
and stormed inside. It was 677 Third Avenue all over again. The
building could not be held, and in the few minutes before the
remains of the door gave way, Sergeant Burdick led his men out
through a hole in the back wall. The opening was barely a foot
and a half wide; each big patrolman, having squeezed through
with considerable difficulty, had to drop some eighteen feet to the
ground. But they all made it. Fighting off a crowd of hangers-on
who tried to intercept them, they made their way to the Eighteenth precinct stationhouse on East Twenty-second Street. It
was not the Broadway Squad's day, however. Within an hour the
stationhouse was attacked too, and the force had to flee once
more, this time back to headquarters.

The upshot: another defeat for the police. So far they had
failed everywhere. The mob seemed invincible, the armory its
richest prize of the day—and armed with the guns there, it might
well prove invincible from this point on.

So it seemed. But the police were not quite through. The
several squads that had fought the mob in Third Avenue, though
repulsed, had managed to withdraw in fairly good order. And
when the mob turned its main strength against the armory, a
number of these squads were able to unite. Somewhere around a
hundred men, bruised and weary but fighting mad too, now counterattacked down Second Avenue.

The timing was fortuitous. A large part of the mob—no doubt including all its boldest spirits—had jammed inside the armory. The crowd left outside was scarcely more than a rabble, and it broke and scattered as the police advanced. Rioters inside, drawn out by the yells of alarm, found themselves running a gauntlet of locustwood clubs. Most of them turned and ran inside again, passing the word that the police were back in force. Suddenly the prize became a trap. The first of the mob inside the building had discovered that the weapons were kept in a drill hall on the third floor. Now it was crowded with scuffling, jubilant men and women snatching rifles, muskets, and bayonets out of the racks and breaking open cartridge cases. Some were tossing weapons out the windows to friends in the street. Some, hearing the wild commotion below and fearing that the armory might be recaptured, barricaded the drill-room doors for a last-ditch stand. And then, true to mob form, others busily ransacking the lower stories panicked and set the place on fire. The warehouse was an old wooden building, tinder-dry. The flames began to spread out of control immediately, and erstwhile rioters tumbled out of every door and window. Those who came out unarmed were allowed to flee unmolested. But any who carried guns were clubbed down unmercifully by the police cordon. Few in the drill hall escaped at all. Many jumped from windows, killing or maiming themselves on the hard pavement. Most were trapped behind the barricaded doors. They died there, trampled, smothered, or burned alive as the flames ate greedily through the floor beneath and the walls crashed in.

Weeks later, when the city got around to clearing away the debris, more than fifty barrels were filled with human bones and carted off to Potters' Field. It was as close as anyone ever came to counting up the toll.

So great was the confusion gripping New York now, so widespread the disorders great and small, that the catastrophe went almost unnoticed at the time. Charles Chapin, for example, barely mentioned it in his account. Even while the battle for the armory remained in doubt, other reports were coming into headquarters, dumping another hard decision in Commissioner Acton's lap.

The ten thousand who attacked the armory were only part of the mighty mob in Third Avenue. Other crowds had swung off into side streets, carrying terror and violence across the whole breadth of Manhattan Island. Most of this was planless and wanton. But beyond doubt there still were leaders struggling to assert control. And sometime around the middle of the afternoon several of these marauding groups surged back together and headed south down Broadway. Now, once more the mob moved with bold tactical purpose. This time it was nothing less than an all-out drive on central police headquarters itself. Again it was detectives circulating among the rioters who got the word to Mulberry Street. It was no doubt vague and fragmentary; the detectives had to do their work in circumstances of immense danger and difficulty, and the mob itself could not have been wholly sure of what it meant to do. But apparently there was talk, too, of carrying on into the Wall Street financial district, plundering the banks there, and seizing the Federal subtreasury. About the same time, reports came into headquarters of the crowd menacing the mayor's home on Fifth Avenue.

Acton was scarcely ready for a pitched battle. He had fewer than one hundred and fifty fit men at hand, and the oncoming mob in Broadway was estimated to number at least five thousand, perhaps as many as twice that. But he had very little choice. Police headquarters could not be allowed to fall without a fight. And Wall Street in the rioters' hands would mean unutterable chaos—a sure death blow to the city's tottering morale. Number 300 Mulberry Street was a fine new stone building, strong enough to stand a siege if it should come to that. Acton could hold his men there in readiness. Or he could go out and attack the mob.

He chose to attack.

Chapin called the decision a "forlorn hope." He was present at the time, on duty in the telegraph bureau, and so probably reflected the prevailing opinion. In plain, blunt fact, there was not much reason for optimism in anything that had happened up to now. But Chapin also wrote that, "The decisive battle, which must be won or all was lost . . . must not take place upon the narrow streets for the police would be crushed by the mere weight of numbers." So apparently the defeats earlier in the day were laid, in part at least, to the poor locations in which the police had had to fight. For whatever it was worth, Broadway was a wider, more spacious avenue.

Acton had three police inspectors from whom to select a

leader for his striking force. They were Daniel C. Carpenter, James Leonard, and George Dilks—all competent, experienced career officers. (A fourth, Inspector John Folk, was occupied with duties in Brooklyn.) Daniel Carpenter was elected. Possibly he volunteered, for Chapin quoted him as saying, "I'll go, and I'll win this fight, or Daniel Carpenter will never come back alive."

About one hundred and twenty-five patrolmen were lined up in Mulberry Street. According to Chapin, Carpenter said only, "Fall in, men, fall in." And Commissioner Acton then ordered him quietly to "make no arrests." Some other accounts say that Carpenter told the men, "We are going to put down a mob and we will take no prisoners." More likely, in the confusion, excitement, and conflicting information seething about headquarters, no one could be quite sure of anyone's words, then or afterward. A reporter named David Barnes, writing for the New York *Times*, thought that the police were totally unaware at this point of the mob coming down Broadway. Carpenter's mission, Barnes would report later, was simply to disperse the rioters at Mayor Opdyke's residence; hence the encounter in Broadway was wholly accidental.

Whatever actually was said, beyond doubt, was both brief and grim. Carpenter's detachment then stepped out smartly, turned left into Bleecker Street, proceeded two short blocks, and wheeled right into Broadway. Even if Barnes's version was correct, what followed could not have been a complete surprise. The policemen had heard the roar of the advancing mob some time before they reached the corner. Now they saw it ". . . filling the whole street as far as the eye could reach," wrote Chapin, "moving tumultuously forward. . . . Armed with clubs, pitchforks, iron bars, and some with guns and pistols; most of them coatless and hatless, shouting as they came, they presented a wild and savage appearance. . . ."

Behind the mob, burning buildings sent twisting pillars of smoke high into the sky. Ahead of the advance, storekeepers hastily shuttered their shops and fled. Ahead, too, hurried a horde of frightened pedestrians, many of them Negroes. Some pushed or pulled carts piled with whatever possessions they had had time to snatch up. Omnibuses and carriages wheeled frantically into side streets, where drivers and passengers alike abandoned them and ran. On came the mob, led by a man waving a big American flag. These people thought of themselves as patriots, or wanted to appear so. At the leader's side strode another man bearing a huge plank with the mob's scrawled battle cry: NO DRAFT!

Inspector Carpenter was a cool customer. Halting his force, he detached two companies into the side streets left and right, with orders to hasten north to Fourth Street and then converge on Broadway to strike the mob in the rear. "He waited until they had reached the positions assigned them," wrote Chapin, "then shouted, '*By the right flank. Company front, double quick.* *Charge!*' "

The mob had stopped also, in apparent surprise at the appearance of an attacking force. A hundred or so of the rioters had turned aside into the LaFarge House, a hotel at Amity Street, to chivy the Negro servants there. The rest, after a few moments of indecision, rolled forward again behind a barrage of bricks, stones, and gunshots. Some patrolmen fell. But Carpenter, running several paces out in front of his first rank, met a huge tough who sprang ahead of the mob to meet him. The tough swung furiously at his head with an iron bar, missed, and was sent sprawling by the inspector's nightstick. To a patrolman named Thompson went the honor of capturing the mob's flag; its NO DRAFT! standard went down, as another with the good Irish name of Doyle knocked its bearer staggering. The ranks came together with a roar, and it was close-quarter fighting then, the mob's mass and savagery against the disciplined courage of the police. Discipline told—locustwood clubs rising and falling and rising again almost in unison, bloodied now and terrible; the close-packed, yelling crowd still surging in to break and bear them back. Then the two flanking groups plunged in from Fourth Street. ". . . The battle ground had been well chosen," Chapin wrote. "The confusion and uproar became terrific—the mass surged hither and thither; now rolling up Broadway and again thrust back; or shoved up against the buildings, now seeking to escape from the murderous storm of blows. . . ."

It lasted perhaps fifteen minutes. At the end, the mob's retreat became a rout. They fled back up Broadway and down every alley and side street, "closely pursued by the police, whose clubs never ceased to fall as long as a fugitive was within reach.

N.Y. Historical Society

"*THIS SIR FORCIBLE FEEBLE IS HIMSELF CHIEFLY RESPONSIBLE FOR THE OUTRAGE ...*" New York's Democratic Governor Horatio Seymour. *(p. 119)*

"...AND CRUSH THIS DAMNED ABOLITION DRAFT INTO THE DUST." The scene in Third Avenue as an artist for the *Illustrated London News* visualized it, no doubt with some imaginative license, but with considerable accuracy as well. *(p. 71)*

N. Y. Historical Society

THE RIOTS IN NEW YORK: THE MOB BURNING THE PROVOST MARSHAL'S OFFICE

N. Y. Historical Society

"AN UNLIKELY FIGURE FOR A HERO..." Neverthe-less, staunch *Tribune* editor Horace Greeley refused to be cowed by the mobs which threatened to hang him. *(p. 95)*

"I BEG OF YOU TO LISTEN TO ME AS YOUR FRIEND..." Typical of public disgust with Governor Seymour's performance was this cartoon by Thomas Nast of the *New York Times.* *(p. 117)*

N. Y. Historical Society

"Broadway," Chapin's story concluded, "looked like a battle-field thickly strewn with prostrate forms."

Miraculously, Carpenter did not lose a man. For all that, it had not been a cheap victory. Training and discipline had been the only difference. Many of the rioters had fought with great bravery, giving as good as they got, and scarcely a patrolman had come off unwounded. A score or more were injured seriously enough to be carried or helped back to headquarters, and from there to the hospital; some of them would be out of action for a long time to come. Downed rioters were left where they lay, the injured with the dead. It was the rule that would be followed from here on—no quarter asked on either side, and no comfort given to the enemy. But the mob took care of its own. Under cover of darkness, some hours later, every fallen rioter was carried off by his comrades or his family. Even the dead disappeared. It was presumed that they were buried in unmarked graves somewhere in the city's slums and shantytowns.

Having tended to his wounded, Carpenter reformed the rest of his force and marched it across town to Fifth Avenue. But the crowd at Opdyke's home had dispersed, and the neighborhood seemed quiet. So he marched back to headquarters, meeting no other rioters or any sign of resistance along the way.

For the time being, at least, the threat of anarchy had ended. This first decisive victory by the police was a thing of incalculable importance for its psychological value alone. As Chapin observed, the rioters had now been "impressed with a certain fear of the representatives of the law." But the mob had more heads than Hercules' hydra, more lives than a cat. Nothing was settled. The masses broken up still were men and women full of sullen hatreds, the hatreds smoldering more bitterly now with the sting of added grievance. And the police could not be everywhere at once.

Night closed down, sticky and uncomfortable, over a city already darkened by a hanging pall of smoke. Some twenty buildings had burned to ashes or been gutted. At least that many more still blazed. Several volunteer fire companies had followed the Black Jokes into the mob. Most had not. They stuck, went on answering the almost incessant alarms with a courage and devotion to duty that too often went unnoticed. But nearly everywhere they still were hampered, in some cases driven off, by crowds that seemed determined to let New York burn.

Manhattan Island south of Fifty-ninth Street lay in a virtual state of seige, the mob setbacks on Broadway and at the armory notwithstanding. Marauding bands roved at will even far uptown. By dark practically all of the police reserves had reported to 300 Mulberry Street. But many of the force's rank and file already were out of action, wounded or near exhaustion after the day's hard fighting. Early in the evening Inspector Folk led about a hundred patrolmen in from Brooklyn. An uneasy quiet still prevailed there, and it was reckoned that they could be spared, though only temporarily. All the same, they were most welcome. For most of the night the police would be on their own.

Military help was promised, but complications had developed; the army would be a little late.

Chapter 11 | Generals Fall Out

HARVEY BROWN, BREVET BRIGADIER GENERAL, United States Army, had put in a strenuous afternoon and evening. Brown's position was a somewhat anomalous one, and he was not happy in it. He was officially the military commandant of the city of New York, by direct order of the Secretary of War. But the calling of all available troops to the battlefield at Gettysburg had left him, in effect, a general with no command at all save for the dubious Invalid Corps. Known as an able though hot-tempered officer with an unfortunate habit of blunt speech, Brown was said to feel bitterly about the transfer from field duty which had brought him to New York. Like most professional Army officers, he considered it something of a dead end. He had, in fact, threatened to retire at the time, but had thought better of it.

It was typical of the frustrations irking him that Mayor Opdyke's call for military help had gone not to him but to his nominal superior, Major General John E. Wool, commanding the Military Department of the East. In all probability the slight was unintentional. Opdyke, a civilian, knew little of Army protocol. And the question of military authority in the city was a somewhat cloudy one at best. Since Wool maintained his headquarters in the St. Nicholas Hotel, to which the mayor had transferred his own office quite early in the day, it may simply have been a matter of convenience. The thing was unimportant, anyway, save for the train of touchy feelings it set alight.

Probably more annoying still to a man of Brown's temperament, a separate plea for assistance had been sent directly to Major General Charles W. Sandford of the New York National Guard.

John Wool was a distinguished soldier with a military record going all the way back to the War of 1812. In 1847 his skillful selection of the American position at Buena Vista had contributed to one of the great victories of the Mexican War, a service for which Congress had awarded him a letter of thanks and a ceremonial sword. In 1861 it was Wool who had held Fortress Monroe for the Union Army when Confederate forces occupied Norfolk and Portsmouth, and Wool again who reoccupied those cities upon the Confederate withdrawal. He had headed the Military Department of the East since January of 1863. But John Wool was an old man now—either seventy-six or seventy-nine; the records are conflicting—and many of his superiors in the War Department considered him a senile bumbler. He had acted on the mayor's request with reasonable promptness, however, directing the commander of Fort Hamilton in New York harbor to send a company and a half (about one hundred and fifty men) into the city as soon as possible. On his own initiative he had also contacted Rear Admiral Hiram Paulding, commandant of the Brooklyn Navy Yard, who promised detachments of seamen and Marines. And in addition, Paulding presently ordered all naval vessels at the Yard to take stations in the East and Hudson rivers, ready for action if necessary.

General Sandford, reacting on his own to Opdyke's plea, had established himself and his staff in the U.S. arsenal at Seventh Avenue and Thirty-fifth Street. From there he had dispatched messengers, placed ads in the afternoon newspapers, and ordered handbills printed calling in all members of the city's militia not yet mobilized. Obviously it was not going to be a very rapid process. Besides, most militia units already had been sent off to Gettysburg too. But one National Guard regiment was ready for immediate service, as it happened. This, the Tenth, had mustered that same morning in the Federal Arsenal at Worth and Elm streets under orders to embark for Pennsylvania. Those orders were canceled. But since the arsenal held a considerable store of military supplies, it was Sandford's decision that two companies of the Tenth be held there on guard duty. Two more were marched hastily off to garrison still another arsenal located in Central Park, leaving only about fifty men free for other assignments. Sandford ordered them to join him on Seventh Avenue. The active help for the police thus far was nil.

In all this flurry of messages and orders it appears that Brown was the forgotten man. No one had thought of contacting him at all. It was around one o'clock in the afternoon before he heard of the rioting, and then the news came only by indirection. No doubt stung, he proceeded at once to the St. Nicholas Hotel. And there—apparently with a better grasp than Wool of the scope and seriousness of the trouble—he urged that troops be sent immediately from *all* of the harbor forts, every man and artillery piece that could be spared. He also asserted his right, as military commander in New York City, to lead those troops himself. To this, he recalled later, General Wool assented "reluctantly," adding the proviso that Brown "co-operate" with General Sandford.

That undoubtedly chafed too. Nevertheless, Brown went vigorously to work. By nightfall, after a long and tiresome round of the various harbor commands, he had ordered up detachments from forts Sandy Hook and Richmond in addition to Hamilton; had ordered out two steamboats to bring them in; and had then reported to Commissioner Acton at 300 Mulberry Street.

As he may already have suspected after the interview with Wool, the intraservice difficulties were about to begin.

General Sandford was not at Mulberry Street. No troops had arrived there, either. And none did. After some three hours with nothing done—it must have been growing very late by then—Sandford finally appeared. Whether he had yet received any orders from General Wool or any word from him at all is not clear. But he plainly considered himself the ranking military officer in the city, after Wool, and was in no mood to compromise about it. In his opinion, he stated flatly, the U.S. arsenal on Seventh Avenue was the important point; it must be held at all costs, and the troops should be concentrated there. Brown disagreed. Strongly seconded by Thomas Acton, he argued that cooperation with the police was essential and that police headquarters, centered in its network of telegraph lines, was the only spot from which combined operations against the mobs could be directed with the necessary intelligence and dispatch. In spite of the breaks which had cut off the uptown precincts, most of this network remained intact. It still was vulnerable to repeated sabotage by the rioters, of course. But in any case, it was the only system of rapid communication available.

Sandford refused to budge. The discussion grew heated, attitudes on both sides more prickly. Neither Brown nor Acton was given to soft words, and Sandford had a reputation as a crochety and arrogant man, fiercely jealous of his prerogatives. Like Wool, he was a man well advanced in age. Like Brown, he had some reason, real or fancied, to be embittered by past disappointments in the course of this War Between the States. He was an attorney by profession but had devoted the better part of his life to the National Guard in New York City. He had headed it for many years. At one time, following the Guard's mobilization early in 1861, he had been the ranking military commander in Washington, D.C., where he seems to have been highly regarded by old General Winfield Scott, premier soldier of the Republic at the time. There apparently was some likelihood, for a while, that he might be given command of the Army of the Potomac instead of Irvin McDowell. But Scott's influence had faded, and with it Sandford's chances, whatever they might actually have been worth, had faded too. Since then the war had passed him by. But he was a major general, and a stiff-necked one at that; Brown was only a brigadier. On that difference in rank the conference split hopelessly.

Seth Hawley, Commissioner Acton's chief clerk, was present and did his best to sooth flaring tempers. Afterward the *Times*'s David Barnes, for one, would express praise for his tact and common sense in a difficult situation. But it became clear that no agreement was possible. At last Brown told Sandford bluntly that, as he put it later, "I did not understand myself to be under his command—but co-operating with him." The meeting ended there. Sandford walked out. It appears that he went straight to General Wool—so Brown would claim later, at any rate—and spent some time urging his point of view on the old man. And the next thing heard from the St. Nicholas was a terse order:

> All troops called out for the protection of the city are placed under the command of General Sandford, whose orders they will strictly obey.
>
> JOHN E. WOOL
> MAJOR GENERAL, U.S.A.

Some peacemakers, then and later, doubted that the general really meant to go that far and insisted that he still was aiming at some compromise. But the order was clear enough on the face of it. When Harvey Brown read it, what little patience he had left blew up in a furious burst of temper. He declared violently that he washed his hands of the whole affair, that he would resign his commission on the spot. And he might have done so but for Seth Hawley. Somehow Hawley contrived to calm the angry general down and pick up the pieces of what threatened to become a tragic fiasco.

At best, though, the upshot was a night-long interval of fuzzy confusion in which it became almost impossible to pin down the whereabouts of the various military detachments or to say with any certainty what they did. Instead of resigning, Brown simply reasserted his right to command all troops in the city and placed himself, and them, at Acton's disposal. Later he would deny that he had disobeyed any order; perhaps *ignored* was a more appropriate word. General Wool, probably more confused and bewildered than anyone else, seemed content to let matters ride and took no steps to enforce his order for the time being. But for a long and worrisome while, seemingly, there were grave doubts on Mulberry Street that the officers from the harbor forts would report there. Eventually they all did; all but one hapless lieutenant who brought his men ashore in the midst of the imbroglio, marched them to the Seventh Avenue arsenal and reported there in all innocence. And there they stayed; Sandford refused to release them.

Afterward there would be long and bitter recriminations, charges, and countercharges by Brown, Wool, and Sandford. But few informed civilians ever doubted that Brown had acted properly, regardless of the military protocol involved. Charles Chapin, for one, called General Wool's order a "great blunder" and made no effort to hide his contempt for Sandford, who, he wrote, ". . . locked himself up with the few members of the Militia he could gather together, in the Arsenal and took no part in any of the subsequent operations, excepting at the very last."

One small party of Marines from the Brooklyn Navy Yard landed at South Street sometime during the evening. On their way to police headquarters they were menaced by a crowd of looters and had to fire a volley to disperse them. Much later another mob returned to Fifth Avenue and stoned Mayor Opdyke's home, breaking nearly every window in it. They were driven away by an unidentified infantry detail on guard there. Both incidents were minor, and no other military units got into action throughout Monday night.

In the meantime, as Chapin noted simply, "the rioters were not idle . . ."

Chapter 12 | "We'll Hang Old Greeley . . . "

LONG BEFORE DARK, MOBS HAD BEGUN TO TURN THEIR WORST FURY against the city's Negroes. The attack on the Colored Orphan Asylum was only an early sign, perhaps not even the first one. The mere appearance of a dark face in the streets was provocation enough. Peter Heuston was dark. He was a full-blooded Mohawk Indian from upstate. But rioters mistook him for a Negro and left him on the sidewalk so brutally beaten that he would die in Bellevue Hospital four days later.

By nightfall, as drunkenness burned away the last shreds of restraint, black folk in neighborhoods throughout the lower East and West sides were being hunted like animals. Down in the Bloody Ould Sixth, a score of Negro families was routed from tenements around Leonard and Baxter streets near the Five Points. Crook's, a well-known restaurant, was wrecked because someone in a roving mob happened to remember that the waiters were all colored men. They were beaten up but somehow escaped with their lives—lucky, at that. In a section just off the Bowery, known as New Bowery, several Negroes were chased to the roof of a building. Their pursuers put the torch to it and waited, howling in insane glee while flames drove the poor fugitives to the eaves, then over the eaves, and at last burned their hands so they could hang on no longer. One by one they fell to the ground and the crowd flung itself on them, stamping and clubbing, and so they died. Things were worse, if possible, in the Fourth Ward. There some of the vicious waterfront gangs joined in a spree of plundering, burning, and murder in which not even the seamiest of the dives were safe. But there too the Negroes were the prime quarry. A bawdy house on Water Street was invaded, the girls stripped and tortured because some in the mob thought that they had hidden a colored servant. Behind a vanguard of screaming Irishwomen, another great mob streamed out of the Five Points for a raid on the notorious old Arch Block on Broome Street. The brothel kept by Sue the Turtle was ransacked, its stock of liquor handed around and drunk up. Big Sue's girls scattered and fled into the night. But the Turtle herself, too ponderous to run, was beaten so savagely that she too died some days later.

Undermanned and hard-pressed, the police still did what they could. Captain John Jourdan of the Sixth precinct led a force of sixty patrolmen through the worst of the troubled areas, dispersing crowd after crowd in near-constant skirmishing. Captain Jacob Warlow of the First precinct, along the Hudson River on the lower West Side, and tough George Walling of the Twentieth, on the lower East Side, also had patrols in action throughout the early hours of the night. Inspector Carpenter, the victor of Broadway, kept a roving squad sweeping the waterfront. But there simply were too many rioters.

Around eight o'clock word was telegraphed to police headquarters that another huge throng was marching south down Fifth Avenue. It must have seemed, nightmarishly, that the events of the morning were about to start repeating themselves. And at the moment there was no strong force available to head this new mob off. (About then, General Harvey Brown and Commissioner Acton were waiting fretfully for some message of encouragement from Sandford or the harbor forts.) Somewhere in the Twenties the mob turned east, then south again into Third Avenue. It reached Astor Place and swung off Third into the Bowery. Rolling on south, gathering strength and fury as it went, it reached Chatham Square, turned once more, and went roaring through Park Row toward City Hall Park. This mob, too, marched behind a swaggering leader who waved an American flag aloft. It was organized, and it knew where it was going. The target, it became apparent, was the New York *Tribune* building, located on Printing House Square, just beyond City Hall Park. As the rioters tramped along Park Row in Old Glory's wake, thousands of rough voices began to thunder out the frightening cadence of a parody on a popular Union marching song, which was itself a parody on the *Battle Hymn of the Republic:*

We'll hang old Greeley to a sour apple tree,
We'll hang old Greeley to a sour apple tree,
We'll hang old Greeley to a sour apple tree,
And send him straight to hell. . . .

Others were there before them, with the same idea. The crowd of surly idlers that had hung about City Hall most of the day was still there. It was a large crowd now, and still surly. A police detail was stationed at the Hall itself, but it was not strong enough to clear the park. The crowd, however, had not yet become violent, though part of it had spilled over into Printing House Square to jeer and hoot in front of the *Tribune* building.

Earlier that evening a visitor had dropped in—James Gilmore, a onetime cotton broker turned ardent Abolitionist and a close friend of Horace Greeley's. As he told the story later, *Tribune* employees had tried for some time to get Greeley to slip out the back way. Sidney Gay, the managing editor, was quoted as declaring that, "This is not a riot, but a revolution." And Greeley had agreed, adding as he looked out over the square that he thought there was a good chance they meant to hang him. But he refused to leave.

The crowd had grown more raucous. There were cries of "Down with the old white coat that thinks a nigger is as good as an Irishman."

"The old white coat" was Horace Greeley. Everyone knew that; the garment was one of his noted eccentricities. He was an unlikely figure for a hero—moon-faced, white-whiskered, and untidy. But he was no coward. Again Gilmore and Gay and others had begged him to leave, even to flee the city. Another visitor had added his pleas, this one Theodore Tilton, editor of Henry Ward Beecher's Abolitionist weekly, the New York *Independent*. And at last Greeley had announced that he would go, but only out to dinner. Said he peevishly, "If I can't eat my dinner when I'm hungry, my life isn't worth anything to me."

With that he had put on his hat, taken Tilton by the arm, and walked boldly out into the square, as Gilmore said: ". . . hat pushed back, specs hanging on his nose and his face wearing its expression of unshakable benignity . . ."

Unmolested by the crowd, apparently unrecognized, he and Tilton had walked a short way down Park Row to Windust's

Restaurant. They were still there. And as the new mob fanned out into City Hall Park, the crowd joined it with a roar.

Together they rolled across the park, across Printing House Square, and into the *Tribune* building. A lone policeman, a sergeant named Devoursney, had stationed himself at the front door. He beat off the first few rioters with his nightstick, but bystanders shouted at him to run for help rather than throw himself away in a hopeless cause. He took the advice, as *Tribune* men scuttled out the back door and ran down Park Row. But this was not to be a mob victory either. Exultant rioters scarcely had begun to wreck the premises when a phalanx of bluecoats double-timed into the square out of Nassau Street. It was Captain Warlow and his First-precinct force, reached by telegraph from headquarters just as they returned to their stationhouse from another patrol. The melee was short and sharp, for this mob appeared to lack the stomach for punishment some of its predecessors had shown. In a matter of minutes it was streaming back across City Hall Park in pell-mell disarray. There it collided headlong with Inspector Daniel Carpenter and his flying squad from the waterfront, now joined by some of Folk's Brooklyn men; they too had been rallied by telegraph. David Barnes claimed later that Carpenter roared, "Up, Guards, and at them!"—the Duke of Wellington's battle cry at Waterloo—to sound the charge. The inspector, it seems, had a nice knack for quotable words in the pinch. But it was a mopping-up now, not a fight, and the mob took a bad hammering before its remnants escaped helter-skelter into the surrounding streets.

True to form, the rioters had set several fires in the *Tribune* building. But the action was over so quickly that patrolmen were able to dash inside and smother them before they spread. Damage to the presses was slight. And since most of the employees pluckily returned to their jobs within the hour, the paper did not miss a single edition.

Among the casualties of this skirmish, police found an old man, the proverbial innocent bystander, who had been felled by a patrolman's club in the confusion. Taken to Mulberry Street, where a surgeon dressed his head wound, he asked repeatedly whether it would leave a scar. Finally he was told, somewhat apologetically, that it would. "I'll wear it proudly," he declared—

a stout citizen whose name deserved to be remembered but was not.

But Horace Greeley and the *Tribune* were the objects of a near-psychotic hatred by the city's Copperhead factions. And there could be no doubt now, indeed there never had been, that such factions were active among the rioters. About ten o'clock the mob, or another one, returned to Printing House Square to try its luck again. In the meantime, Warlow and Carpenter and their squads had been called away on new alarms and patrols. But they had left a police guard at the *Tribune* building. Lighted lanterns had been placed in all the windows, too, illuminating the square so brightly that no surprise attack was possible. In the face of such obvious preparedness, this second threat was somewhat abortive, and the mob soon retired. Though random disorders continued everywhere, large-scale fighting was over for the night.

Central police headquarters still was out of touch with many of the precincts north of Sixtieth Street, though repair crews of the telegraph bureau were out and working. Frequently they traced and mended the cut lines at considerable risk from roaming gangs. Fortunately, however, the rioters' incursions into the isolated areas were comparatively few and minor. On West Eighty-sixth Street, sometime before midnight, the home of postmaster Abram Wakeman was looted and burned. Earlier there were scattered outbreaks of violence as far away as Harlem, a good many of them probably the work of neighborhood rowdies excited by reports of the widening breakdown in law and order. But occasionally throughout the rioting there would be outcroppings of purely political enthusiasms that contrasted oddly with the general lust for bloodshed and destruction. One of these occurred in Madison Square, where a large and noisy crowd demonstrated for some hours in front of the posh Fifth Avenue Hotel. The nervous management barricaded its doors with piles of luggage and prepared basins and pitchers of boiling water for pouring out of upper-story windows onto the attackers' heads. But there was no attack. Next day a *Tribune* reporter who happened to be there would describe a scene touched with a kind of fiddling-while-Rome-burns madness:

In the Fifth Avenue Hotel there was an immense crowd all the evening of the upper ten. They were about as decided in their expressions as their poorer neighbors outside, who seemed to think that General McClellan was present, and kept calling for him. The fashionable cursed the Abolitionists, and when the news of the attack on THE TRIBUNE office came, *expressed their great approbation.* "It has been a curse to us, and the main cause of our trouble," said one. "That's so," repeated others, and, to settle the matter, numerous cocktails were called for. It might be impertinent to say so, but the *bon ton* seemed *somewhat under the weather.* They were particularly severe upon the Administration, and *very hard upon the "damned Abolitionists."*

The weather, lowering and humid since early afternoon, broke in a furious thunderstorm about eleven-thirty. Rain fell in blinding sheets. It steamed on the hot sidewalks and sluiced inches deep through the gutters. It quenched the fires that still burned all over town; later some commentators would claim that all the lower part of New York City might have been consumed but for that rain, and some preachers would liken it to an Old Testament intercession. It did, at least, put a stop to the worst of the rioting. The thugs and the looters and their women scattered to hunt cover. Some hurried home to rickety hovels or stuffy tenements. Some sought handy dives and gin mills, to spend the balance of the night carousing. And some, beyond doubt, would spend it in back rooms around Paradise Square and off the Bowery and along the waterfront, planning new violence to keep the mobs' momentum going. The trouble was not over. No one thought that it was.

At 300 Mulberry Street, battered, bone-weary patrolmen accepted the respite gratefully. Headquarters was filling up with refugees, too, both white and Negro—burned out of their homes, destitute, scared, and bewildered, with nowhere else to go. More would keep coming. Ultimately they would jam-pack the big stone building. They would bed down as best they could, in cells, on benches, on cots, or on the floors, and their care would pose additional problems for the city authorities. Already Sergeant John Young, chief of detectives, had taken on extra duties as emergency commissary head. Before it ended he would dispense an estimated fifty thousand gallons of hot coffee and sandwiches and other food past counting. Chief Clerk Seth Hawley had drawn the job of organizing a citizens' Volunteer Police Reserve. Men of Captain James Todd's Twenty-fourth precinct, the Harbor Police, were busy bringing additional firearms from municipal arsenals on Blackwell's and Riker's islands. There would be little rest for any department head this night, and none at all for Thomas Acton and General Brown. The first two companies of regular infantry from the harbor had reported in around eleven o'clock. Other help was on the way—regular infantry and Invalid Corps units. Good news, but it meant added problems too—details of bivouacs, meals, and liaison to be arranged. Though General Sandford still sulked in the armory at Seventh Avenue, word came of growing strength there, too, as militiamen reported in.

Implicit in all this was the feeling . . . it was not fear exactly, and certainly not panic, but a chilling awareness that what was happening was bigger than a riot or a series of riots; bigger even than an organized protest against the draft. Not many were ready to put the thought into words, apparently, as Gay of the *Tribune* had. But the thought was there: no telling how far this might spread or where it would end. Sometime near midnight Mayor George Opdyke conferred with Acton, then dispatched an urgent telegram to Secretary of War Edwin M. Stanton in Washington. It asked that all New York regiments be returned to the city posthaste from Pennsylvania.

III The Second Day

Chapter 13 | Alarms and Suspicions

WILLIAM JONES WAS HIS NAME, by coincidence the same as the one first drawn to launch the draft on Saturday morning. This Jones was a colored man. He lived on Clarkson Street, a short and grubby thoroughfare ending at the Hudson River about midway along the West Side dock district. He would be mentioned briefly in the public prints, for the first and last time in his life, only because his death signaled the start of the new day's warfare.

The area was a slum with a large population of Negroes. Many had fled. Some, perhaps, were among the refugees who crowded police headquarters on Mulberry Street or the station-houses of the Eighth and Ninth precincts, which were closer. Some crouched in cellars or hidey holes about the neighborhood. Many were taken in and protected, not only here but all over Manhattan, by white families whose courage and compassion would stand out among the few bright spots in the dark doings let loose upon the city. But William Jones had not fled. He stole out, early in the morning that still was warm and muggy after the storm, to buy a loaf of bread for breakfast. And a mob of prowling troublemakers caught him. Someone threw a rope around his neck. Someone else tossed its end over a handy tree limb. Eager hands took hold and heaved away. The women were the worst: over and over again that would be the story told by shocked witnesses of the rioting. A fire was lighted beneath the dying man and they capered around it, shrieking as they pelted the body with stones and sticks and clods. Tiring of that, the mob went on. A block north, at Washington and LeRoy streets, it caught and lynched another colored man, named Williams. But the police

were out early too. A roving patrol routed the mob before the
body could be burned and went on to cut down what was left of
Jones. It was said that they found his charred loaf of bread still
clutched under one arm.

Thus Tuesday began.

It found a city bewildered, benumbed, by no means sure just
what was happening to it. Early editions of the newspapers when
they appeared on the streets did not wholly clarify the picture. In
all of them the rioting was front-page news, of course. Headlines
varied from the *Herald*'s understatement, POPULAR OPPOSITION TO
THE ENFORCEMENT OF THE CONSCRIPTION, to the *Tribune*'s matter-
of-fact THE RIOT IN THE NINTH CONGRESSIONAL DISTRICT. Most
papers reported the various mobs' movements and the main
clashes with police in remarkably complete detail, and by and
large, with reasonable accuracy as well. But on the editorial
pages they all stayed very much in character.

The *Tribune* appeared to understand more clearly than any of
its competitors that New York was facing an all-out emergency.
Predictably, Horace Greeley's paper was also quick to see evidence of forces at work more sinister than spontaneous public
resentment. The real mob, it declared, had been built around a
tough-striking corps of about three hundred who had "a previously understood purpose, and were carrying out their atrocities
by the aid of a certain amount of rough discipline." And it went
on to say, somewhat incoherently but with a meaning that could
not be missed:

> No person who carefully watched the movements of this
> mob, who noticed their careful attention to the words of cer-
> tain tacitly-acknowledged leaders, who observed the unques-
> tionably preconcerted regularity with which they proceeded
> from one part of their infernal program to the next; and the
> persistency with which the "rear guard" remained and fought
> off all who dared to check any part of the destruction that
> everywhere marked their work, can presume to doubt that
> these men are acting under leaders who have carefully elab-
> orated their plans, who have, as they think, made all things
> sure for their accomplishment, and that they are resolved to
> carry them out through fire and blood, this day's crimson
> work fully attests.

Monday night had put Greeley's dander up, and he was not through even then. Said another editorial:

> It is known that for some time past Governor Seymour has held out the promise to this treasonable Irish mob, that he would remove the Police Commissioners.
>
> They had been told that this step was to be taken yesterday, and it is believed in certain quarters that Governor S. did really intend to take this step yesterday, but the mob anticipated the act, and commenced their work of riot at an hour too early for the Governor to get out of bed. . . .

Not many were ready to go that far, at least not yet. Henry J. Raymond's New York *Times* frequently was bracketed with the *Tribune* as "radical" by opposition papers. But the *Times*, though it expressed the strongest indignation against the rioters and urged that they be put down without delay, by military force if necessary, had nothing to say about Copperhead conspiracies.

Predictably, also, the Democratic press displayed an almost undignified enthusiasm in denouncing the national Republican Administration as the cause of all the trouble. Many papers seemed absurdly eager to defend and placate the masses who made up the mobs. The *Daily News* even professed to see a parallel between the rioters in New York City and the Union heroes at Gettysburg:

> The men who have gone from among us to the war, who today guard the Capital and hold Lee and his men at bay among the Maryland hills, are just such men as those who have struck terror through our peaceful streets, of like passions, swayed by like motives, to be kindled with the same patriotic fire.
>
> Will the insensate men at Washington now at length listen to our voices? . . .

The *World* decried the mobs' excesses, frowned on violence, and urged that the constitutionality of the draft law be tested in the courts. But then it asked rhetorically:

> . . . Does any man wonder that poor men refuse to be forced into a war mismanaged almost into hopelessness, perverted almost into partisanship? Did the President and his cabinet imagine that their lawlessness could conquer, or their folly seduce, a free people? . . .

The *World* also reported a small sidelight of the previous night's attack on the *Tribune*, which it found vastly amusing. Horace Greeley, according to this story, had fled from his office when the mob approached, dived under a table in Windust's Restaurant, and cowered there until peace was restored. James Gordon Bennett's *Herald* picked up the story too, with obvious relish in a rival's embarrassment. But Greeley actually had hidden in Windust's refrigerator, the *Herald* claimed, chortling that it was "a strange place for a vegetarian" to select. (In subsequent editions of the *Tribune* Greeley would deny all this indignantly.)

The *Herald*, too, was prone to take a tolerant view of the rioting. Referring to the early rout of the Invalid Corps detachment on Third Avenue, an editorialist noted:

> Excuse must be made for the conduct of the crowd by the glaring fact that a number of their kindred had been shot down in cold blood by their sides while fighting in defense of the same principle [i.e., resistance to the draft].

Herald news columns carried a unique version of the attempted raid on Mayor Opdyke's home. It made Justice George G. Barnard of the New York Supreme Court the hero of the incident, and the whole thing more of a somewhat rowdy political demonstration than a mob outbreak. Barnard lived in the neighborhood and, it was said, went immediately to the spot and addressed the rioters. "Being recognized, the crowd gave three cheers and demanded a speech. It was almost impossible to distinguish what the Judge said, but he was understood to DENOUNCE THE DRAFT AS AN UNCONSTITUTIONAL ACT, AS AN ACT OF DESPOTISM . . . whereat there was tremendous cheering. . . ." Barnard then admonished the people not to break the law but to disperse and go home, said the *Herald*, and this too was received with great applause. Then, the account continued:

> In the midst of the excitement, a great concourse proceeded to the residence of Gen. McClellan in East Thirty-first street, to give him an ovation. The throng halted opposite the house, WHERE THEY GAVE LOUD AND PROLONGED CHEERS FOR "LITTLE MAC," but ascertaining that he was in New Jersey they left, proceeding down Fifth Avenue shouting and hurrahing.

This report is puzzling, in that other chroniclers of Monday's events did not mention Barnard's presence on the scene at all. And most of those who noted the *Herald*'s story afterward were inclined to see his friendly reception by the mob as significant of political bias among the rioters. For Barnard was a well-known Tammany Hall stalwart, later to be notorious as a corrupt tool of Boss William Marcy Tweed. And the enthusiasm for McClellan corresponds strikingly with the similar demonstration on Monday night at the Fifth Avenue Hotel. It would also seem to lend point to the *Tribune*'s earlier charge that pro-Secessionist forces were hard at work in the general's behalf.

There would be other puzzling aspects of the rioting before it ended. Down in Washington that Tuesday morning the first reports were fragmentary and confusing. Sometime during the day or evening Navy Secretary Gideon Welles would record some dark thoughts in his diary:

> We have accounts of mobs, riots and disturbances in New York and other places in consequence of the Conscription Act. Our information is very meagre; two or three mails are due; the telegraph is interrupted. There have been powerful rains which have caused great damage to the railroads and interrupted all land communications between this and Baltimore.
>
> There are, I think, indubitable evidences of concert in these riotous movements, beyond the accidental and impulsive outbreak of a mob, or mobs. Lee's march into Pennsylvania, the appearance of several Rebel steamers off the coast, the mission of A. H. Stephens to Washington, seem to be parts of one movement, have one origin, are all concerted schemes between the Rebel leaders and Northern sympathizing friends —the whole put in operation when the Government is enforcing the conscription. This conjunction is not all accidental, but parts of a great plan. In the midst of all this and as a climax comes word that Lee's army has succeeded in recrossing the Potomac. If there had been an understanding between the mob conspirators, the Rebels, and our own officers, the combination of incidents could not have been more advantageous to the Rebels.

Chapter 14 | Riot into Rebellion

THROUGHOUT MONDAY NIGHT'S DRENCHING RAINSTORM James Crowley and Eldred Polhamus of the telegraph bureau had led repair crews in a dogged battle to keep the lines working. It had been a struggle, and would be. In addition to the breaks on Third Avenue, poles were down and wires cut on First Avenue between the Seventeenth and Eighteenth precincts, in several places on Twenty-second Street, and on Ninth Avenue between the Twentieth and Twenty-second precincts. Charles Chapin later wrote that, "The mob had already . . . rendered useless over 12 miles of wire, and how much more would be destroyed none could tell."

Communications in lower Manhattan had faltered badly at times. Nevertheless, they had stayed open. And now, as Tuesday morning wore along, the telegraphers on duty at Mulberry Street were scribbling out new messages telling of mobs on the move again.

Word of Jones's murder came in, and of Williams'. Far uptown on East Eighty-sixth Street the stationhouse of the Twenty-third precinct was attacked. The area had been thought safe; only the lockup keeper had been left there when the reserves were mustered. He fled; the station was wrecked and burned. On West Eighty-sixth the home of Assistant Provost Marshal General Nugent was burning, too. On West Thirty-second Street a Negro shoemaker with the unlikely name of James Costello was threatened by an Irish bully named Maney. He had a pistol and shot Maney. But a crowd incited by the Irishman's wife overpowered him, hanged him from a lamppost, and set his home on fire, then chased his family into a tenement at the rear. Losing them there and finding no other Negroes in the place, they turned the white tenants out and burned it anyway. Over in Printing House Square a great, shouting mob—the third inside of twelve hours—gathered to vent its hatred on the New York *Tribune*. That episode, at least, turned out better. Horace Greeley's friend James Gilmore was a prominent Republican who wielded considerable influence in Washington. He had visited the St. Nicholas during the night and prevailed upon General Wool to have a quantity of old army muskets sent from Governor's Island and turned over to *Tribune* employees. At his instigation, also, Admiral Paulding had sent a gun crew with a howitzer from the Navy Yard. It was wheeled into position at the building's entrance, the seamen at quarters around it. The mob took a long, hard look and retired in some haste. But Greeley, arriving at the office around noon, was not pleased with either howitzer or muskets. It was said that he protested vigorously: "Take 'em away, take 'em away. I don't want to kill anybody, and besides they're a damned sight more likely to go off and kill us."

Much more serious in its implications than such random incidents was the information that large numbers of men and women were busy barricading Ninth Avenue northward from Thirty-seventh Street. Worst of all was a message that reached headquarters earlier, around six A.M.: another mighty throng was massing in Second Avenue, apparently for an assault on the Union Steam Works at Twenty-second Street. The works had been spared on Monday when mob leaders elected to go after the arsenal instead. In the meantime, a police guard had been stationed there. But more than four thousand army carbines and some two hundred thousand rounds of ammunition were still in the building, for harried authorities had found neither the time nor the manpower to remove them.

The indefatigable Daniel Carpenter drew the assignment. During Monday someone, probably Seth Hawley, had had the foresight to commandeer a small fleet of wagons and omnibuses for quick transport in just such emergencies. Shortly after six o'clock, two hundred patrolmen climbed into them and clattered east down Twenty-first Street at a gallop. Turning left into Second Avenue, past the blackened ruins of the New York State Arsenal that still stank of wet ashes, smoke, and charred flesh, they saw the mob ahead. It was a big one, bigger than yesterday's on Broadway—filling street and sidewalks in a tossing river of humanity from Twenty-second Street all the way north to Thirty-second. Still the attack had not begun. The omnibuses pulled up, and the police jumped down and formed a double rank to block the street. The mob sullenly pulled back. It appeared to lack leadership, to have no common drive or purpose as yet. But ". . . Dirty, bedraggled, ferocious looking women were mingled with the crowd," Charles Chapin wrote, "urging the men on to action." A good many of the men held guns.

Yet the mob retreated. There were hoots and catcalls and shouted threats from the crowd and from the windows of tenements on both sides of the avenue as Carpenter ordered his men forward. Still the vast throng rolled backward, keeping its distance, though it did not break. The slow, grudging ebb went on all the way to Thirty-second Street. It began to appear that the show of police force would be enough to do the job. At Thirty-second Street that ended abruptly.

A scattering of shots marked the mob's sudden resolution. It was ragged and ineffective. In this encounter as in others to follow it would be remarked again and again that the possession of firearms, which might well have made the mobs unconquerable, actually had scant effect. Many observers put it down to lack of skill. More probably it was the result of the indiscriminate looting by which these rioters had armed themselves. They had taken whatever they could lay hands on—pistols of various makes, types, and ages; military and sporting rifles snatched up along with army surplus muskets of ancient vintage and widely dissimilar calibers. It was not an era of standardization even in military firearms, or in their ammunition either. Cartridges—modern paper ones, old cap-and-ball types, rimfire, or whatever—could be fired only in the guns for which they were specifically designed, regardless of calibers. Caught up in such frantic scramblings as the melee in the armory, many a rioter had no doubt been unable to match weapons with ammunition. The circumstance may have been New York's salvation.

But along with the scattered fusillade came a barrage of missiles from rooftops right and left. Brickbats and cobbles were the mob's natural weapons, and their aim was better. The blue ranks wavered as men went down. The mob stormed forward. Hot work; but again the police lines held; again no hoodlum could stand up for long to the smashing nightsticks. Still the missiles rained down from the rooftops. Shouting above the uproar, Carpenter detached fifty patrolmen and ordered them into the buildings to clear out rioters there. Doors hastily slammed and barricaded were broken down. Policemen fought their way up the stairs. As on Broadway the day before, no arrests were made, no quarter given. Heads were cracked and the rioters abandoned their hoarded brickbats and broke in panic. Some jumped to the street below or were pushed over in the savage crush of close-quarter fighting, and so died. Some struggled to the stairways and fled. The roofs were cleared.

In the street there was a lull, and the mob drew back. But it was not yet routed. Having made up their minds to fight, these people were a tough lot. Possibly a day and a night of unbridled plunder and carousing had filled them with a heady sense of power in the mass. And in the jammed street hundreds of them—thousands—had not been able to come to grips at all with their adversaries. This undoubtedly was a main reason why relatively small forces of police were able to beat odds that seemed overwhelming in clashes such as this. But it meant also that the great masses of rioters were slow to taste the nightsticks, and hence, unless they panicked, were not easily dispersed.

As the mob hesitated now, milling in confused fury, a yell went up. Soldiers! Soldiers were coming.

A hundred and fifty militiamen were marching down Thirty-fifth Street, led by Colonel H. J. O'Brien of the Eleventh New York Volunteers. Afterward it was not entirely clear how they had come to be there. Because they were militia, most contemporary writers assumed that General Sandford had sent them from the Seventh Avenue arsenal. There were indications, however, that they probably were a mixed force hastily raised by O'Brien on his own. The Eleventh, in fact, was a brand-new regiment still in the process of being recruited. It was headquartered at Tammany Hall; and O'Brien, himself a man of uncertain background and no particular military attainments, appears to have been a purely political appointee.

In any event, Inspector Carpenter grasped the opportunity

to take the mob from front and flank at once. He ordered his patrolmen forward again. But the sight of military uniforms goaded the mob to renewed fury too. In the excitement and the noisy, moiling confusion, perhaps many of the rioters had no clear notion of what was happening now, simply felt themselves threatened from a new quarter and reacted blindly. But also— and this would be noticed more than once as the rioting went on—soldiers inspired these people with far less awe than did the police. They knew the potency of the locustwood nightsticks, and they had learned through harsh experience that the patrolmen would not hesitate to use them. But most regiments, the militia in particular, were local boys. Many of them came from the same neighborhoods as the rioters, were laboring-class Irishmen too, and among the mobs there was a stubborn reluctance to believe that they would fire on their own kind. (Respectable New Yorkers had similar misgivings at first, as they had had about the police also, and for the same reasons.) So now, with a roar, a large mass of rioters boiled into Thirty-fifth Street toward the troopers.

O'Brien wheeled his force into company front. If he called on the mob to halt, no one seemed to hear him in the hubbub. They did not halt, at any rate. He gave the order to fire, and a volley crashed, and then another. They were hurried and poorly aimed, and only infuriated the rioters. But somewhere Colonel O'Brien also had picked up a pair of six-pounder field pieces manned by a detachment of artillerymen under a Lieutenant Eagleson. He ordered Eagleson to fire. Point-blank, the guns belched a whistling sleet of canister and grape into the close-packed crowd.

The effect could not have been less than frightful. That an undisciplined mob stood up to it and still kept coming seems scarcely credible. Nevertheless, the six-pounders bellowed again through the ebbing powder murk; and then a third time; and yet again. Six rounds in all swept the street, and the mob scattered in shrieking rout, leaving sidewalks and pavement littered with the dead and dying. A story would be told and retold afterward— how one of them was a young woman with a baby at her breast, how she fell and was trampled almost beyond recognition in the stampede, but the baby was found alive and unhurt beneath her body. Whether it ended in an orphanage, no one ever said.

There were other unanswered questions as an aftermath of the battle in Second Avenue. It appears that Carpenter presently regrouped his patrolmen and led them off on a sweep of other troubled East Side districts. What Colonel O'Brien did is less clear, raising the suspicion of misunderstanding and perhaps even of controversy between the two men. Almost all contemporary accounts leave the colonel at the scene of his victory. Some imply that he reported with his militiamen to the Seventh Avenue arsenal. Charles Chapin said only that he "marched them off the ground." But Chapin, who was present at police headquarters this whole time, and personally close to Thomas Acton, raises some ugly doubts about Colonel O'Brien's fitness. His journal added flatly that O'Brien "subsequently offered his services to Cmr. Acton, but being in an intoxicated condition the offer was refused. Whether he disbanded his handful of men or they disbanded themselves is not known."

Among the police casualties of this Second Avenue fight, or of another which followed shortly afterward, was a detective by the name of Slowly. While circulating among the rioters, he was recognized, attacked, and soundly mauled before he could take shelter in a nearby house. Curiously, though the sixteen detectives on the force mingled constantly with various mobs, and many must have been known by sight to underworld characters, Slowly was the only one ever recognized. His injuries were slight, however. He was back in action almost immediately.

Curiously, too, this affair in Second Avenue ended in a puzzling anticlimax. The Union Steam Works seems to have been forgotten, though it had been the mob's evident objective. Daniel Carpenter apparently left no men to reinforce the small police detail guarding the place, and O'Brien obviously did not. Nor was anything done about removing the carbines stored there. It was a grave oversight, for the mob wanted those carbines. And the mob returned. Where it found the fresh masses and the implacable will to rally, no one knows. But it did rally. And it had found new leaders now—a shaggy, one-armed giant and a slim, pale youth filled with fire and hate. It came back with startling suddenness, almost on the heels of the retiring police. Headquarters was caught by surprise, had neither time nor any force on hand to counter the move. When no relief column appeared, the guard detail could do nothing but retire, leaving the building in the mob's hands. This time the mob had discipline and organization and a better plan than senseless plunder and destruction. They started no fires blazing. There was no mad scramble for guns and cartridges. Most of the carbines were not even broken out of their cases. Instead, some five hundred men settled down inside the building. The intent was plain: to hold it as the mob's own arsenal and headquarters. There was an arrogant self-confidence here, a frightening thing. For they obviously believed that they could do it. They *meant* to do it; all at once this began to look like no rabble, but men determined and formidable, turning from blind riot toward knowing, calculated rebellion.

There were other ominous signs about the city. Crowds still worked diligently to throw up barricades in Ninth Avenue. It was nothing new in gang warfare in New York; both Dead Rabbits and Bowery Boys had fought from barricades during the riots in 1857. But this activity in Ninth Avenue worried many people. Afterward, and probably at the time as well, statements were made that "the mob were introducing the revolutionary methods of Europe." There it was again, *revolution:* a word no man scoffed at, this angry year of 1863. And still the efforts to cut the telegraph lines continued, more or less at random, yet still suggesting some shadowy leadership bent on hamstringing the police. Chapin, who was in a position to know, thought that they might have succeeded had not many of the mobsters lost sight of the goal in drunkenness and looting.

For the moment, though, nothing was more important than recapturing the Union Steam Works.

Around noon Inspector George Dilks reached the spot with another force of two hundred patrolmen, very nearly the last of Mulberry Street's uncommitted reserves. The Works was a sturdy five-story factory. With their newly won arms the mob might have stood a long and bitter siege there. They chose instead to meet the police hand to hand in the street outside. The one-armed man raged like a berserk in the forefront, followers massed around him in inspired fury. Nightsticks failed to stop him. His own flailing bludgeon beat back every patrolman who stood up to him, until at last several went after him with service revolvers. He was shot down, and still the mob fought on. The other, younger man rallied them time after time, wielding knife and club with reckless courage. A nightstick finally sent him reeling. He fell

against an iron fence and there he hung and bled to death, his
throat pierced by a paling. Part of the mob broke then and ran.
But others defended the building with a disciplined ferocity the
police had not faced before. In the end they took it floor by
floor, the last of the mob clubbed down in a final stand on the
roof. A physician from the neighborhood, acting the good Samari-
tan during the final stages of the fighting, reported later that he
dressed more than a score of head wounds within an hour. He
saw none of the men again but reckoned that every wound was
fatal.

The police brought wagons up this time and emptied the
Union Steam Works of its arms. They were taken to headquarters
under heavy guard. One lesson had been enough.

At some time during the brief lull after this battle, curious
policemen found the opportunity to examine the mob's two fallen
leaders. Neither ever was identified. The big one-armed man, indeed, seemed no more than a typical slum tough—a laborer, possibly, or a minor criminal of no great renown among his fellows
until some latent rage in him flamed up to become the stuff of
leadership. The corpse of the slim young man impaled on the
fence touched off a greater flurry of speculation when the story
got about. He did not appear to belong with the mob, certainly.
Much was made of his features, described as pale and "aristocratic," and of his hands, which were too soft and well cared for
to be the hands of a laboring man. Underneath the "dirty overalls
and filthy shirt" he wore, according to one writer, were ". . . fine
cassemere pants, a handsome rich vest and a fine linen shirt."
Whence he had come, what fanatic loyalties or twisted hatreds
had brought him into the alien mob, could only be guessed at:
the sort of morbid-romantic mystery dear to the nineteenth-
century mind. Inevitably, of course, some would suggest that he
was a secret agent of the Confederacy. But most of the guessing
would come later. Journalists had more urgent news to cover at
the moment, and the police had other concerns than dead rioters.
Most of the bodies were carried off after a while by loyal comrades, the young man's with the rest.

Tradition forever afterward would hold that it was buried in a
secret, unmarked grave in one of the dank tunnels beneath a Five
Points tenement.

Chapter 15 | "My Friends . . . "

GOVERNOR SEYMOUR ARRIVED IN NEW YORK TUESDAY MORNING. It might have been a city in the throes of an enemy invasion that he approached as his ferry chugged across the harbor toward the Battery. Great coils of smoke still twisted lazily up to join the dark drifts hovering above the skyline. Up the East and Hudson rivers lay the tall shapes of deep-water sailing ships at anchor, warped out into the stream from slips and piers on the waterfront for fear of prowling gangs. Among them moved flotillas of smaller craft carrying refugees to Brooklyn or New Jersey. Governor Seymour's ferry was not crowded; few passengers were going to Manhattan today. But it would be crowded on the return trip. An exodus was under way, though the governor saw only part of it from the water. Panicky citizens were heading north to the mainland, too. Railroads, those whose tracks had not yet been torn up, were backing long special trains into depots; they pulled out with coaches loaded to the platforms. Well-to-do families scrambled for every carriage and hansom cab that was for hire, no matter how exorbitant the rates. Earlier that morning a gang had tried to burn the wooden bridge over the Harlem River. They had failed, the timbers too wet from last night's rain. But it was one more apparent attempt to isolate the city, adding to the panic.

It was said that the governor's face was haggard as he stepped ashore.

He was there in response to a message from Mayor Opdyke, but the reception committee was strictly partisan. William Marcy Tweed was on hand with a few lesser Tammany officials, no Republicans, and no one else of note. The greetings were terse.

Tweed and the governor stepped into a waiting carriage and headed up Broadway, flanked by a small cavalry escort. This far down toward the Battery the street bore few scars left by the mobs. Plenty of poorly dressed people thronged the sidewalks, however. In places they had milled together into small crowds. This was one of the lower Manhattan precincts that had given Horatio Seymour an overwhelming majority in last March's election. William Marcy Tweed was popular here also—he had been born on Cherry Street, over in the Fourth Ward—and both men drew cheers as the carriage passed.

At the St. Nicholas Hotel there was a brief conference with Opdyke and then an announcement: the governor would speak from the steps of City Hall.

A crowd was waiting in City Hall Park. One crowd or another had been hanging about there, in fact, since the start of the rioting. The park was not large, forcing some of the late arrivals out into Broadway. The ovation for Seymour when he appeared was something less than thunderous. This was the mob, there could be no doubt. There were bandages in evidence, bruised faces, and other marks of recent battle. And the general mein was sullen. A file of Army infantry troopers stood with fixed bayonets across the front of City Hall. From the steps other soldiers could be seen at the far side of Printing House Square, where details stood guard at the *Tribune* and *Times* buildings. It was quite obvious that the crowd resented the soldiers' presence. But the governor's record was in his favor. They would listen to him.

It was not one of Horatio Seymour's better performances.

"My friends," he called them, and "Fellow citizens . . ." He assured them that, "I come not only for the purpose of maintaining law, but also from a kind regard for the . . . welfare of those who, under the influence of excitement and . . . supposed wrong, were in danger not only of inflicting serious blows to the good order of society, but to their own interests. . . . I beg of you to listen to me as your friend and the friend of your families. . . ." He went on like that at some length. He was all conciliation. He had sent his personal adjutant general to Washington to try to have the draft stopped. He was sure that it would be; he virtually promised that. He reminded them of past labors in their behalf. . . . Now and then he was interrupted, not always by cheers. The draft may have aroused these people in the beginning, but it did not seem to be the draft that annoyed them now. There were loud cries of "No sojers!" and "Send away the bayonets!" He pleaded with them to go back peacefully to their homes and their jobs. They milled about and muttered resentfully among themselves and shouted again and again: "Send away the bayonets!"

The speech ended. William Marcy Tweed had stood in plain sight at Seymour's back all through it. But he said nothing—he seldom spoke in public—and no one else had anything to add. George Opdyke was there too. He had accompanied the governor, both men walking over from the St. Nicholas as a gesture of confidence and solidarity. But while Seymour spoke Opdyke had remained inside City Hall, well aware that his presence would only inflame these people. Sometime later the mob finally was dispersed by Inspector James Leonard and a police detail sent from Mulberry Street.

Back at the St. Nicholas, Horatio Seymour showed a little more iron. He issued a proclamation declaring New York City to be "in a state of insurrection," ordering the rioters once more to desist and resume their orderly pursuits, and calling on all good citizens to assemble at six designated centers, where they were to place themselves at the disposal of officers duly authorized to help in putting down disorder. It is perhaps worth noting that among the latter was the name of Captain I. Rynders. The captain was getting old now. He was no longer a U.S. marshal nor a power in city politics. He was scarcely a shell of the bully boy who once had loosed the fury of the mob upon poor Edwin Macready and the Astor Place Opera House. Before the present trouble ended, in fact, he would be appealing to the authorities for a special military guard to protect his own home from the rioters. (The request would be denied.)

Mayor Opdyke also issued a proclamation. It was a singularly weak one, the gist of it a plea to the proprietors of all stores dealing in firearms which might be seized by rioters to shut up shop until order should be restored. Most such places probably had been plundered already or closed by the owners of their own volition.

Though both documents were dated July 14, they apparently were written too late to catch the next day's editions of the news-

papers, for they did not appear in print until Thursday, the six-
teenth. It made little difference; the mobs were not going to be
stopped by proclamations. Next day, for all that, New York's
Democratic press would react to the governor's presence by
hewing raucously to the party line. The *Daily News* would sum
its feelings up in one large headline, for example: *THE REPUBLI-
CAN PARTY RESPONSIBLE!*

And the *World* would declare somewhat fatuously:

> Happily for the city, and for the country too, the Execu-
> tive of the State has arrived among us in time to assert the
> authority of the laws of New York and every loyal citizen will
> breathe more freely this day with a sense of returning confi-
> dence and hope.
>
> But we should be indifferent to the highest interests of this
> great community if we permitted this formidable crisis to pass
> by without using a brief plainness of speech with the real,
> though indirect authors of the terrible scenes we have been
> seeing. . . .

Horace Greeley, already on record with his opinion of the
executive's part in events, would show considerably more restraint than he often did. The *Tribune* would report the speech
verbatim and let readers draw their own conclusions. And down
in Washington, Secretary Welles would, as usual, confide *his* reaction to his diary: "Governor Seymour, whose partisans consti-
tuted the rioters and whose partisanship encouraged them, has
been in New York talking namby-pamby. This Sir Forcible Feeble
is himself chiefly responsible for the outrage. . . ."

As for the rioters, they went right on.

By early afternoon the reports on Mulberry Street showed the
police force to be holding its own, if only barely. The mobs' main
thrusts, in Second Avenue and at the Union Steam Works, had
ended in defeat. Some other developments warranted cautious
optimism. Most of the troops moving into the city were pinned
down by guard assignments, and so had been slow to see actual
fighting. But all arsenals and other government buildings appeared to be reasonably secure. In spite of some early panic in
Wall Street, business was going on there more or less normally.
Armed guards had been provided for clerks carrying money and
securities through the street. A strong detachment of regular in-

fantry and a National Guard artillery battery were on duty at the
United States subtreasury building. All approaches to the Brooklyn Navy Yard, target of a rumored mob attack, were covered by
the guns of the old receiving ship *North Carolina*, the corvette
Savannah, and several sailing gunboats. The ironclad *Passaic* and
the steam gunboat *Fuchsia* patrolled off the Battery, guns run out
ready to sweep any street where rioters might show themselves.

Not all of New York's poor had joined the mobs, either,
though it had seemed so for a while. A party of policemen marching down the Bowery after the battle at the Union Steam Works
was cheered loudly by crowds gathered on the sidewalks. "The
place was soon after quiet," reported a witness, "and the crowds
soon afterwards dispersed."

All over the city, however, other crowds had prowled and
rioted since daybreak. Even while the fighting swayed back and
forth in Second Avenue and Governor Seymour preached good
will and conciliation at City Hall Park, police squads had coped
with dozens of outbreaks great and small. In the Twentieth precinct Captain George Walling had started his day by hurrying to
the aid of a small party of soldiers beset by an angry throng in
Pitt Street. He had then proceeded up the Bowery, dispersing
several mobs. Within an hour he was marching north again, to
Allerton's Hotel on Eleventh Avenue between Fortieth and Forty-
first streets. A mob had sacked and burned the place; the fire had
spread to the City Cattle Market beyond; then someone had
turned the fear-crazed cattle out of their pens to stampede
through the streets. That mess attended to, Walling's men had
been dispatched across town to Fifth Avenue and Forty-seventh
to drive off another mob busily pillaging residences in the vicinity. They had backtracked then to Thirtieth Street near Seventh
Avenue, where rioters had set a Negro church burning and attacked the fire company that answered the alarm. From there
Walling had marched against still other crowds reported to be
looting hardware stores and gunsmiths' shops along Third Avenue. Thus far his day had been typical.

Overall it was a spotty picture, mobs not without their suc-
cesses, too. Following the recapture of the Union Steam Works,
Inspector Dilks and the bulk of his party joined an infantry pla-
toon in a grueling house-to-house battle against mob stragglers

holed up in a block on East Twenty-first Street. In the meantime, the Eighteenth precinct stationhouse on East Twenty-second was wrecked and burned. All but three of its normal complement had been sent to help Dilks, leaving the place practically undefended. Another mob warned the residents of a tenement block on Second Avenue between Thirty-fourth and Thirty-fifth streets that their homes would be burned that night—then treacherously started the fires within the hour. A Negro running to escape was caught and hanged. Down in the Sixth precinct a menacing crowd collected in front of the stationhouse at Baxter and Franklin streets. This station, too, was seriously undermanned at the time, though a number of Negro families from the area had taken refuge there. Several of these refugees offered to defend themselves if given weapons. A harried desk sergeant issued nightsticks, and about forty Negro men, taking a stand in the street outside, faced up to the rioters so grimly that they finally slunk away without a fight. Earlier in the day, however, a detachment of the luckless Invalid Corps was routed when it ventured on a foray against the barricades in Ninth Avenue. The bodies of several slain troopers were savagely mutilated with their own bayonets. Again witnesses told of women whose ferocity outdid their men's.

About one-thirty in the afternoon a disorderly multitude swept down Forty-first Street to the Weehawken Ferry building at the Hudson River. A saloon next door was owned by one O'Bryan, a Republican politician of some small local prominence who seemed to be, as one observer said later, "obnoxious to the crowd." They looted his bar of its potables, tore up the fixtures, drenched the wreckage with turpentine, and set it on fire. The flames quickly spread to the ferry building, then to a scow tied up at the pier nearby. When firemen of the Chatham Volunteer Hose Company Number 14 came running, they were not allowed through the street at first. But this was a comparatively good-natured mob. Someone managed to explain that the firemen owned the scow, whereupon they were permitted, fairly enough, to try to save their property while the ferry building burned to ashes. The Metropolitan Gas Works stood close by, and for a time the mob appeared bent on burning it too. But the engineer in charge, a Colonel A. J. White, stepped boldly into the street with a strenuous plea for mercy and common sense. He so impressed the rioters that they decided to spare the Works after all, and in a little while went roaring off in fine, high spirits—taking the plant's whole eighty-man work force with them.

The elusive figure of John Andrews of Virginia appears here again for a few moments. The mob's leader was described as a big man mounted on "a fine cavalry horse, fully caparisoned." He was garbed in a bright red shirt and brandished a saber as he ". . . galloped up and down the street all the while, apparently engaged in giving orders and instructions to his followers." So said a number of witnesses, and most of them thought that he was Andrews.

It must have been one-thirty or thereabouts, also, that Colonel H. J. O'Brien returned to Second Avenue. It was a quiet and nearly deserted street by that time, though still littered with brickbats, broken clubs, and other battle trash. The mob had carried off its dead. Somewhere out of sight its wounded nursed their hurts. But a mob dispersed is still people, and these were angry people. The man who had turned cannon on them that morning was foolhardy to have come back.

Colonel O'Brien lived in the neighborhood, which made it worse: he was known here. And somewhat belatedly, one would think, it had occurred to him that there might be reprisals against his family. If he had not been drinking, as Charles Chapin said that he was a little earlier, then he was a very brave man indeed —though far too rash for his own good. He was alone, on horseback, and armed with saber and pistol. He still wore his Eleventh New York Volunteer regimentals. And he was recognized, as he could hardly help but be. Word ran through the neighborhood. Nevertheless, he reached his home unmolested. It was empty. Neighbors, or it may have been a note left in the house, told him that his wife and children had gone off to stay with relatives in Brooklyn until the trouble blew over. Relieved, he started away. But a crowd was gathering now. Angry murmurs followed him: there went O'Brien; he was a cop-lover, a murderer; he turned cannon on women. . . . A man ran into the street, seized his stirrup, and tried to drag him from the saddle. O'Brien kicked out, and the man retreated. But others blocked the street. Some began to throw stones and brickbats. The colonel pulled up, dismounted, and went into a saloon on the corner of Second Avenue and Nineteenth Street. No one followed him in, but outside the crowd grew. There were shouts: "Come out, O'Brien, damn you!" and "Get him! Kill him!"

After a while he did come out. Perhaps a shot or two of whiskey had buttressed the courage that had brought him back here in the first place; perhaps he simply had nerved himself to the bold front that still might cow the crowd. He came out with pistol in one hand, saber in the other, and started across the sidewalk toward his horse. The crowd parted. They backed off to let him through, but grudgingly, egging one another on: "Get him! Kill the damned . . ."

Someone ran at him from behind and knocked him down. The rest were on him instantly—fists and feet, clubs and cobblestones, and whatever else they had. He never got up again. Tales were told later—how they tied a rope around his ankles and dragged him to and fro about the street, and when that palled they beat him again, and after all that he still lived. There was a story that a Catholic priest intervened long enough to administer the last sacrament, for O'Brien was an Irish Catholic, like most of his tormentors. And then, according to one version of this story, the priest callously went off about his business and the mob closed in again. Finally they turned him over to the women, who dragged him into his own backyard and went to work on him with knives, and it took him all the rest of the long, hot afternoon to die. Thus the various stories.

A week later the New York *Tribune* would print a letter from an anonymous reader who signed himself "Eye Witness," telling it somewhat differently. There were no women in the mob. O'Brien was beaten with clubs and musket butts after being taken from behind. At the end a man crushed his skull with a cobblestone.

And then, "Eye Witness" would conclude, the mob went off cheering loudly for Jeff Davis.

Chapter 16 | Barricades and Brooks Brothers

"ALL THIS TIME," WROTE CHARLES CHAPIN, "the fight was going on in every direction, while the fire bells continually ringing increased the terror which was, every hour, becoming widespread." The vast majority in the mobs probably neither knew nor cared that their governor had come to town. Chapin added, ". . . the draft now seemed to have been forgotten by the rioters in their thirst for plunder and blood. . . ."

One great crowd tramping down Twenty-ninth Street was diverted into Lamartine Place, near Eighth Avenue, by the cry that a fine, large home there had once been "Horace Greeley's boarding house." It happened to be true; the house actually belonged to a cousin of Greeley's named Gibbons. It was enough for the mob. Men and women swarmed joyously inside to smash and pillage. They were hard at it when Police Captain James Bogart led a detachment of the elite Broadway Squad up to take them in the rear. This crowd was tough and fiercely determined to hold on to their loot. A savage melee surged through the street, policemen hard-pressed to hold their own until a party of militia appeared and blasted an indiscriminate volley into the confusion. It struck down patrolmen as well as rioters, at least one of them wounded fatally. The crowd, also hurt but still full of fight, drew off in a slow retreat down Twenty-ninth Street. At Ninth Avenue it turned north and took shelter behind the barricades there.

Those barricades had worried police authorities all day. A series of them blocked the avenue from Thirty-seventh to Forty-fifth Streets. The mob had worked with furious energy and determination. Each was a formidable tangle of broken telegraph poles and lampposts, overturned carts, wagons, even omnibuses, and anything else at hand. Some had been laced together with wire torn from the telegraph poles. Similar barriers blocked most of the side streets. It was quite plain, as one observer wrote, that the rioters "had chosen these premises for their own, and meant to hold the area." Clearly, the barricades had to be taken. But it was well into the afternoon before police headquarters could assemble a force strong enough to risk an attack.

The available patrolmen under captains Walling and J. C. Slott were mustered at the Twentieth precinct station on West Thirty-fifth Street by about three o'clock. But Commissioner Acton also had asked General Brown for troops, and they were slower to report. It was after five when they arrived—two companies of regular infantry under a captain named Wesson. According to Chapin, General Sandford had promised some National Guard units, which never appeared at all. It was considered essential, however, that the attack be made while there still was daylight. So, about six o'clock, the combined force moved out.

In the opening phase of the operation that followed there is a strong hint that captains Walling and Slott may have started out with some reservations about their military allies. The soldiers—mostly men of the Invalid Corps up to now—had not precisely covered themselves with glory thus far, for a fact, especially from the viewpoint of tired policemen who had carried the brunt of the fighting almost without rest since Monday morning. Having arrived in Ninth Avenue, at any rate, the patrolmen closed ranks and advanced to spearhead the assault. The troops were held in reserve, it appears, and took no part in this first onset. But the rioters were several thousand strong. They had had most of the day to prepare their positions, were well armed with muskets, rifles and pistols, and had piled up large stocks of bricks and paving stones besides. A crackle of gunfire and a storm of missiles drove the police back. There was a hurried consultation, and then the troopers deployed in a skirmish line, laying down a heavy fire against the first barricade as well as windows and rooftops on both sides of the street beyond. These were combat veterans. Many of them were Connecticut boys, it seems, for a contemporary chronicler wrote somewhat emotionally: "All praise be it

said to these noble sons of Connecticut from the war; they understood their work most thoroughly. . . ." The fire was accurate and
galling, and under its cover the police moved forward again. A
special squad armed with axes led the way. As they hacked at the
barrier, a second wave of patrolmen swarmed through and over it
with nightsticks swinging; the troopers followed with a bayonet
charge, and the defenders broke; the barricade was taken. Resistance at the next one was considerably less spirited. One by one
the rest fell, too. It took a good two hours to carry them all. But
when the fighting ended, Ninth Avenue was a mob fortress no
longer, ". . . and although some innocent ones suffered from care-
lessness, by extending their heads from windows, or from other
exposed positions"—again quoting the chronicler above—"yet
there was but a small average of life lost to what there would
have been had this matter been left in less experienced hands."

That night Horace Greeley left his desk at the *Tribune* with
the announced intention of taking the horse car to his home on
Nineteenth Street, as was his nightly custom. (Some lines still
were running, though many had been put out of business by the
mobs, and the service everywhere was slow and subject to inter-
ruption.) Again it was his friend James Gilmore who recalled
how he and Sidney Gay apprehended him and prevailed on him,
virtually by physical force, to get into a closed hansom cab instead.

But not many had Greeley's crusty courage or his placid faith.
To the average New Yorker there seemed very few signs that law
and order were winning or that they would win. Many rioters
appeared to think the city already theirs, and many a discouraged
citizen probably agreed. It was obvious by this time, of course,
that almost any pitched battle could be won by the police, and
now by the soldiers as well. But the riots were becoming a kind of
guerrilla warfare, and mob resources seemed limitless. As Chapin
explained: "Had there been a single band of rioters, however
large, or well organized, a force of police and military properly
armed, could have been concentrated to have dispersed them.

"But the police were compelled to move from point to point,
to fight and conquer, only to march away to another battle
ground, and which while it was wearing out body and soul, had
but a temporary effect upon the mobs. . . ."

There were about five thousand saloons scattered throughout the worst of the riot-torn neighborhoods. None of them closed on Tuesday night. (None had closed on Monday, either, or would close later.) Curiously, it does not appear that anyone in authority even requested that they do so, though there was abundant evidence that whiskey had contributed to many of the worst mob outrages. Drunken gangs still sought Negroes in particular. More and more colored families were fleeing their homes, some to the precinct police stations, others trying to get out of the city altogether. And some who made it would never return. Many tried pathetically to carry off the most prized of their poor household goods. A witness told of crowds that gathered in Fifteenth Street to curse and jeer and pelt some of them with brickbats as they loaded these things into handcarts. Rioting went on all night. Scattered fires burned from the Battery to the Harlem River. Tonight there was no saving rainstorm to put them out. A large planing mill at Third Avenue and One Hundred and Twenty-ninth Street was totally destroyed. Another huge mob—possibly many people in it who had listened to Governor Seymour that morning—converged on Printing House Square and was beaten off in yet another attack, the fourth, on the *Tribune* building.

Frightening rumors ran through the city. One said that rioters had seized several livery stables and horse-car barns and were organizing a cavalry brigade to sweep the police from the streets. There was scant substance to it. A few mob leaders were, in fact, seen, or it was said that they were seen, on horseback. And one rioter was known to have stolen a horse from the Red Bird Stage Line's stable when a mob attacked the place during Tuesday morning. There was even slimmer evidence to back up another rumor—that rioters planned to free the Confederate prisoners of war held at a Union prison in Jersey City. Nevertheless, the prison director, one Dr. Dougel, took it seriously enough to telegraph his superiors and request that the prisoners be transferred to David's Island, where a Navy gunboat could help guard them. More ominous were still other stories that spoke of the violence as religious—nothing less than a Catholic revolution in the making. A mob was heard hurrahing lustily for the Pope while they sacked a Methodist mission in the Five Points. Other mobs were seen

bearing placards: *DOWN WITH PROTESTANTS!*
The city had its thousands of the gullible, the scared, and the merely
stupid who were ready to swallow this sort of scare-talk, for the
vast majority of the despised slum folk *were* Irish Catholics, and
everybody knew it. Yet many of the stories contained a germ of
truth. Deep-down resentments in the rioters, unchained now,
were lashing out in all directions: Protestants identified as the
enemy, along with the rich, the Negroes, and the Republicans.
Quite early in the rioting, Mayor Opdyke and others had appealed to Archbishop John Hughes, New York's ranking Catholic
prelate, to make a public statement urging his people to obey the
law and take no part in mob violence. For reasons of his own the
archbishop had declined to intervene, lending credence to even
the wildest of the rumors.

Great stretches of the city lay in darkness, save for the fitful
glare from burning buildings. The sky was overcast, and few
householders cared to show lights lest they attract the attention
of some roaming gang. Rioters had smashed the gaslights in many
streets, too, leaving whole blocks as black as caverns. Looters
were busy everywhere. Sometimes they were well organized.
Captain Walling's patrolmen, marching to disperse the mob in
Fifth Avenue that morning, had noticed a crowd of women and
children with empty sacks and market baskets waiting at Sixth
and Forth-sixth for the signal to join in the plundering. Any number of witnesses told of streets full of rioters burdened with clothing, silverware, bulky articles of furniture, even paintings, and all
sorts of odd bric-a-brac. In the frenzy of compulsive greed, much
of this looting made little sense. At the Gibbons home in Lamartine Place ". . . one burly, ferocious looking Irishman had under
his arm a huge bundle of music. . . ."

Now, in the concealing dark, such crowds grew even bolder.
Heretofore private residences had been hit hardest. Strangely, the
larger stores and fine shops had not suffered a great deal, except
those dealing in firearms or other items of possible use as weapons. But about nine o'clock a message was telegraphed into police
headquarters from the Fourth precinct, warning that a mob was
about to attack the Brooks Brothers clothing store on Catherine
Street.

Fifty patrolmen sent to the rescue burst upon a scene smack-

ing of macabre slapstick comedy. The mob was already in control. Three police officers who tried to stop them had been beaten
up and driven away; the display windows had been smashed, the
front doors broken down. The big building blazed with light,
every gas jet in it flaring brightly. Showers of haberdashery were
being tossed from upper windows. And the street below was a
mass of shaggy thugs happily trying on modish Brooks Brothers
suits and of frowsy women scurrying off into the night with arm-
fulls of fancy shirts, cravats, and underwear. They all seemed to
have forgotten the police. Taken by surprise, they gave way as
the charging patrolmen clubbed through to the front door. But a
rioter leaned from a second-story window and fired a pistol, and
the slapstick abruptly turned ugly. "Many of the rioters were
armed," wrote Chapin, "and the police seeing that the time had
come to lay aside the club, now drew their pistols and poured a
deadly volley into the crowded body. . . ." (It is not clear whether
this was a deliberate new tactic or one perhaps taken in desperation by policemen whose patience and physical stamina alike
were wearing thin.) The mob scattered. Some fell to their knees
and begged for mercy—a sign of weakness not often seen until
now. But others were trapped inside the store as the patrolmen
rushed in. Some of these fought bitterly, and there were casualties on both sides. There was one last, brief flash of slapstick as
well. Several thugs, cornered in the second story, tried to escape
by sliding down a rope through a trapdoor in the floor. Policemen
waiting at the bottom clubbed them senseless as they landed, one
by one. Several others were driven into a rear room and surrendered there without further resistance. These, it appears, were
the first large-scale arrests made since the start of the general
rioting.

There might still have been trouble, however, for parts of the
mob tried to rally in Catherine Street again, as so many others
had rallied before. But Inspector Daniel Carpenter arrived about
that time with his flying column, and they fled, many still decked
out in the height of Brooks Brothers' fashions. Sometime later a
detail of troops was sent to guard the store, and the police
marched their prisoners off to Mulberry Street. They were, observed Mr. Chapin dryly, "a motley, cowed gang."

Thus Tuesday night: another victory but no real peace, nor

any prospect of rest for the city's weary defenders. At midnight a telegram was delivered to the St. Nicholas Hotel:

Washington, July 14

To the Hon. George Opdyke
Mayor, New York City

Sir:
    Five regiments are under orders to return to New York. The retreat of Lee now becomes a rout, with his army broken and much heavier loss of killed and wounded than was supposed. This will relieve a large force for the restoration of order in New York.

EDWIN M. STANTON
SECRETARY OF WAR

It was heartening news. Another twenty-four hours would pass, though, before the regiments could get there.

IV   The Third Day, and the Fourth

Chapter 17 | "Give Them Grape and Plenty of It"

FOUR-THIRTY A.M.: A DEAD AND EERIE TIME IN THE CITY, a grave-yard hour. The clippity-clop of a coach horse's plodding hooves echoed hollowly in Third Avenue, rubble strewn after all the fighting that had raged there, but dark now and empty save for the lone hansom cab jogging south. The chance of a fare seemed dim. But the two nondescript figures hunched side by side on the driver's seat were not ordinary coachmen. They were James Crowley and Eldred Polhamus of the police telegraph bureau, and a fare was the last thing they wanted at the moment.

They were tired men. Few besides themselves ever would know the full story of their two days' and two nights' struggle to keep the bureau's lines open. Charles Chapin, a telegrapher himself, might have told it. It was a pity that he did not. All he said, with the professional's matter-of-fact brevity, was that "it would be readily appreciated by a telegraph man. . . ." Disconnected bits and pieces of it would come out later in other men's accounts. Ever since Crowley's near lynching in this same Third Avenue on Monday morning, both he and Polhamus and no doubt other men as well had worked almost without rest. Their difficulties had been discouraging, the risks far worse than that. Disguise, subterfuge, and their own gritty courage had been virtually their only protection. And there had been neither the time nor the facilities for proper repair work, even had the roaming mobs permitted it. Instead, they had wrought near miracles of ingenuity and make-do, splicing broken wires and stringing them unobtrusively down dark alleys and through backyards, supporting them on fences, housetops, trash barrels, or whatever else they could find in lieu of the poles torn down by rampaging rioters. Once Polhamus had had the boots charred completely off his feet while he traced a loose wire through the smoldering ruin of a burned-out building. Once Crowley, cornered by a suspicious crowd, had escaped a bad beating or worse only because a Catholic priest had chanced along to intercede for him. On occasion both men had mingled with the mobs, pretending to be rioters themselves. That had had its hazards too; swept up in an unexpected clash with police patrolmen, both had come near being brained by nightsticks. Another time they had talked their way out of a tight spot by posing as a pair of farmers from Westchester. So far, one way or another, they had got the job done.

A favorite guise was this present one of hack drivers. It enabled them to get about quickly from place to place, yet was not too likely to arouse the mobs' dubious interest. But hacks were customarily for hire, and that could lead to complications too. As now:

At Houston Street, five rough-looking characters stepped out of the shadows and hailed them. There was not much they could do but pull up. The five, obviously members of some gang on the prowl, climbed into the hack and ordered them to drive on. Up on the high seatbox Crowley and Polhamus exchanged glances. This same thing had happened once before. That time the passengers had proved bleary with whiskey, and it had been no great trick to deliver them straight to the front door of police headquarters and have them clapped into cells before they realized what was going on. By pure chance they were on their way to 300 Mulberry Street now, too. With luck and a little nerve they might repeat the coup. But this morning's passengers were more alert, and either grew suspicious or changed their minds enroute. Some way short of Mulberry Street one of them stuck head and shoulders out of the hack, brandished a large pistol, and ordered the drivers to turn around and head back uptown. Neither of them was armed; they could only obey and hope to play out the pretense. At a saloon in the Tenth Ward the hoodlums ordered the hack stopped. They piled out, commmanded the two drivers to get down also, and all trooped into the place like boon companions. It turned out that that was what they were, like it or not. Polhamus and Crowley were slapped boisterously on the back, praised boozily as "good fellows," treated to lemonades and at length allowed to go. In parting one of the men pressed fifty cents hack fare on them.

It was an incongruous beginning for another tragic day.

Wednesday would be the hottest day of the year, the torment of its stifling heat made worse by the smoke and stench of burning. Long before dawn the police department's weary grind began again. Another large mob marched down Fulton Street with the evident intention of setting a torch to Fulton Market. Sometime Tuesday evening, it was said, a Negro had fled there and market workers had taken him in. But detectives circulating in the district learned that the punitive mob then meant to go on to the ferry house at the foot of Fulton Street and burn it too, so that no more troops from the harbor could land there. Inspector Leonard and a force from headquarters scattered this crowd after a mild skirmish. But by daylight sporadic outbreaks were cropping up as before, all over town. It would be another bitter day for the Negroes, and for many a white as well.

Ann Derrickson was white—a quiet, hard-working housewife, by all accounts. She lived at 11 York Street, had always got on well with her neighbors. But Ann Derrickson was married to a Negro sailor, and they had a little boy. Early Wednesday morning a gang of Irishwomen from the vicinity caught the child as he played in the street outside his home. These women had run with the mobs, and hate had burned all the softness out of them. They saw the little mulatto boy as a "nigger's brat"—they screamed that as they pounced on him, a witness remembered—and they would have killed him had Mrs. Derrickson not come flying from the house to stop them. Then they turned on her. The boy squirmed out of the scuffle unhurt, and a passing police detail drove the harpies away before they had quite finished with the mother. Not in time, though; she would die in Bellevue Hospital several weeks later.

This long, hot Wednesday would be a make-or-break day for the city authorities. Weariness, wounds, and the strain of unceasing demands on dwindling resources had brought the police department's fighting spearheads very close to collapse. No one admitted it, not even later. But Charles Chapin's recollections convey a little of the atmosphere of desperation at 300 Mulberry Street. "The morning of the 3rd day opened with both parties pretty well worn out," he wrote, "and altho' the rioters had many dead and wounded to mourn over they were not yet conquered.

"Forty-eight hours without sleep or rest was telling upon even the wiry Mr. Acton, but he would confess to no fatigue.

"Every moment that could be spared was devoted to the comfort and encouragement of the wounded police and military, who were tenderly cared for at the Head Quarters, while he saw that ample provision was made for the comfort of the still active members. . . .

"With the small force at command the prospect was a gloomy one and the return of the absent militia [from Pennsylvania] was anxiously looked for. Still there must be no wavering. . . ."

There was none. But it was apparent that the Army units available now would have to take over the heaviest part of the day's work. At nine o'clock, the morning still young, a horde of some five thousand was reported hanging and burning Negroes in the district around Eighth Avenue and Thirty-second Street. The force hastily assembled and dispatched by General Brown included a small cavalry troop, some infantry of the Eighth Regiment of Volunteers, and a battery of howitzers from the Third New York Artillery, U.S. Volunteers, all under the command of Colonel Gershom Mott of the regular Army. The report had not been exaggerated. As the column's vanguard marched down Thirty-second and turned into Eighth Avenue, they saw three Negroes dangling from lampposts above a sea of heads and tossing arms. The clothing of one body was afire, and women pranced about all three, hacking and slashing at them with knives while their menfolk yelled and cheered them on.

The mob recoiled at sight of the soldiers; and Colonel Mott, spurring out ahead, cut the nearest body down with a sweep of his sword. At that a man dashed out of the mob and tried to drag him off his horse. The colonel ran him through. But others advanced, cursing and threatening. Then, as Mott cantered back to his column, the whole mob surged forward behind the usual shower of bricks, stones, and gunshots. The infantrymen met them with fixed bayonets. A saber charge by the cavalry detachment rolled the mob backward. But it closed ranks as the impetus of the charge died and came roaring to the attack again, forcing infantry and mounted men alike back into Thirty-second Street in a solid, fighting mass too furious to be stemmed. There had been time, however, for Captain John H. Howell of the artillery to unlimber a pair of howitzers and wheel them into position at Seventh Avenue, loaded with canister and grape. As the troopers fell back in good order and opened out to give the guns a clear field of fire, he shouted at the mob to stop. Fair warning: they should have known he meant it. But if these hard-bitten masses knew about yesterday's carnage at Second Avenue, they were past caring. They saw soldiers retreating; perhaps they thought the day was won, if a mob can think at all. With their jeers of defiance dinning at him, the captain gave the command to fire.

Six rounds; it had taken that many yesterday and it took six today, the gunners loading and firing with disciplined precision, before the mob broke under the punishment and scattered back into Eighth Avenue. There most of them went streaming north to vent their spite in easier depradations.

This was typical. The mobs' tenacity remained as hardy as ever. A little later in the morning more rioters attacked Jackson's Foundry on Twenty-eighth Street between First and Second avenues. But an artillery battery was on duty there too, and after a brief taste of canister this crowd drew off and broke up. Part of it wandered across town to plunder and burn a block of homes on Seventh Avenue. The rest waited until the soldiers had withdrawn, then reassembled in Twenty-eighth Street and burned a half-dozen houses along Second Avenue, though they did not venture to move against the foundry a second time. Up and down the East Side other buildings were on fire, Negro victims being hunted, rioters clashing with squads of troopers or police. When Colonel Mott marched his victorious detachment away from Eighth Avenue, he left the bodies of the three murdered Negroes on the sidewalk, apparently under the impression that the police would remove them to the morgue for identification. But the soldiers scarcely had gone before mob stragglers were back to carry off their own fallen. They strung the bodies up again, and there they hung for most of the day—grisly reminders that the mob's hate and fury were implacable. The police had learned, and now the military was learning too. These armies out of the slums could be beaten, smashed, and scattered—but they sprang up again like the parts of a vast Antaeus crushed to earth, and came back stronger than before. "As the day wore on," Chapin recalled, "matters continued to wear a threatening appearance. At the same moment came news of mob gatherings, and calls for help, from entirely opposite points. But the scenes of this day were scarcely different from the preceding ones," he added wearily.

Had anyone been in a position to view the overall scene with anything like detachment (no one was), he might have wondered at some of the troop assignments. There was a great deal of confusion, inevitably; probably many misunderstandings, as well. But one suspects that there was influence brought to bear in various quarters, too. Thus the famous Fifth Avenue Hotel, favorite refuge of what the *Tribune* called the "bon ton" and scene of the noisy demonstration for General McClellan on Monday night, soon resembled a citadel. A sturdy wooden platform had been erected ten feet above the floor of the grand ballroom, from which a strong military detail could fire down upon invading rioters while safely out of reach themselves. The soldiers were quartered in the hotel bar, possibly a grievous hardship for the gentleman accustomed to drink to the downfall of the Abolitionists. The Fifth Avenue was not molested, however, and the troopers had a rather pleasant tour of duty.

At the same time, shipyards along the East and Hudson rivers got no guards at all, though many of them were engaged in U.S. naval construction which made them obvious targets for any mobs with militant Copperhead leanings. An example was the big Webb and Allen establishment, stretching along the East River front from Fifth to Seventh streets. Around midmorning Wednesday, a large, rough crowd swept into the place and ordered the management to close down. The big yard bell was rung as a signal to knock off. Workmen were forced to arm themselves with hammers, crowbars, and other tools, and marched off as mob conscripts. Webb and Allen were among the oldest and largest shipbuilders in the nation, with a distinguished history that went back to the early years of the century. Donald McKay of East Boston, known on all the seven seas as America's premier builder of flash clippers, had learned his trade as a Webb apprentice. The

Webbs themselves, first father and then son, had launched some of the best of the staunch Atlantic packets and tall-hatted Cape Horn flyers that made the Yankee merchant marine supreme throughout the 1840's and 1850's. The *Dunderberg,* a big iron ram for the Navy, was nearing completion on the yard ways now. And some in the mob evidently began to regret having let her live. Presently loyal workmen turned up at the yard again. They had slipped away to bring word that the rioters were coming back, this time with their minds made up to burn the *Dunderberg.*

The warning reached Mulberry Street barely in time. Shortly after noon, four hundred troopers of the Seventh Regiment, Old National Guard, quickstepped down Sixth Street and overtook a thousand hooligans striding purposefully along behind several leaders mounted on horseback. It was an array less warlike than it looked, however. Disconcerted at being taken from the rear, the rioters broke up and fled without a fight, leaving behind a strewn windrow of turpentine bottles and various other flammables. So the threat of arson had been real enough. The troopers marched on to Webb and Allen's and left a permanent guard there. The Navy's big new ram was saved—one of the day's few bloodless victories.

Governor Seymour had stayed on in the city, headquartered like Mayor Opdyke at the St. Nicholas Hotel. The crisis had sunk personal dislike and political difference for the time being, though in fact there was not a great deal that either executive could do anymore. Both had had opportunity to play the leader, and neither had quite measured up. The fighting men would save New York now, or lose it, on the battleground of its own streets. With Major General John E. Wool heading up the Military Department of the East from a suite at the St. Nicholas also, the place should have been an important command post. It was not, despite the appropriate air of snap and purpose. Wool's adjutant, Major C. T. Christiansen, bustled busily with paperwork and careful detail, after the manner of military adjutants. Troopers stood guard smartly at the entrance, couriers came and went, and somehow it all managed to be meaningless. What went on, no one really understood, and never would. Orders were issued, apparently a great many of them, though it was not always clear to whom. Afterward General Brown would deny that he ever re-

ceived most of them, and even Major Christiansen would disclaim
any knowledge of others. Nevertheless, they had the splendid
ring of authority, some of them. Viz, one on Monday to the effect
that ". . . patrols of military and police should be sent through the
disaffected districts," and a follow-up on Tuesday: "To-day there
must be no child's play. . . ." There was something querulous and
empty and slightly pitiful about such orders: an old soldier fum-
bling to take hold of a situation that was beyond him. At seventy-
nine, John Wool had come a year or so too far down the long trail
from 1812 through Buena Vista and Fortress Monroe into this
metropolis in revolt.

He was not the only confused man in New York. Ordinary
citizens who found the time to read their newspapers that
Wednesday felt themselves caught up in angry little feuds that
popped and sputtered alongside the main event. The *Daily News*
continued to see the mobs as decent working people, wholly justified if perhaps a little overzealous in their wrath against an Administration guilty of every sin an evil government could devise.
Agreeing only a trifle less vociferously, the *World* pleaded for
gentleness and forbearance in putting down the disorders and
urged the authorities to shun the use of firearms. Clubs, the
World's editorialist pointed out—with a degree of accuracy, if
somewhat too indulgently—had proved adequate for the job.
Today, too, the *World* had found another villain to share the
blame for New York's ordeal. The editorial continued:

> This is no time for veiled or for uncertain speech. The very
> moment bids us ope our mouths. . . . We charge it, therefore,
> plainly upon the radical journals of this city that they, and
> chiefly they, have educated the people of New York to the
> pitch of passion and the extremes of desperate feeling which
> have gleamed out so luridly and so terribly upon us in these
> last sad days.

No one could miss this slap at the *Tribune* and the New York
Times. But Henry J. Raymond of the *Times*, inclined in the beginning to reserve judgment, had had a bellyful by this time, of
lawlessness and fuzzy thinking both. Thundered the *Times*
sternly:

> This mob is not the people, nor does it belong to the
> people. It is for the most part made up of the vilest elements

of the city. It has not even the poor merit of being what mobs usually are—the product of mere ignorance and passion. They talk, or rather they did talk at first, of the oppressiveness of the Conscription Law; but three-fourths of those who have been actively engaged in violence have been boys and young men under twenty years of age, and not at all subject to the Conscription. Were the Conscription Law to be abrogated tomorrow, the controlling inspiration of the mob would remain the same. It comes from sources quite independent of that law, or any other law—from a malignant hate toward those in better circumstances, from a craving for plunder, from a barbarous spite against a different race, from a disposition to bolster up the failing fortunes of the Southern rebels. . . .

In that last, Raymond was lining up with Horace Greeley. The mob must be crushed at once, he concluded. And with reference to the use of cannon against the rioters—which had horrified many people—he had but one piece of advice for the military: "Give them grape and plenty of it."

Nothing had been heard from the New York City Common Council since its refusal to convene on Monday. It appears that individual councilmen, though, had been very diligent behind the scenes. Incredibly—or perhaps altogether naturally, considering New York's long tolerance of municipal venality—most of them seem to have shown less interest in quelling the riots than in lending their good offices to constituents among the rioters. The machine, built on political favoritism, lubricated with graft, and dedicated to taking care of its own through thick and thin, had run the city for too many years. Like a blind mechanical monster, it simply went on running now. Two weeks later, in an open letter published in the New York *Herald*, General Harvey Brown would complain bitterly of ". . . pressure from high dignitaries for the withdrawal of troops from certain wards," and praise Thomas Acton for his integrity in resisting it. Nevertheless, the pressure went on without letup, even while hapless Negroes were being murdered and mobs ran rampant through many of those selfsame wards.

On Wednesday afternoon the Council finally saw its duty as a civic body. It met just long enough to pass an ordinance empowering the city to borrow two and one-half million dollars to set up a fund out of which the three hundred dollars substitute fee would be paid for any poor draftee who requested it. (Later on the sum would be boosted to three million, seven hundred and fifty thousand.) Newspapers reported the Council's action in subsequent editions, but few of them made very much of it. The *Times* had spelled it out: appeasement was not going to restore peace now.

Chapter 18 | "The Mob Ain't Commenced Yet"

IN THE MIDST OF WAR THE NEWS OUT OF NEW YORK CITY had slighter impact around the Union than it might have had. The newspapers were almost unanimous in calling the disturbances "draft riots," and it went without saying that most communities had troubles of their own on that score. There was rioting in Boston, where the slums teemed with underprivileged Irish too. Unrest simmered and would shortly break into open violence in Troy, New York, and other cities great and small. Conscription and its attendant bloodshed, burnings, and near rebellion were an old story in the Pennsylvania coalfields. As far west as Chicago, General Ambrose Burnside had the Military Department of the Ohio seething with resentment of his heavy-handed suppression of Copperhead treason, as he called it. Little crossroads towns all through Illinois, Indiana, and Ohio stewed in militant opposition to the draft on the one hand and nervous panic over tales of Secessionist plottings on the other. Where such local turmoils loomed large, New York's woes seemed far away and not very newsworthy; wasn't everybody doing it, after all?

Journalists down south in the Confederacy would be pleased to get the word of Yankees at each other's throats, of course, but they didn't have it yet. The news would take longer still to cross the Atlantic. But in England public interest in the American civil war had run high from the very start. By August the English press would be devoting large amounts of space to accounts of the rioting in New York. (Long before that, though, there would be harder evidence of England's concern. Friday editions of the

New York *Tribune* would note briefly that a British man-of-war was on its way to safeguard the interests of British subjects in the city.)

In Washington the war itself was bigger news, and closer to home, besides. Yet, official Washington was concerned. Though the Congress was not in session, national affairs had kept a good many of its members in the capital, and some of them were quick to speak up for martial law in New York City. There were those in Mr. Lincoln's cabinet who agreed. Gideon Welles wrote in his diary that, "General Wool, unfitted by age for such duties, though patriotic and well disposed, had been continued in command there at a time when a younger and more vigorous mind was required. In many respects General Butler would at this time have best filled that position. . . ." He meant Benjamin Franklin Butler: no great shakes as a soldier, to be sure—a political general through and through—but a rabid hard-war man and a tough administrator who had lately presided over occupied New Orleans with such stiff-necked severity that angry Southerners would forever afterward know him as "The Beast." In the capital's radical Abolitionist circle, many were of Welles's mind. Led by Senator Edward Morgan, though, most New York Republicans opted for their own Major General James S. Wadsworth. There was some logic in the idea. Wadsworth was a gentleman farmer from upstate, a hero of the recent victory at Gettysburg, and the man Horatio Seymour had defeated for the New York governorship in the last election. (He had refused to go home and campaign for the office on the grounds that it was not fitting for a soldier to do so.) There would therefore have been a wry political irony, and possibly some solid advantage, too, in his appointment.

Abraham Lincoln vetoed all such suggestions. It would be time enough for the Federal government to step in, he said, "when the State fails to do its duty." If there were political considerations involved here, the President could see them perhaps a little more clearly than some of his advisers. There was no hasty action. Instead, a telegram was drafted and sent off:

War Department
Washington, D.C.

July 15, 1863

Governor Seymour:

Eleven New York Regiments have been relieved and are at Frederick [Maryland] and will be forwarded to New York as fast as transport can be furnished. Please signify anything you may desire to be done by this department. Whatever means are at its disposal shall be at your command for the purpose of restoring order in New York.

EDWIN STANTON
SECRETARY OF WAR

That laid the cards on the table. If it *was* rebellion going on up there, it would be crushed. But Seymour was the man on the spot; let the responsibility be his. Copperhead Democrats would be presented with no opportunity to scream persecution over a military dictator in the Union's largest city.

Help promised still was help deferred, though. New York fretted in heat, uncertainty, and the dread of violence. If there was any improvement in the situation as Wednesday dragged along, few saw any signs of it.

Andrews of Virginia turned up, haranguing a crowd again. Two men on horseback rode up to another crowd at the corner of Thirty-third Street and Third Avenue. They called for three cheers for Jeff Davis. The crowd hurrahed. These were rumors, but they pointed up the great, underlying fear: that the rioters had a purpose relentlessly Secessionist, that they had leadership, above all that they were organized. And incidents more solid than mere rumor kept cropping up to lend substance to the fear.

A man walked into Mr. A. C. Alvord's printing shop at Number 15 Vandewater Street in the Fourth Ward. He was alone; there was no disturbance in the street outside, no report of a mob in the vicinity at the time. Afterward no one was able to describe the man very well. He wore "a red shirt, blue pants and a blue cap," that was about all. He asked for Mr. Alvord, and when Alvord appeared he ordered him coolly to shut down the shop. Apparently he was reasonably civil about it, made no threats. At that point in the rioting he did not have to. He left the place but came back a short while later to satisfy himself that it *was* shut down. And it was; he accompanied the proprietor on an inspection of the premises to make sure. He talked freely, everyone present agreed; even mentiond that he once had worked for Alvord himself (though none of the employees seemed to remember him). In the course of the conversation someone ventured to comment on the report, widely circulated around town by that time, that the Seventh Regiment of the New York National Guard was on its way back to the city to put down the rioters. The man bridled at that.

"We were not organized yesterday but are today; and we're going to see who's to be put down and who is not," he retorted. "The mob ain't commenced yet."

Braggadocio, perhaps. But there was a flavor of cocksure arrogance about the whole incident that impressed the *Tribune*, at least. A *Tribune* reporter would write it all up next day, adding that similar calls were made on a number of other printing plants in the city at about the same time. Like Mr. Alvord, most of the proprietors obeyed orders and closed up. Several of them recalled "a sort of badge" worn by their callers and took for granted that they were mob leaders. No one knew why printing establishments had been singled out. The *Tribune* man did not hazard any guesses. But the hint of mysterious purpose was unnerving.

Throughout Tuesday and Wednesday, relations between Major General Sandford and Brigadier General Brown remained where they had ended Monday night: that is to say, precisely nowhere. The two had not met again. There had been no real effort at cooperation or even at any workable liaison between 300 Mulberry Street and the arsenal on Seventh Avenue. General Wool had done nothing concrete to end the impasse. Brown, of course, had been busy, increasingly so as Army units reported in from the harbor forts and got into action. In the general confusion of Tuesday, Sandford's activities are more difficult to pin down. But while the crochety old lawyer-militiaman brooded over his bruised prerogatives, he probably was not as idle as some of his critics inferred. Still the local militia had seen very little action up to Wednesday and had won even less distinction. No doubt many of the units were slow to assemble at the arsenal. And some, like the Tenth New York, were occupied with necessary if not very glamorous guard duties. On Wednesday afternoon, however, the militia finally arrived at the ball.

A force issued from the arsenal, formed ranks, and marched

eight blocks down Seventh Avenue to Twenty-seventh Street, where a large and menacing crowd had gathered. Afterward commentators did not have much to say about this encounter, if it could be called that. There was no clash. The crowd fell back before the show of force. But apparently it did not disperse. Charles Chapin, no admirer of General Sandford, was among the few who mentioned the occurrence at all. He wrote that ". . . after making an imposing demonstration the force was marched from the ground leaving the mob in full possession of the field." He called it "unfortunate," and a "retrograde movement" which only emboldened the rioters. But the militiamen, amateur citizen-soldiers anxious to show their mettle, were probably emboldened as well. And that was doubly unfortunate, for there was a vast difference between a fight and a demonstration. Presently they found that out.

Toward six in the evening the militia marched again. This time they were about two hundred and fifty strong, and commanded by a Colonel Cleveland Winslow. According to some sources, the force included "enrolled citizens" in addition to parts of two troops known as the Hawkins Zouaves and the Duryea Zouaves, so it appears to have been something of a grab-bag column. It was a gaudy one, at any rate, as it stepped out toward First Avenue to put down a mob reported congregating between Seventeenth and Eighteenth streets. These Zouave companies were a phenomenon of the times, immensely popular among many militia enlistees because of their colorful uniforms and general air of raffish swagger. As was the custom among such volunteer units, they frequently were named for the prominent citizen who sponsored or commanded them. But they called themselves Zouaves after the French colonial troops from Algeria, first brought to world attention during the Crimean War in 1854 and widely admired for their ferocity and exotic native dress. In the American version this latter suggested some ceremonial lodge regalia rather more than military garb, what with its voluminous pantaloons, bright sashes, jackets vivid with embroidery and gold braid, and a variety of outlandish headgear. Regardless of these fripperies, not at all looked down on by military thinking of the 1860's, Zouave regiments could be as brave as any. Many of them served the Union with great valor, once they had been blooded in battle—*seen the elephant*, as soldier slang expressed it. This force of Colonel Winslow's had seen no elephants. But jingling along in the rear were two small brass howitzers attached to the Hawkins Zouaves. Cannon had made the difference before. No doubt they would again.

As the weary patrolmen of the Metropolitan Police could have told these militiamen, mobs varied considerably in temper and the will to fight. It was their misfortune that this one they were about to catch was a Tartar.

It was a large mob, perhaps as large as any since Monday, and it showed no disposition to be awed by the advancing uniforms. This was strictly the militia's show. General Sandford had not deigned to ask support of Brown or Acton; no police were on hand and none appeared. For once the department's own communications system seems to have broken down, for nothing was known on Mulberry Street of this mob's gathering. And it proceeded to handle the Zouaves unmercifully. They fought well enough—the infantry first with rifle and bayonet against clubs, knives, and the inevitable rain of brickbats and cobbles. When at length they fell back under the surging weight of superior numbers, Colonel E. E. Jardine of the howitzer battery was ready. But a mob could learn, it appeared, and suddenly this one had a better tactic than its predecessors' suicidal rush into the cannon mouths. At Jardine's order to fire, toughs flung themselves flat on the pavement or scattered into doorways on both sides of the street. And in the intervals between rounds of canister screaming harmlessly down First Avenue, an answering rattle of musketry began to grow from windows and rooftops. Rioters had armed themselves with guns before, but few had used them very skillfully. These fellows were different; some of them appeared to be sharpshooters. It was said afterward that they concentrated their fire on the officers. It was past six o'clock now, and the garish Zouave trappings made good targets in the failing light. Troopers began to huddle and mill together. Weekend soldiers whose drill had prepared them for no such trap as this, they lacked the disciplined toughness to go in and clear the buildings hand to hand as police patrolmen would have done. And the enemy grew bolder as the cannon fire slackened. Colonel Jardine fell, shot through the thigh by a man who was seen to step deliberately into the

A GORILLA ON THE LOOSE DRAGGING COLONEL O'BRIEN'S BODY THROUGH THE MUD

SACKING BROOKS CLOTHING STORE

THE DEAD SERGEANT IN TWENTY-SECOND STREET NEGRO QUARTERS IN SULLIVAN STREET

N. Y. Historical Society

"AT THE SAME MOMENT CAME NEWS OF MOB GATHERINGS,
AND CALLS FOR HELP, FROM ENTIRELY OPPOSITE POINTS . . ."
Sketches of various riot incidents as seen by artists for *Harper's Weekly.*
(p. 138)

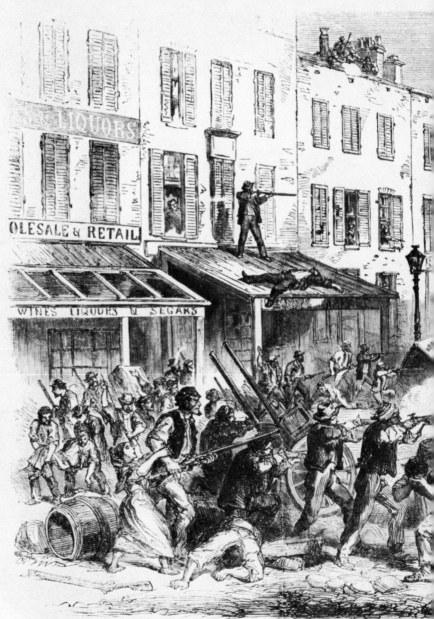

THE RIOTS IN NEW YORK: CONFLICT BETWEEN THE MILITARY AND THE RIOTERS IN FIRST-AVENUE

"*IT WAS A LARGE MOB...AND IT SHOWED NO DISPOSITION TO BE AWED BY THE ADVANCING UNIFORMS.*" Another sketch from the *Illustrated London News*, and very likely the way it looked. The militia came off badly in this First Avenue clash. (p. *148*)

N.Y. Historical Society

POLICEMEN RECOVERING STOLEN GOODS   "THE POPULAR TUMULT"—ONE OF THE "PEOPLE"
FROM THE SHANTIES IN YORKVILLE

N.Y. Historical Society

RIOTERS CHASING NEGRO WOMEN AND CHILDREN THROUGH THE VACANT LOTS IN LEXINGTON AVENUE

*"BUT THE SCENES OF THIS DAY WERE SCARCELY DIFFER-
ENT..."* Another page of sketches "from life," as seen by the *New York
Illustrated News.* (p. 138)

street, steady his musket on a companion's shoulder, and draw a careful bead. The situation was hopeless, Winslow realized at last, unless police or veteran troops could be brought in to drive the rioters into the open and give the howitzers a chance. Apparently with some such thought in mind, he sent a runner off for help and gave the order to withdraw until it got there. He had waited a shade too long, though. The mob poured out of conceal-ment in vindictive frenzy, and the retreat fell apart in panic. The howitzers were overrun, the gunners beaten down. Zouaves and enrolled civilians abandoned their fallen comrades and ran, with the mob roaring in pursuit. There was no quarter. The hunt spread relentlessly down the avenue and off into every side street, and not many got away.

Colonel Jardine did, by an unlikely piece of luck no fictioneer would have dared invent. Somehow, while rioters trampled over and around them, he and two wounded officers of the Duryea Zouaves crawled more than a block to Second Avenue, where they tumbled into the basement of a building near Nineteenth Street. Two women who lived there were not mob sympathizers, as so many were not, even in the meaner districts. They helped the fugitives into a dim corner and contrived a hiding place by piling firewood on top of them. Still the mob came back and found them after a while. One man recognized Jardine; there had been some casual friendship between them in the past, perhaps a favor done, and so he stood over the wounded Zouave and held his fellows off. But before they left they clubbed the other two officers to death.

Like so many of those who happened to emerge for a moment from the faceless obscurity of the mobs, this man never was named publicly. Possibly Jardine held his tongue out of gratitude. But the small incident hints at the personal relationships—there may have been many—inextricably tangled and caught up in the divided loyalties of this civil insurrection.

The militia's debacle led to a long and arduous night action between the victorious mob and a strong detachment of the Twelfth Infantry sent out from police headquarters under cap-tains Putnam and Franklin. Both were later cited by General Brown as "meriting especial praise." Sometime before this force reached the scene, rioters had trundled off the Hawkins Zouaves' two howitzers as prizes of war, and the threat of a mob armed with artillery of its own aroused some consternation for a while. In the confusion of their triumph, however, the rioters had apparently neglected to seize any ammunition for the guns. Too, these people who had spent their lives in the city slums probably were ignorant of artillery. Had they possessed even small quantitites of looted gunpowder, they might have crammed the howitzers' barrels with nails, bolts, or old scrap iron, which was all that canister amounted to anyway. But whatever it may have been at first, mob organization clearly was beginning to break down now. The captured howitzers never were turned on the city's defenders, in any case. Nevertheless, the relief column had no easy time of it. Savage skirmishing went on for blocks in all directions, the rioters ferociously refusing to break and run even under heavy punishment. Many were dug out of last-ditch pockets of resistance in tenement cells and on rooftops only by dint of bitter close-quarter fighting. In the end the mob took a bad mauling, for the soldiers were not gentle with them. A reporter for the *Herald* would tell of it next day: "The pickets brought in a large number of prisoners, dirty, ragged and sullen in appearance but sullen and determined in demeanor. With a jerk and a twist from their captors they soon found themselves located in a secure place. They were then tied up something like trussed fowls, and left to meditate at their leisure."

The *Herald* had had about enough, was beginning to sound a bit weary of these rioters it had defended earlier as plain folk with a legitimate grievance. But at the end of this third straight day of vicious fighting there still was little sign that the mob's spirit was flagging.

Their victory had not been allowed to stand, nevertheless. And though Wednesday had been a long and wearing day in the brutal heat, there was apparently a strengthening conviction among the forces of the law that they were gaining the upper hand. Later some writers would quote Thomas Acton as declaring at this point that the backbone of the disorder was broken. If he said it, which is doubtful, it probably was meant as a prop to public confidence, and in the expectation that help would arrive that night. Mayor Opdyke, too, issued another proclamation:

TO ALL CITIZENS OF NEW YORK:

I am happy to announce to you that the riot which for two days has disgraced our city, has been in good measure subjected to the control of public authorities. What now remains of the mob are fragments prowling about for plunder and for the purpose of meeting these you are invited to form voluntary associations under competent leaders to patrol and guard your districts. With these exceptions you are requested to resume your accustomed daily vocations.

A strangely optimistic document, this. In the face of the day's events, His Honor's reassuring tone scarcely seems justified. And his "invitation" to citizens to take over the maintenance of order in their own neighborhoods smacks somewhat of irresponsibility, if not of desperation. Far too many citizens already had taken the law into their own hands since Monday morning. Besides, the organization of a citizens' Volunteer Police Reserve had been in progress, under the department's own supervision, for more than forty-eight hours now. One is left with the impression that New York's mayor was not looking his best under duress.

Horatio Seymour made no public statement of any kind, even after receiving Edwin Stanton's telegram.

Between ten P.M. and midnight—various reports would differ considerably as to the exact hour—the Jersey City ferryboat nosed into its slip at Canal Street. Aboard was the Seventy-fourth Regiment, New York State National Guard. So the newspapers all called it, anyway. More accurately, as one of the volunteer units previously absorbed into the Union Army, it was simply the Seventy-fourth New York now. No matter; it was the first of the promised regiments from Pennsylvania, and that was the important thing. Some accounts said that it marched ashore to the strains of the regimental band, which sounds unlikely. But it may have, for the Union's was an army much given to its bands. The Seventy-fourth were mostly German-American boys of Dan Sickles' Excelsior Brigade. They came almost directly from Gettysburg, had taken a fearful beating in the overextended line south of Cemetery Hill on July 2, and had left a great many brave men dead there. It was a gaunt and jaded shadow of a regiment, to tell the truth, but it had looked the elephant in the eye and knew it, and riot in New York would hold no terror after that. The troopers came ashore in full field kits, ready for action. Officers had been sent to greet Lieutenant Colonal Thomas Holt, the regimental commander, and guide him through the dark streets to police headquarters. General Brown was taking no chances of another such foul-up as Monday night's; none of these new arrivals would report mistakenly to General Sandford if he could help it.

No reports tell of any crowds gathering to cheer the Seventy-fourth. There was no mob there to contest their landing. But across the East River about that same time there was a glow of burning in the sky. The long-drawn tension in Brooklyn had burst into flames; the mob there had commenced.

Chapter 19 | Mr. Chapin's Vigilantes

DURING THREE HECTIC DAYS SINCE MONDAY MORNING, more than four thousand messages—reports of mob movements and orders for the police and military detachments that tried to cope with them—had crackled in and out of the telegraph bureau's big basement room on Mulberry Street. Three operators, Charles Chapin, John Duvall, and James Lucas, had handled the whole traffic, which meant that they had had no more rest than anyone else at headquarters. And all the while, like the others there, they had fought off the same worries that plagued every householder in the city. Almost apologetically, having recorded the events of Wednesday, Chapin's narrative adds that, "I must now turn to matters of a purely personal character."

The department had done what it could to protect its own. At the height of the crucial fighting for the Union Steam Works on Tuesday, Commissioner Acton himself had ordered the wires cleared for a message to the Fifth precinct station: "Send to Dr. Purple at 183 Hudson street to go as soon as possible to Inspector Leonard's house," it had said. "Baby very sick." An escort of patrolmen had hurried to fetch the doctor and someone took the trouble to note that he arrived in time and the baby later recovered. But everyone connected with hated authority was subject to special attention by the mobs. The mayor's home had been attacked twice. Provost Marshal Nugent's had been burned. So had Postmaster Wakeman's and others'. Charles Chapin's position might easily be worse than most, for Thomas Acton happened to be his landlord.

The house was located on Eighty-fourth Street near Second

Avenue, well north in the Yorkville district. It was a frame building set in a block of similar construction, hence very vulnerable to
fire. Moreover, an apartment on the second floor was occupied by
a police officer known as "Bull Run" Brown, back on the job after
having joined the Army, been wounded in action, and discharged.
Brown, a tough and conscientious policeman, was markedly unpopular with Yorkville's rougher elements, several of whom he
had had occasion to jail at one time or another in the past. He was
assigned to duty on Mulberry Street also, leaving both wives
alone in the house. The two men had talked things over with deep
misgivings, but there was nothing they could do about the situation. As late as Wednesday, and in fact much later, central headquarters still was out of touch with the northern sections of the
city. Crowley, Polhamus, and their doughty repair crews had
their hands more than full keeping vital telegraph lines operating
in lower Manhattan. Wires north, torn down by rioters on Monday morning, remained down. Transportation had come to a virtual standstill. But sketchy reports of looting and destruction in
the northern precincts filtered through. So far the forces at Mulberry Street, still stretched very thin, had been unable to respond.
"We well knew," wrote Chapin, "that the women were in great
distress of mind if not in actual danger. . . ."

Late Wednesday afternoon, however, he learned that a picked
force of police was going to try to run a Third Avenue horse car
through to Yorkville and Harlem on a reconnaissance. He asked
and was given permission to go along.

Third Avenue still was clogged with the wreckage of derailed
cars and gaunt with burned-out ruins. There had been no opportunity to clean it up, and street-department labor crews had been
among the first to join the rioters, anyway. More than once the
police car had to be halted while debris was dragged off the
tracks. Gangs still roamed and looted along the avenue as well.
"Altho' stopped several times, and obliged to fight the way thro',"
Chapin recalled laconically, "we succeeded in accomplishing our
object." At Eighty-fourth Street he dropped off the car, and the
reconnaissance party proceeded on toward Harlem.

He found his home undamaged, though several men already had appeared and roughly ordered Mrs. Chapin to turn
Mrs. Brown into the street. This she "was courageous enough to

refuse to do," Chapin reported, "and word then came that they intended to burn the house, which must be vacated within 24 hours." For answer, the two plucky women had gone to work on some homely defense measures. They had kept kettles full of water simmering on the stove, ready for dousing over attackers if the need arose, and tied stout cords to heavy lead fishing sinkers in case the hot reception was not enough. (What these amounted to, ironically, were crude versions of the slung-shot so highly favored by New York thugs themselves.) Having barricaded the doors, they were waiting nervously for whatever might happen next. As yet, nothing had. But mobs of toughs already had sacked and burned some other houses and stores in the area roundabout —proof that the threat was real. Neighbors were beginning to talk of banding together in a vigilance committee. And here it appears that the arrival of Chapin, the man from police headquarters, was fortuitous. "I at once proceeded to organize such a body which soon included 150 of the best citizens in the vicinity," he wrote, and added modestly that "they made me the virtual leader."

The bold front was enough, and Mr. Chapin's vigilantes were not called upon to fight. But they were honest men sick of bullying and threats, and they meant business. Under his direction they set up a system of around-the-clock patrols, which brought riotous goings-on in Yorkville to a stop. It was no small matter, though. Many of them would have memories to pass along to children and grandchildren for years to come, of long, sleepless nights lightened by "hot coffee, crackers and red herrings" dispensed at Chapin's house; and of wary scoutings down dim streets that might have blazed up in mob ambush any moment, though they never did. Some incidents were funny. There was the woman seen skulking down Eighty-fourth Street one midnight. She hiked up her skirts and ran like a deer when challenged—and was revealed as no woman at all, but a mob spy reconnoitering the street. Some could tear at a man's heart. A shadowy figure was chased and captured one morning just at dawn—a frightened Negro fugitive trying to get to the Astoria ferry landing at the foot of Eighty-sixth Street. He had been hiding out from rioters for two days, was so crazed with fear and suffering that they had a hard time convincing him he was safe at last.

All in all, Chapin found the experience "most severe."

Out here beyond the reach of police protection, other plain folk waited and watched, fearfully but with courage, too, for the trouble to run its course. Horace Greeley owned a farm near the village of Chappaqua. Mary Greeley and their daughters Ida and Gabrielle were there alone, though far removed from riot in the city streets. Or so one would think. But the stormy Abolitionist editor was well hated even there. A gang of drunken rowdies from nearby Sing Sing started out to raid the farm one night. They got as far as the front gate, found it barred and a neighbor by the name of Edward Quinby stationed there. Quinby was a Quaker and would not fight. But he told a story of a gunpowder train laid across the path, ready to blow the first intruder into his component atoms. "Heed my warning, my brethren," he told them. "Horace Greeley is a peace man, but Mary Greeley will fight to the last." It was a good story. The rowdies thought it over and departed.

In other communities the mobs had their way, however. And some, at least, still seemed bent on the strategy of keeping New York cut off from outside help. On Wednesday telegraph stations on the Harlem Railroad were burned at both Williams Bridge and Melrose. The operator at Williams Bridge was an enterprising employee who promptly arranged to set up a temporary installation in the back room of a local store. But "a Copperhead" called on the storekeeper with the blunt warning that he "would send for the mob and gut the store" if the offending instrument was not removed at once. It was.

There was no effective communication between authorities in New York City and most of these northern districts until Sunday. The police reconnaissance party with which Chapin had managed to reach Yorkville went on to Harlem. But on their return trip, the mob on Third Avenue evidently had been alerted and was waiting with reinforcements. The car was intercepted, thrown off the tracks, and burned. The policemen fought their way to the nearest precinct station. But once again Third Avenue was closed. Chapin, busy with his vigilante committee, probably did not learn of this till later. He was needed where he was, in any case. But by Sunday he was growing concerned about his continued absence from Mulberry Street. That morning news came that the first steamboat up the river since the start of the rioting would touch at Eighty-sixth Street on its way to Harlem and would then head back for lower Manhattan.

"Having established a protection and feeling that my house was now comparatively safe," he wrote, "I was anxious to return to Hd Quarters . . . and I gladly took passage on her, tho' scarcely able to stand upon my feet."

Though he did not know it yet, the rioting was over.

Chapter 20 | The Last Battle

THE SEVENTH REGIMENT OF THE NEW YORK NATIONAL GUARD had gone off to save the Union in April, 1861, the long-ago start of what was supposed to be a brief storybook war. It had been a dandy regiment indeed, even the privates young gentlemen of the city's best social circles, impeccably military in tailor-made uniforms with pipe-clayed crossbelts. Delmonico's had put up box lunches to sustain them on their way. In Washington they had marched to the White House with band playing and standards unfurled to salute the President as saviors—the first regiment into the capital following the firing on Fort Sumter. In keeping with the times, though, the saviors had been thirty-day enlistees. Most of them were safe home again before First Bull Run. But the Seventh had stayed in being as a regiment and had gone back. If it had won no great renown since then, at least it had learned a little something about war. It had kept its reputation as a dandy, kid-glove outfit, too. And it still was New York City's very special pride.

The Seventh landed at Canal Street about four o'clock Thursday morning. It was paraded to police headquarters by a roundabout route, apparently to impress the populace with the happy fact of its arrival. At so early an hour it is unlikely that many citizens were in the streets to be impressed. But neither were any rioters. New York was a worn-out, quiet city. The flare-up over in Brooklyn had been quelled almost as soon as it began. A crowd of disgruntled laborers had burned several grain elevators along the waterfront, but there had been no general uprising, and police and firemen quickly got things under control again.

By ten A.M. the Sixty-fifth New York and the artillery battery of the Eighth, another regiment in the state's German-American Excelsior Brigade, had followed the Seventy-fourth and the Seventh into the city. They too were paraded through some of the districts where rioting had been most violent. Still no incidents occurred. And more regiments were on the way. The mobs' last slim hope of winning New York was gone.

The fact, if it was realized, touched off no display of public jubilation. Strangely, not even the Republican press had had very much to say about the troops on their way to the city's relief, and would indulge in no flights of thankful rhetoric now that they were on the scene. There were few cheers, even for the dandy Seventh. Mayor Opdyke's optimistic proclamation was received with little comment. All the newspapers in their editions of Thursday, July 16, seemed chary of reporting the rioting at an end or near an end. The *Tribune*, very much preoccupied with its account of the goings-on at Mr. Alvord's printing plant on Wednesday, featured a bleak headline: *THE MOB FULLY OR-GANIZED.*

The *World* hewed stubbornly to its editorial line that ". . . the masses of the people of New York . . . have been stung by the madness and irritated by the chicanery of the administration . . ." But enough was enough; the paper was beginning to sound just a bit tired of apologizing for the rioters. Not so the *Daily News*, which reacted to Wednesday morning's clash at Eighth Avenue with a bitter and irresponsible attack on Captain John H. Howell, commander of the howitzer battery in that affair. He had fired without provocation into a crowd of innocent women and children, according to the indignant version served up by the *News*. The *Times*, on the contrary, was firm in its own conclusion: "We have no doubts that there are . . . agents direct from Richmond, now in the city, who are using both energy and money in feeding the flames that have for three days darkened and for three nights reddened the sky of New York. . . ."

A dispatch from Washington announced President Lincoln's decision against martial law for New York City. It also quoted Provost Marshal General James Fry to the effect that the draft was indefinitely suspended because a legal question had arisen regarding its application to thirty-day volunteers. The statement happened to be quite false—pure rumor and nothing else—but every paper carried the item. None of them gave it much space, however. After all the city had suffered, even the Copperheads seemed to lack heart for trying to blow it up into any very meaningful victory.

But Thursday's most sensational development would not break as news until the next day.

Around eleven A.M. a closed carriage pulled up in front of an undistinguished residential building at Number 10 Eleventh Street. Four men got out. They were detectives of the Metropolitan force: Thomas Dusenbury and John McCord, both of whom had been in on the first hints of trouble brewing on Sunday evening, and two others named Radford and Farley. Apparently acting on a tip from some secret informer, they entered the building and burst into a room on the second floor. Some reports said afterward that they surprised their man in bed with his mistress. Some said they found him hiding under the bed. As veterans on the force, they probably recognized the woman at once. She was a Negro, Josephine Wilson by name; had been a practicing New York harlot for the past twelve years; and had in fact risen to be the madam of her own middling-fashionable fancy house on Green Street. They knew her companion, too. He was John Andrews.

They took him without a fight. As the *World* would tell the story on Friday, the four detectives posed as emissaries from Andrews' friends. The police knew of his hiding place, they told him, and they had come to take him to a better one. It seems a thin story on the face of it. But perhaps it was plausible enough to a man like Andrews, who had been a minor police character even before the rioting. He went quietly, at any rate. In the carriage on the way to Mulberry Street they informed him that he was under arrest—whereupon, it was said, he blurted in traditional outlaw fashion that they never would have taken him alive had he known what they were up to.

One of Horace Greeley's reporters appears to have interviewed the prisoner at some length shortly after he arrived at headquarters. Andrews, he wrote, was about thirty-five years old, blue-eyed and brown-haired, with a full, sandy beard. He spoke with a strong southern accent. The *Tribune*'s story implies that he was a cool specimen, quite articulate and self-possessed. He readily admitted having addressed the mob on Third Avenue on Monday but denied that there had been anything wrong in that. He had delivered the identical speech, said he, to a "Peace Meeting at Cooper Institute" only a week or so earlier. (And he may well have been telling the truth. New York City had seen a rash of such "peace meetings," at Cooper Institute and elsewhere, for months past. Though many of them had been violently Copperhead in tone, none of the local authorities had shown any undue concern.) But, Andrews insisted, he had not spoken in public since Monday. This the *Tribune* man denied. Forgetting his editorial objectivity for a moment, he wrote somewhat smugly that any number of witnesses were prepared to swear otherwise. He also commented on a cut on the prisoner's temple—a possible memento of mob combat—but gave Andrews' own explanation: that he had slipped and fallen in his cell. Concluding with a brief summary of the very little that was known about the man's background, the story on Friday would note that in 1860 John Andrews had been president of a club in the Eighth Ward, made up of "most of the notorious thieves, pimps and gamblers in that ward."

The *World*, adding nothing of importance to the *Tribune*'s information, would make no effort to defend Andrews. His colored mistress seemed to offend the *World*'s man exceedingly: "Had the crowds whom he offered to lead known the facts, the practical amalgamationist would probably have met with a very different reception. . . ." Later, various other contemporary writers would add the hearsay that Andrew had a wife and family back in Virginia but had deserted them and come to New York as a result of some mysterious scandal.

And there, in sum, stood John U. Andrews—an unsavory character, clearly, and no doubt a rabid Copperhead as well. Whether he was more than that, no one could say. Now that he was in custody, his very stature as a suspect seems suddenly to have become hazy. Save for the *Tribune* and the *World*, New York newspapers would pay no great attention to him next day. The usually alert *Herald* would not report his arrest at all. The *News* would ignore it, perhaps designedly. The *Times* would refer to it only casually. Actually, the man had not figured prominently in any riot news after Monday. None of the many reports of his later activities were more than vague and unsupported rumor. Yet somehow a sinister, half-legendary aura appears to have grown up around him during three days of lawlessness and terror. Possibly it was simply that the mobs' leaders had all been such dim and nameless shadows. "Andrews of Virginia" filled a sort of vacuum. Here was a tangible figure the ordinary citizen could take hold of and identify—the arch-villain who had loosed a storm of fiery rebellion on the city. *The Bloody Week!*, a cheap paperback collection of eyewitness accounts which was hurried into print within the next few days, would perhaps reflect a public anger whipped close to the lynching point when its anonymous editor fulminated: "Suppose him captured and imprisoned, who shall guard us from the mockery of a sham trial on writ of habeas corpus, and speedy acquittal by a copperhead judge? If we had a Commanding General possessed of energy, a Governor thoroughly loyal, and a Mayor not absolutely paralyzed with fear, this howling fiend, this emissary and spy of the Rebels would have been shot at the head of his rioters on Tuesday, and this community spared the mortification of his subsequent career of crime. . . ."

Whether or not this kind of feeling had anything to do with it, the police authorities did not keep Andrews at Mulberry Street very long. Headquarters was crowded by this time with some seven hundred refugees. Many were injured, many more were destitute, and no doubt all of them saw John Andrews as the author of their misery. Guarding him against reprisals, therefore, may well have been a problem. Whatever the reason, Andrews was put in irons and transferred to a cell at Fort Lafayette in New York harbor by Thursday evening.

Order was being restored now, though slowly and painfully. More troops entered the city during the afternoon, the streets beginning to echo to the tramp of marching feet and the rumble of artillery limbers. Some units were detached immediately to strengthen the guard details at important public buildings. The rest were held at police headquarters, ready for action as needed. Armed detachments of Citizens' Volunteer Police Reserves patrolled various points of lesser danger, taking some of the pressure off weary regular patrolmen. For the first time, city authorities were able to turn their attention to the refugee problem on something more than a makeshift basis. On Thursday morning the children from the Colored Orphan Asylum, housed since Monday in the overcrowded City Orphanage on the Bloomingdale Road in upper Manhattan, were taken down to the Battery and sent by steamer to more adequate quarters in the City Hospital on Blackwell's Island. A fifty-man police escort covered the move, for no one could be sure as yet that the streets were safe. And many of them were not, quite. Thugs and looters still prowled, reluctant to give up the pickings that had been so easy for a while. A gentleman standing on the corner of Twenty-fourth Street and Ninth Avenue was accosted boldly in broad daylight Thursday afternoon. "You have got $300 and I have not," the thug shouted, knocking him down with a club. Bystanders ran to the rescue and the thug fled, still without his three hundred dollars.

Incidents of this kind were small and isolated. On Thursday several of the idled street railway and omnibus lines began to get back into operation on a limited scale. Yet when night came the mob still showed the power and the savage resolution to draw itself together one more time and strike, like a great, wounded animal, with bitter ferocity.

This time it was a large crowd near Gramercy Park, at Second Avenue and Twenty-second Street. Again it found confusion among the commanders of the city's defense. The first word of this gathering, apparently, reached General Wool at the St. Nicholas. Either he or General Sandford—it was never settled which —ordered Colonel Mott, yesterday's victor at Eighth Avenue, to take a force of city militia out and restore order. Wool and Sandford still were standing on their prerogatives. Nothing had been learned from Wednesday evening's fiasco, and again Mulberry Street was neither told of what was going on nor asked for help. Official reports of what *did* go on were fuzzy and contradictory, in retrospect. But there was no hiding the fact that the militia took another beating. A sergeant was killed and the rest of the force driven from the scene in panicky disarray. The largest group of fugitives, about twenty-five, was pursued for several blocks to Jackson's Foundry, on Twenty-eighth Street. There they managed to make a forlorn, near-hopeless stand, beating off repeated efforts by the enraged rioters to set the building on fire and drive them out. Finally another relief column from Mulberry

Street, again commanded by the efficient and hard-working Captain Putnam, arrived to break the siege. Still the rioters retreated only after a broadside from a battery of field guns made a shambles of the street. In a letter published by the New York *Herald* two weeks later, Commissioner Thomas Acton wrote of this encounter that the troops and a supporting detachment of police "recovered the body of the dead sergeant and following up the mob inflicted severe chastisement. . . . The loss of the rioters was great," Acton added significantly, "and seemed for the first time to break down the desperate spirit of the mob. . . ."

Even then they did not give up easily. Once more, as on Wednesday night, the final stages of the fighting dragged out in a nasty, grueling business of snipers chivied one by one out of hiding places in the streets and buildings of the district. There were indications that it ended with Captain Putnam's troopers aroused to such a pitch of fury that they threatened to get out of hand at times. In the course of it another suspected ringleader, one Martin Moran, was taken on Third Avenue near Twentieth Street. He had been firing from cover and deliberately picking officers as targets, apparently with considerable effect, for the angry soldiers were all for hanging him on the spot. Discipline was reestablished with some difficulty, and Moran finally was handed over to the police. The *World* would report the incident on Friday along with the arrest of Andrews of Virginia—the whole account under the hopeful headline *PARTIAL SUBSIDENCE OF MOB RULE.*

The *World* was guilty of understatement, for mob rule was over. The battle near Gramercy Park was the last one. It remained for a great many pieces of wreckage to be picked up, of course, and some would be fitted together again only with a vast amount of trouble, toil, and hard feelings. But that was a problem to be dealt with in its own good time.

At two o'clock Friday morning Thomas Acton lay down on a cot in his office for a little sleep, his first since he had reported for duty at six A.M. on Monday. He probably slept well. For him, as for most New Yorkers, the long nightmare had ended.

Chapter 21 | Victors and Vanquished

GIDEON WELLES'S DIARY FOR THE WEEK FOLLOWING THE RIOTS mentions a conversation at the Navy Department with ". . . Senator Morgan and Sam J. Tilden of New York, in relation to the draft." The senator being a Republican and Mr. Tilden an influential Democrat, their joint visit would appear to hint at some sober bipartisan second thoughts as a result of the uprising. "The gentlemen," wrote Welles, "seem to believe that a draft cannot be enforced in New York."

In fact, though troops remained in the city for several weeks, the New York enrollment offices reopened to remarkably little overt resentment. But the draft was not destined to be much of a success from any sensible point of view. Virtually no one liked it, including the politicians of both parties who ran local governments throughout the Union. And because the Act allowed each district credit on its draft quota for all voluntary enlistments by residents, the various states, counties, and communities soon were vying with one another to vote lavish bounties for all men willing to enlist. Such volunteers frequently could claim total rewards running as high as a thousand dollars or more. The prospect of easy profits attracted hordes of unscrupulous opportunists who presently set themselves up as substitute brokers and made a lucrative business of packing Army rolls with all manner of jailbirds, ne'er-do-wells, and even mental incompetents. For a few dollars' cash and a skinful of cheap whiskey, such riffraff were easily persuaded to sign over their bounty claims to the brokers and join up. And miserably poor soldiers most of them made. Sharper crooks simply collected their own bounties, then deserted at the first opportunity, made their way into some other locality, and did the whole thing over again. Many a bounty jumper contrived to work the dodge several times before being caught at last. The Army itself was the only loser by the system. But one practical result was that relatively few poor men had to be drafted against their wills. Of more than a million whose names were drawn in all the northern states, only about forty-two thousand ever wound up in uniform. In the circumstances, then, the number of New York draftees who actually benefited by the Common Council's somewhat panicky generosity never was publicized, and was not very material, anyway. Obviously, the rioters had been a little before the fact in raging against an injustice that would prove worse in theory than in practical application.

There are few indications, though, that even the most thoughtful observers saw in the riots a symptom of far deeper, broader discontents. Even in retrospect it is difficult to define them precisely. At the time, no doubt, it would have been impossible. For one thing, they were rooted in the nature of a young America not given much to introspection. It was an America now gripped in a headlong current of change, and the current was running more swiftly and with far greater power than anyone could guess. The war itself was part of it. The Emancipation Proclamation and the end of slavery were parts of it too. So were the slums, the sweat shops, and the factories booming with swollen wartime business—themselves the harbingers either of promise or of a new kind of serfdom brought by an industrial revolution that was taking the nation down a long road far beyond the point of any turning back. In their great, dim mass these things were *felt* rather than consciously thought over and understood. Anthracite miners in Pennsylvania, reacting to the draft with night ridings and murders, were in reality groping toward the principle of trade unionism and the right to bargain for a better deal. That too was grasped only imperfectly as yet. In New York, long years of corrupt politics and pandering to the mobs had bred a contempt for lawful processes more dangerous than the anger that finally let it loose. Mixed up in all this was the vague stirring of a conviction that old mores and old ways no longer served; that poor people ought somehow to have things better than they did. Whatever the hope, in the 1860's violence seemed the only way to bring it true.

Violence was a deep strain in the American character, anyway. The Union had been born violently. It had pushed its frontiers westward in blood and strife and hardship, as it would for years to come. And if one side of that coin sometimes came up looking sublimely heroic, as at Gettysburg, its reverse was too often something a great deal uglier. In December of 1862 the Army of the Potomac had wrecked and looted Confederate Fredericksburg, Virginia, quite as thoroughly and wantonly as any New York neighborhood raped by the rioters in 1863. The one could be excused on military grounds—or was, at any rate—while the other was altogether criminal. Yet for all their strident demagoguery, the *World* and the *Daily News* had expressed a certain twisted logic in declaring there was kinship between mobs that could stand up to canister and grape in the city streets and still keep coming and "the men who have gone from among us to the war."

None of this meant that the riots would open anyone's eyes to the evils of poverty and misery in New York's slums or that anything much would come of it if they did.

New Yorkers who could afford it were generous enough. They contributed liberally and without question to a Colored Relief Committee which opened an office almost before the rioting was over and dispensed large sums to Negro families victimized by the mobs. Before the end of July a measure was introduced in the Common Council to appropriate fifty thousand dollars for rebuilding the Colored Orphan Asylum. It was opposed only by a staunch Irish-American named A. F. Warburton, who maintained that since the orphanage had been burned by Irish rioters, the honor of old Erin demanded respectable Irish citizens be given the opportunity to provide a replacement out of their own pockets. The Wall Street financier and man-about-town Leonard Jerome sponsored still another relief fund for the families of policemen, militia, and volunteer firemen killed or injured during the riots. Subscriptions totalled 54,980 dollars, of which nearly 23,000 was distributed immediately and the balance invested to provide a permanent fund for the future. But in all this openhandedness it simply did not occur to anybody that similar moneys spent in improving the slum conditions that had helped to spawn the mobs might be a good investment too. It was not a time of social reform.

New York did not mend its wicked ways as a result of the riots, or of anything else. Its Haves continued to hold what they had and to amass more and to show it off in glittering ostentation. Its Have-nots went on stewing in squalor. Tammany's grip on city politics was not shaken and would not be until the Tweed Ring's cataclysmic downfall in 1872, still a long way off. Meantime, New York sin carried on as gaudily as ever. In 1866 a Methodist bishop thundering from the pulpit in St. Paul's Church decried the presence of twenty thousand prostitutes in the city. Whereat John A. Kennedy, recovered from the beating the mob had given him and back at his post as superintendent of police, expressed his grief at such a "monstrous statement" and endeavored to set the record straight. New York had but six hundred and twenty-one whorehouses, ninety-nine houses of assignation (establishments of somewhat higher social standing), and seventy-five "concert saloons of ill repute," said he—in all, not more than thirty-three hundred harlots of varying degree. He granted that possibly there were "other" presumably amateur and unsupervised doxies roaming about, perhaps quite a few of them, though he, of course, had no means of knowing about that. But he gave it as his considered opinion that New York was, on the whole, behaving itself quite morally.

Captain George W. Walling, the epitome of the tough and honest cop, rose to be superintendent of police in his turn—the only one of the riots' rank-and-file heroes to achieve high station. Thomas Acton finished out his term as commissioner, returned to his brokerage business, and lived for many years as a well-to-do and active New Yorker. He served in various other appointive offices from time to time, in the course of them was frequently quoted or mentioned in the public prints, and generally comes through as a genial and widely respected man about town. The New York public, though, seems never to have appreciated fully what a service he had done them during those four critical days in July of 1863. One gathers that he was just as happy to have it so. Mayor George Opdyke finished out his term also. Thoroughly soured on public office, he never again ran for anything.

It appeared for a while that Horatio Seymour's reputation had come through the crisis unscathed, as he went on to become the Democratic party's nominee for President in 1868. Then, however, his softness toward the rioters five years before came back to haunt him. Republican campaign literature crucified him with quotations from his speech to the mob at City Hall Park, and General Ulysses S. Grant beat him handily. He never again was a power in politics.

By an odd twist in postwar political confusion, reform Republican Horace Greeley was fated to be another Democratic Presidential candidate—also against Grant, in 1872. It was an ill-starred ending to a career that had been, in its own way, brilliant. He too was beaten. He died, a pathetically discredited and broken man, not long afterward.

The Irish in New York, as in all America, ultimately were destined for better things than poverty, slums, and riot. It is a matter of history that they lifted themselves, by hard work and their own bootstraps, to a position of honor and respectability in their adopted land.

But these were still to come, things unforeseeable as the Union plodded on through twenty months more of a war that might have been won at Gettysburg but was not. Rebellion in the New York streets would be remembered only as one battle on the bloody, muddy road through Chickamauga and the Wilderness, Petersburg and Atlanta, and all the other battlegrounds with storied names, to an ending at Appomattox Court House and, finally, peace. Out of it all would grow a destiny greater than any man could dream of in the midst of war. It would not be made by a people lacking courage for the long ordeal.

And so they faced the future. . . .

Epilogue

EPILOGUE: AFTERMATH

EDWIN STANTON KEPT HIS WORD. By Saturday, July 18, ten regiments of the Union Army were bivouacked in New York City. At least two of the later arrivals, the Twenty-sixth Michigan and the Fifty-fourth New York State Volunteers, a Rochester outfit, were as tough and seasoned as the Seventy-fourth. By that time, though, the fighting was virtually over, combat efficiency less important than the show of Federal force. The soldiers brought, if not martial law, then something close enough to get the job done. There was peace, whether New York liked it or not.

Some did not. On Friday a *Tribune* reporter, preparing for his written stint in next day's paper, had walked through a few of the seamier districts, examined the lowering face of defeat, and was far from sure that peace would last:

> Through the low groggeries in the avenues and side streets, groups of men lounged about the doorways and stoops, ready for any mischief. The bitterest feeling was expressed against both police and military. Large numbers are in possession of arms, stolen from the armories and gun stores, with which they threaten to shoot from their windows at night every obnoxious person who may pass by. Many have laid aside their arms for want of ammunition; and instead have filled corners in their rooms with stones and bricks. . . .

Defiance had flickered up now and again through most of Friday morning. A story in that same edition of the *Tribune* told how a crowd of roughs had set upon Captain John Howell as he rode up Seventh Avenue in a private carriage. Howell was the officer stigmatized by the *Daily News* the day before for turning

173

his artillery on the innocent poor. He had denied it vehemently, but of course in vain; people who read the *News* believed what they wanted to believe, and he was fair game. The crowd stoned him. The carriage was damaged, the captain himself hit and injured by a brick. Luckier than Colonel O'Brien on Tuesday, he had managed to hold the boldest of the assailants off at pistol point while he whipped his horses to a gallop and got away. But such things were enough to keep citizens in a jumpy frame of mind.

On Friday morning, too, Archbishop John Hughes finally had broken his silence. Notices distributed about the city had called the Catholic faithful to the square in front of his residence at Madison Avenue and Thirty-sixth Street. The archbishop, an old man badly crippled by rheumatism, had spoken from a chair on his balcony above the street. His words were rather like a father's scolding a misbehaving brood. He had been grieved by some of the bad things he had heard, he told them. "Is there not some way by which you can stop these proceedings and support the laws, none of which have been enacted against you as Irishmen and Catholics?" He had warned them sternly: "No government can save itself unless it protects its citizens. Military force will be let loose on you. The innocent will be shot down and the guilty will be likely to escape. Would it not be better to retire quietly? . . ." And they had, some three thousand of them who had gathered there to listen. The strong detachments of police and soldiers on hand to maintain order had not been needed. But some newspapermen present, noticing the dearth of battle scars in the archbishop's audience, doubted that many of these people had been rioters at all. By Friday the speech was too late, anyway. "It might have saved lives and much destruction," wrote one, "had it been delivered two days before. . . ."

On Saturday the mistaken impression that the draft had been suspended was cleared up in no uncertain terms. Virtually every New York paper printed the full text of an order from Washington, dated July 17:

> The operations of the draft lately ordered in the New England and Middle States, though in most instances completed or now in progress without opposition, have in one or two cities been temporarily interrupted.

Provost Marshals are informed that no orders have been issued countermanding the draft.

Adequate force has been ordered by the government to the points where the proceedings have been interrupted.

Provost Marshals will be sustained by the military forces of the country in enforcing the draft, in accordance with the laws of the United States, and will proceed to execute the orders heretofore given for the draft as rapidly as shall be practicable, by aid of the military forces ordered to co-operate with and protect them.

JAMES B. FRY
PROVOST MARSHAL GENERAL

That seemed to settle that; there would be no further misunderstandings, or false hopes either. The order occasioned less grumbling than it might have, even in the Copperhead press. The storm had passed and there was peace: sullen, bitter and uneasy —still, peace.

All the same, even in respectable circles frayed nerves and short tempers boiled up in furious little eruptions here and there. On Saturday afternoon a local provost marshal, Captain John Duffy, dined at Delmonico's with a friend on the Common Council, the Honorable Bernard Hughes. During the meal, as the New York *World* got the story later, Hughes made some remark "which the provost-marshal considered as favoring the rioters." Jumping up from the table indignantly, he called a policeman and had Mr. Hughes arrested—a shocking breach of decorum at fashionable Delmonico's. But when Delmonico himself intervened in a well-meant effort to smooth over the difficulty, his attitude appeared to irk the provost marshal too, for a few minutes later, ". . . having denounced the proprietor of the place as a disloyalist in a very vigorous manner [Captain Duffy] was also arrested." Both men were allowed to cool off for a while at the nearest precinct station and then released.

In the wake of four days of strife and strain came some other repercussions which could not be laughed away quite so easily. Records show that the troops sent from the war front had all been under orders to report directly to General Harvey Brown, indicating at least tacit approval by the War Department of his own contention that he was the military commandant of the city.

Nevertheless, his falling-out with a superior officer was a sin the U.S. Army scarcely could overlook. On Friday he was replaced, abruptly and without explanation, by Brigadier General E. R. S. Canby. The militia's General Sandford, bursting with vindicated dignity, seized the occasion to issue a long general order declaring in part that ". . . the peace of the city would have been restored in a few hours but for the interference of Brevet Brigadier General Harvey Brown, who, in disobedience of the orders of General Wool, withdrew the detachments belonging to the general government. . . ." It was a petty and pointless outburst, serving no useful purpose. But old John Wool had the bad judgment to sit down and dash off a self-righteous letter to Governor Seymour, agreeing with everything Sandford had said and adding some crochety accusations of his own. It was embarrassingly bad judgment, as things turned out, for by the time the letter was made public, a few days later, Wool too had been relieved of duty, by Major General John A. Dix. But hot-tempered Harvey Brown lost little time in lashing back to defend himself. And thus brought into the open, the brouhaha between the three generals —with Metropolitan Police commissioners Acton and Bergen presently jumping in on Brown's side—sputtered on for a couple of weeks or more in angry public statements and open letters to the press. It is unlikely that a city struggling back toward business-as-usual paid much attention.

Saturday was the last day on which rioting was front-page news. By Monday, July 20, accounts of "the late riots" had been pushed back to page two or deeper in all papers. New Yorkers, a resilient breed, soon would get used to the spectacle of military patrols tramping through their streets and soldiers standing sentry-go on every strategic corner. In the meantime, as labor forces straggled back to jobs—many to be kept busy, no doubt, cleaning up debris they themselves had helped create—the police were able to turn to the workaday chores involved in a re-established law and order.

One of the first projects was a massive hunt for the plunder carried off by rioters. Search parties of patrolmen and detectives, backed up when necessary by squads of soldiers, swept through the Five Points, the Fourth Ward, and all the dingy mews and shantytowns along the waterfronts. Among other things, they

seized almost eleven thousand firearms, besides iron bars, slung-
shots, and similar gang weapons past counting. Of richer loot
there was a hoard to rival the spoils from an argosy. The press
would exclaim over it for days: "Mahogany and rosewood chairs
with brocade upholstering, marble top tables and stands, costly
paintings and hundreds of delicate and valuable mantel ornaments are daily found in low hovels. . . ." About ten thousand
dollars' worth of merchandise was returned to Brooks Brothers
alone. A single grubby little den in lower Manhattan yielded fifty
fine suits, another a large gunnysack full of cravats and socks.
Groceries and foodstuffs by the bag and barrelful turned up,
along with such random items as tobacco, children's toys, even
boxes of birdseed. "Every person in whose possession these articles are found," the *Times* remarked, "disclaims all knowledge of
the same, except that they found them in the street, and took
them in to prevent them being burned." The police were thorough: "The entire city will be searched, and it is expected that
the greatest portion of the property taken from the buildings
sacked by the mob will be recovered. . . ."

But a huge amount of other property had been wantonly destroyed, of course, and the buildings that lay in charred ruin were
beyond recovery, too. A considerable number of disgruntled owners held the city of New York responsible. By the end of July
damage claims were piling up rapidly. Some were for trifling
amounts. (One Hugh Crombie was listed as claiming twenty-one
dollars for unspecified losses, a Philo F. Barnum wanted fifty-four
dollars, and so on.) But others ran to several thousands. Totaled
up, they would reach a figure of approximately three million dollars by the time they all were in. And at least one of them struck
the New York *Herald* as potentially dangerous in the precedent it
might set. This, filed by the firm which operated the Broadway
and Sixth Avenue stage line, claimed damages of $685.96 cover-
ing business lost because rioters had interrupted the stage service.
If the courts allowed it, grumped the *Herald*, ". . . all the shop-
keepers who closed up during the excitement may likewise file
claims with the Comptroller for 'loss of business . . .'" The paper
sniffed the taint of skulduggery in the air, anyway: "Mr. Brennan
[the city comptroller] has received several anonymous communications already containing information to the effect that many of

the claims which have been filed are gross impositions. Some lawyers are said to be making a good thing of it by drawing up the necessary affidavits and schedules."

How badly the city had suffered would have to be largely guesswork in the final summing-up. Because fallen rioters had almost invariably been carried off and hidden by friends or families, there was no accurate count of total casualties. The police and other reputable witnesses estimated that as many as four or five hundred members of various mobs may have been killed during the actual fighting. Most of them were secretly buried in unmarked graves scattered through the slums. A great many of those wounded in the more furious clashes undoubtedly died later, some, perhaps, after lingering for days or even weeks. Most of them probably received little or no medical attention, and few of the ones who did were likely to have admitted that they were injured while rioting. Taking all that into account, Commissioner Thomas Acton estimated the total mob dead as somewhere around twelve hundred.

A brief item in the *Herald* on July 30, however, suggests that innocent victims may often have been lumped with fallen rioters by mistake:

> In the HERALD of yesterday it was stated that Francis Mc-Cabe, who died from the effects of a musket shot wound, received at the hands of the military during the disturbance at the corner of Thirty Sixth street and Ninth Avenue on the 14th inst., was actively engaged in the riot at the time of his being wounded. We have since been informed that the deceased was accidentally shot while returning from the fire at Allerton's Hotel . . . with Engine Company No. 15, to which he belonged, and that he had no connection with the disturbers of the public peace.

Possibly other such tragedies never came to light. The official records listed eighteen people, eleven of them Negroes, as killed by the rioters. But these were the known dead. There certainly were others. A total of seventy were reported as missing by the time the four days' violence had run its course. Again, many of these were Negroes, and many never were accounted for. There were unverified reports of at least five Negroes chased by mobs into the East River and drowned. Incredibly, considering the no-quarter savagery of the early fighting, the police lost only three men killed. But scarcely a man who saw action came out of it without injuries ranging all the way from slight to very critical. The War Department declined to release any casualty figures at all, which tended to confirm the impression that losses among the troop detachments had been heavy in several of their engagements. Some unofficial guesses put the number of army and militia dead at not less than fifty.

Estimates of the total monetary loss averaged a good round five million dollars. The figure probably was conservative. It covered only property destruction, for one thing, and took no account of lost production or losses in wages and other income during the three days when business in the city came very close to a full stop. David Barnes of the *Times* said that "more than 50" buildings were burned. His count seems far too low, however, for other observers claimed a total that more than doubled his. And most accounts agreed that at least two hundred more buildings were badly damaged or completely wrecked in the course of the fighting and the looting.

No record remains today—perhaps none was kept at the time —of the total arrests made as a result of all this. There may have been hundreds; certainly the prisoner bag grew very rapidly as police and military began to win the upper hand on Tuesday evening, Wednesday, and Thursday. Random newspaper items show that the law caught up with more and more suspects during the days and weeks that followed, as indignant citizens came forward to prefer specific charges or to inform against individuals they had recognized while the rioting was at its height. Some odd fish turned up in the police net as a result. Matthew Scuzack, an eccentric sixty-three-year-old German immigrant, was accused of having furnished the rope used to hang the Negro James Costello on Tuesday. A man who gave his name as Evans and claimed to be a special sheriff's deputy was taken for "making an inflammatory speech" near St. John's Park in the Fifth precinct, urging his listeners "to rise and protect themselves from oppression." No doubt typical of many others was one William Watson, charged with robbery. He was soon exposed as a deserter from a Zouave regiment at the front, his real name Curbin. A Barney McKay, alias McKan, was said to have "marched about the streets with a musket in his hand, calling upon the mob to resist the military and the police. . . ." The *Herald* identified him as a ringleader. But "ringleader" was a word too freely used during this post-riot excitement. More often than not it meant simply any rioter who had happened to be seen with a gun.

A comparative few of the prisoners were held without bail. Most were promptly released on bonds varying from five hundred to five thousand dollars. The amounts appear to have depended much more on the attitude of the presiding judge than the gravity of the charges. Inevitably, there were indications of political influence at work. The same Common Council members who had pestered Thomas Acton to keep his policemen out of their districts even while riots raged there now came forward to spring constituents from jail cells. Sometimes it was done even before they could be booked. A possibly apocryphal story told of one unidentified police magistrate who solved his problem by dismissing all charges on the grounds that the Enrollment and Conscription Act was unconstitutional.

The first use of habeas corpus in connection with the riots was reported in the *Herald* on Saturday, July 18. A man by the name of Morris Boyle, accused of firing from cover at a company of soldiers, had been captured in the Twentieth precinct on Thursday and turned over to Captain George Walling. On Friday morning an attorney appeared with the writ, signed by Judge John H. McCunn of the New York Court of General Sessions. But Captain Walling, the gangsters' nemesis of old, refused to honor it. Boyle was the Army's prisoner, he maintained; therefore he had no authority to release him. Added the *Herald:* "The writ, we hear, bore no seal and was not in the usual form." It was not necessary to explain what already was common knowledge in New York City—that Judge McCunn was a faithful Tammany wheelhorse notorious among even fellow Tammanyites for his favoritism on the bench.

The *Herald* expressed no particular indignation over the incident. Neither, for that matter, did the *Tribune* or the *Times.* Corruption was too old a story in New York.

Copperhead conspiracy among the rioters was a much more intriguing question. It was a subject, besides, on which speculation and partisan prejudice could be aired without restraint. The

Tribune lost little time in opening the controversy. On Friday of the riot week, even as the last seethings of violence simmered down, a headline on the editorial page asked bluntly: *WHAT CAUSED THE MOB?*

Horace Greeley thought he knew. He had thought so from the beginning, had seen signs even before that. His editorial went on to say, its tone portentiously confidential:

> On the Saturday evening before our last State election, a most estimable and trustworthy citizen met an acquaintance well known to us as an active Democrat, and the holder of an important office under Buchanan. Our friend urged this Democrat, because of his professed Unionism, to vote the Republican Union ticket on the Tuesday following. The Democrat declined, still expressing devotion to the Union, but adding, "I *know* that the War for the Union cannot succeed. If there should ever be a prospect of its success, there will be formidable, bloody riots in every city and every considerable village of the Free States, whereby the Government will be so weakened and paralyzed that its advantage will be lost. Rest assured that I speak what I *know*, and do not press me further."

As if by way of emphasis, some later editions of Friday's paper also contained a letter from a reader who claimed that he had "lived with the mob from Monday to Thursday" and could supply positive proof that it was "really the left wing of LEE's Army." The reader neglected to sign his name.

This was pretty irresponsible stuff, even for the loose journalistic standards of the wartime 1860's. Neither Greeley nor anyone on his staff ever publicly named the "active Democrat" of the editorial, and the anonymous correspondent was obviously a crank. He virtually discredited himself when he wrote again a few days later to say that the "plot" actually had been revealed to him in confidence by his Irish cook. Still, there was a tempting impression of inside information here to titillate the many who were ready to believe the worst. The *Tribune* had thrown the subject open for debate, in any case.

Saturday's *World* was first with a rebuttal. "The mobs have been precisely what it is asserted they are not. They have not been at all what it is asserted that they are," it stated somewhat pontifically. Scouting the many tales of "concerted, systematic movement," it characterized the rioting as nothing more than "a spontaneous outbreak of popular passion and discontent. . . . In one point only can we agree with the *Tribune*," it concluded. "The riots will give the greatest satisfaction and hope to the people of the southern confederacy. . . . For this reason, therefore, in common with every true patriot, we regard the riots with profound regret. . . ."

The *World* had printed its share of drivel about the situation during the bloody week just past, but it had something of a point there. Southerners were indeed exulting. Down in the Confederate capital that day the Richmond *Enquirer* published a remarkably detailed rundown of the early riot stories in most of the New York papers. (Incidentally, John Andrews' speech on Monday was mentioned, and he was correctly identified as a Virginian, though without any conspicuous pride in the fact.) Summing up, the *Enquirer* ventured the opinion that, "If General Lee had remained in Maryland, or if he should return there after the waters of the Potomac have subsided, and his reinforcements arrive, these riots will continue throughout the United States." News from the North ran a few days late, however, so that Richmond was not yet aware of the riots' end. Predicted the editor: "When once the mob masters the Government, and forces it to yield in one particular, it soon understands its power and will not fail to use it again. More will be heard from these mobs. . . ."

In South Carolina, where the shooting war had started, the rejoicing was equally vociferous. "After making due allowance for the sensational reports in the New York papers," the Charleston *Daily Courier* considered it "evident that the riot was the most formidable outbreak of the kind that ever occurred on this continent. It will encourage similar demonstrations in other Northern cities." In following editions, its mood growing sunnier still, the *Courier* exulted that, "These open manifestations of hostility to the draft . . . are worth as much to us as a signal victory." There was an assumption in Charleston too that the mobs had had their way: "The black hearted wretch who sits in the seat of power at Washington turned pale at the tidings, and . . . yielding to his unmanly terror, ordered the draft suspended in New York."

Clearly, from any Union patriot's standpoint, this sort of thing came under the heading of aid or at least comfort to the enemy. Elsewhere in the Confederate States there was and would be more jubilation as riot stories filtered through the lines. Naturally; the other side's troubles always make good news, and it was a mean war, with very few holds barred. Nothing in any of the published comments, though, so much as hints that Southerners either dreamed or hoped they had New York allies conspiring to foment armed rebellion. The *Daily Courier* defined the extent of satisfaction in the South quite simply when it said, ". . . nothing delights us so greatly as to hear of Yankees burning, destroying and killing Yankee buildings, Yankee property and Yankee men."

In New York it was not so simple. On Tuesday, August 4, the *World* still was railing impatiently at Horace Greeley's suspicions:

> . . . Not a single man in the slightest degree conspicuous as a politician of New York has been even implicated in these transactions. In every case the persons upon whom the law has laid its hands appear to have . . . drifted into their attitude of resistance to government. Now it is a peddler who falls in with the shouting throng, is borne along with them, appropriates a fine horse and becomes a "lieutenant-colonel of the mob. . . ."

The paper had a point there, too. Yet somehow its continued protestations seemed a shade too vehement. If Fernando Wood was its man "conspicuous as a politician"—a fair enough inference in the circumstances—then the disclaimer suggests that there may have been more talk linking him with the riots than ever had come out in the open. No one really could say whether Wood was or was not the leader of the Knights of the Golden Circle. No one had come straight out and accused the Knights, either, though there had been a deal of talk about them, too. But Wood and his brother Benjamin were avowed Copperheads. And one way or another there *was* a vast amount of disloyalty rampant in the Union that summer. Nobody disputed that.

But Abolitionists were not popular in New York City, and never had been. Besides, Horace Greeley had drummed away too hard at too many touchy issues for much too long to have many friends among his colleagues. James Gordon Bennett of the *Herald* dismissed him with smug scorn:

> The radicals have not succeeded in their conspiracy to make political capital out of the recent riots. The official reports of Generals Wool and Sandford have given these incendiary politicians their quietus. . . . Poor Greeley especially has failed . . . dismally in his pet enterprise of strengthening his party by the riots. . . .

Perhaps it was worth noting that the word "conspiracy" was being tossed about with some abandon.

That appeared on Monday, opening day of the August term of the New York Court of General Sessions, with Recorder Hoffman on the bench and District Attorney A. Oakey Hall present in person to prosecute the first batch of accused rioters. Interested citizens and the idle curious crowded the courtroom at City Hall. But only a small minority of the jury panel had answered their summonses, so the proceedings had to be put over until Wednesday, August 5. There it was—anticlimax right at the start, and only a few spectators turned up on Wednesday. More than forty indictments had been voted by the grand jury. But, reduced to the precise language of the law, the charges seemed strangely dry and matter-of-fact after the reign of terror out of which they had grown. Most of them specified arson or robbery. Six men were named for grand larceny, three for riot. A James O'Neil was accused of assault with intent to kill. Only two, Dennis Carey and Mark J. Silva, were charged as murderers, and the prosecution itself already had conceded to reporters that its case against Silva was dubious. These prisoners all were nobodies—an unprepossessing lot, toughs no doubt, though they looked more like plain poor men in trouble, dressed in their shabby best for their day in court. One searched the list of indictments in vain for the names of John U. Andrews, or the sniper Boyle whose habeas corpus had been denied, or the Martin Moran who had so narrowly escaped a lynching by angry soldiers, or any of the few others who had achieved fleeting distinction, however slight, in the rampagings of the mob. There were no ringleaders here, none of the savage Irish Amazons whose atrocities had horrified the city—above all, no one even faintly resembling a Copperhead plotter or a Confederate agent in or out of disguise.

The proceedings were brisk. But it was the briskness of old and cut-and-dried routine, not courtroom drama. Case after case was called. Defense attorneys rose to request postponements. There were few arguments, only perfunctory objections by the prosecution. Granted, granted. . . . An occasional culprit did stand trial to provide a break in the monotony. Witnesses were called, questioned, and dismissed in routine manner. Judge and jury did their duty. Theodore Arnold, a youth of eighteen, pleaded guilty to robbery; he had been one of the looters of the Bull's Head Tavern and was sentenced to five years in the state penitentiary, the first rioter to be punished. The Zouave deserter William Curbin, alias Watson, drew a ten-year term. Michael Doyle and Joseph Conway were found guilty of robbery—fifteen years apiece. Joseph Marshall was found guilty of robbery also, but sentence was postponed. . . .

That was the sum of it, and a fair summary of all the riot trials as the days of August passed. At one point Mr. District Attorney Hall got to his feet, an urbane and debonair figure, to make the sage observation that there appeared to be an intent by some of the accused to get their cases put over until the next term of court, when Judge McCunn was scheduled to preside. He did not enlarge on the remark, or need to. But, he warned sternly, such maneuvers would not work. If the courtroom spectators responded to this promise with any sign of enthusiasm, no journalist present bothered to report it. A. Oakey Hall was himself a hand-picked Tammany figurehead, a bosom crony of William Marcy Tweed.

Twelve more prisoners were arraigned on Saturday, August 8. Again there were few trials, many postponements. Still the mountain of justice kept laboring as if it might bring forth something more than a mouse. On the following Tuesday it was announced than an additional fifty indictments had been returned by the grand jury. But, as the *Herald* reported, ". . . it has been deemed prudent to withhold for the present the names of those against whom indictments have been found." Why prudent, and who deemed it so? Nobody said. On the one hand, such action might seem to have smacked of Star Chamber methods offensive to a free society. On the other, it could as logically suggest a political cover-up. Nothing in any newspaper reflected even a murmur of public protest. In the same edition, though, the *Herald* continued to see other hobgoblins lurking. "There are many things that as

yet remain secret in regard to the late anti-draft riots in this city,"
it avowed ominously. "Does not this smell a little of the old dodge
to make Frémont a dictator?" Referring here to General John
Charles Frémont's popularity among radical Republicans and his
earlier well-publicized differences with President Lincoln over
military policy in Missouri, the *Herald* was attempting to breathe
life into a very tenuous ghost indeed. But the editorial went on:

> . . . From another source, fully entitled to credit, we have
> also ascertained that, on the third day of the riots, three or
> four of the ablest judges in the city . . . called at Governor
> Seymour's headquarters and offered to issue warrants to arrest
> Horace Greeley and Raymond for inciting the rioters by their
> articles. . . .

The governor, however, had objected that the forces of the
law at the time were "not adequate to protect the accused against
mob reprisals," so nothing came of the offer.

This so-called revelation never was challenged. Greeley and
Raymond probably considered it beneath the dignity of a denial.
The *Herald*'s three or four judges remained forever as nameless
as the *Tribune*'s prominent Democrat and its letter-writing reader.
The repercussions were dying, the thunder rumbling away over
the horizon. If the storm had not cleared the atmosphere much, at
least it was done with.

Few of the postponements ever went to trial. The fifty secret
indictments were, apparently, forgotten in time. By the end of the
August term of court, thirteen rioters had been found guilty of
various crimes, mostly robbery. Subsequent proceedings brought
the total of trials to twenty, of convictions to nineteen. On the
record it was an excellent average for Mr. Hall, and there could
be very little doubt that the nineteen got what they deserved. But
the suspicion persists that they were only the unfortunates who
lacked the funds for clever lawyers or the access to City Hall
connections. The average prison sentence was five years. No
rioter ever was executed for murder.

John Andrews did not appear in court. His name, in fact,
never again was mentioned in a New York newspaper, once he
had vanished into Fort Lafayette. Such utter silence has in itself
the slight flavor of conspiracy. There were no rumors, no further

speculation, not even the perfectly natural question, "What ever happened to Andrews?" He had been, presumably, a prisoner of the Metropolitan Police rather than the Union Army. And it would seem that a sufficient number of witnesses could have been produced to make the charge of incitement to riot stand up, if anyone really had tried. But Fort Lafayette was one of those prisons into which dissidents who ran afoul of Edwin M. Stanton were known to disappear from time to time—usually without the formality of charge or explanation. So far as is known, they all got out eventually, but seldom to plague the Administration further. Perhaps it was a similar obscurity that swallowed Andrews of Virginia, one of the minor lost men of American history.

What with the furor of petty bickerings and backbiting that went on, the question of Copperhead involvement in the riots never was examined seriously, much less settled. It was unfortunate. New York's climate of hot partisan controversy in 1863 undoubtedly fostered all sorts of wild suspicions. Some later romancers have tended to throw a cloak of mystery and intrigue about such figures as the young man with the "fine cassemere underpants" killed at the Union Steam Works, and so occasional speculation has lingered right down to the present. In the course of quelling the mobs, however, both the police and the military apparently satisfied themselves that no Secessionist plot existed, and no one since has turned up any evidence to support the theories of what might have been. Possibly a thoroughgoing investigation by the Federal government would have dispersed the doubts once and for all. But with a war to get on with, the government never found the time or the occasion to hold one. Weighing all the evidence, then—or the lack of it—the outbreak would appear to have been exactly what it seemed: a spontaneous eruption into mob violence by a large underdog population that had proved itself all too prone to rioting in the past. Once under way, the disorders may well have been guided and encouraged by various malcontents with Copperhead leanings, Andrews among them. The many rumors of cheers for Jeff Davis were probably not all unfounded. But of organized conspiracy there never was a sign.

Curiously, though, Confederate agents did carry out a plot against New York a little later. It came to light many years after the war had ended, in the form of a memoir by a young Confederate Army officer named Headley. In the fall of 1864, possibly inspired by the riots of more than a year before, Lieutenant Headley and several fellow agents did indeed invade the city in disguise. They traveled down from Canada, stopped off in Albany for a conference with a man Headley described as "Governor Seymour's secretary," and reached New York without attracting any undue attention to themselves. There they strolled at will through the streets for some days, observed the political parades for rival Presidential candidates Abraham Lincoln and George B. McClellan, and finally left openly by train after setting fires in many of the city's largest hotels, in several strategic locations along the waterfront, and even in Barnum's museum. The fires were all put out with little damage done. Because clues to their incendiary origin were found in the shape of black canvas bags containing the remnants of various flammable materials (Headley himself called the mixture "Greek Fire"), the affair came to be known as the Black Bag Conspiracy. But the perpetrators were safely back in Canada by the time a hue and cry was raised. Significantly, they had made no effort to whip up mob violence while in the city.

To return to July of 1863: Ohio's militant Copperhead Clement L. Vallandigham already had been arrested, tried, convicted of treasonable utterances, and sent through the lines into the Confederacy. It is a matter of record that neither he nor the Confederate authorities took any great satisfaction in his presence there. But during a brief stay in Charleston, be it noted, he had predicted Abraham Lincoln's defeat at the polls in 1864 and the triumph of the northern peace party. He also had urged the Confederacy not to invade the Union. If they did, he declared, dissident elements in the North would inevitably close ranks and rally to the nation's defense. The advice had gone unheeded. Lee did invade; hence Gettysburg. But such sentiments, by so eminent a Copperhead as Vallandigham, do not appear to be the stuff of which conspiracies are built.

An odd and motley clutch of Confederate spies and agents was active in the Union at various times during the war. The names of Rose Greenhow, Belle Boyd, and others come to mind. Very few of them resisted the impulse to write books telling all about their exploits afterward. But no one ever came forward to claim credit for the draft riots of 1863.

On August 14—somewhat prematurely, to be sure—the New York *World* delivered as fitting a valedictory on the riot trials as anyone. "The rioters were alleged to be Democrats," it declared self-righteously, "and Democratic justice rewarded them with stern, impartial chastisement. . . ."

Notes

PROLOGUE: KENNEDY *(pages* xi–xii*)*

The story of the mob's attack on Superintendent Kennedy is based on the one which appeared in the New York *Tribune* of Tuesday, July 14, 1863. Accounts in other papers of the same date agree in all significant details.

CHAPTER 1. JULY 4, 1863 *(pages* 3–12*)*

1. Little is known about the cruise of the *Tacony*. Her actual depradations on the New England coast do not appear to have been very serious. Some time afterward, Governor John Andrew of Massachusetts wrote a letter to Navy Secretary Gideon Welles, apologizing for his accusations of negligence by the Navy Department. Andrew said that he had made his original statements "upon the authority of municipal officers and citizens of Gloucester," which apparently were wildly exaggerated. At the time, however, the panic had been very real.

2. It should be borne in mind that in 1863 the term "Copperhead" was not, per se, one of opprobrium except to radical Republicans and ardent supporters of the war. These people had coined it originally, comparing their political opponents to the venomous serpent, which was said to strike treacherously, without warning. But peace men, opponents of the Administration, and Secessionist sympathizers soon adopted the name openly and even proudly. Many of them wore badges made of the head from a copper penny with the rim cut away.

Thus, there were all sorts and degrees of Copperheads, a good many of them perfectly loyal to the Union in spite of their opposition to the war.

CHAPTER 2. EMPIRE CITY: THE OPULENT SOCIETY *(pages* 13–19*)*

1. The growth of the railroads was not regarded in New York City as an unalloyed blessing. Railroads contributed heavily to the development of industry throughout New England, which threatened strong

competition for New York businessmen. And the war had accelerated this trend. The situation was one reason for the high degree of antiwar sentiment in the city.

2. It is unlikely that the more extreme provisions of the Enrollment and Conscription Act ever affected naval enlisted personnel. Gideon Welles's diary reveals, however, that he protested in vain against the drafting of a number of essential civilian technicians employed in various Navy yards.

3. It happened that the draft threatened the principle of states' rights in a particularly touchy area—the raising of troops. In past wars virtually all regiments in the Federal armies had been recruited by the governors of the various states and retained their identities as state units. A national draft law obviously would destroy this cherished prerogative. As a result, not only Horatio Seymour but also most other governors of northern states opposed it vigorously. (In the Confederate states, where conscription had become the law even earlier, it was not liked either, and for the same reasons.)

4. James Fox recorded his feelings some years after the war in a book entitled *A True History of the Reign of Terror in Southern Illinois*.

CHAPTER 3. EMPIRE CITY: THE DISAFFECTED (*pages 20–27*)

1. In addition to Dickens and Solon Robinson (the actual author of *Hot Corn*), any number of contemporary visitors to New York described the miserable conditions in the city's slums. Some of their works are listed in the bibliography. The best modern account is Herbert Asbury's *The Gangs of New York*.

Hot Corn, incidentally, is a reference to the hot roasting ears sold by slum girls on the New York streets. These "hot-corn girls" were described, and frequently romanticized, by many chroniclers of the early city.

2. The city's most notorious tenement of all time, known as the Old Brewery and located on Paradise Square, had been torn down in 1852–53. In the course of the demolition, large quantities of human bones were found between the walls and in the cellar.

Contemporary accounts leave the impression that slum conditions in the city probably were at their worst during the 1840's and early 1850's. By 1863 they had not improved very markedly, however.

3. The history of the Tammany organization, its influence among the city's poor, and its long record of election and naturalization frauds have been thoroughly documented by a small army of serious historians. Some of their works are included in the bibliography.

CHAPTER 4. THE VIOLENT MEN (*pages 28–35*)

1. Excellent accounts of New York's early riots may be found in Joel Tyler Headley's *The Great Riots of New York, 1712 to 1873*.

2. Kenneth Dunshee's *As You Pass By* is a good, if somewhat romanticized, account of the early volunteer fire companies.

3. The Bowery Boy actually contributed permanently to American folklore in the person of Mighty Mose, a legendary Boy still celebrated as a folk hero.

4. The full story of the Astor Place riots is told in Headley's book.

CHAPTER 5. COPPERS, CLUBS, AND CITY HALL (*pages* 36–43)

1. George W. Walling told of his victory over the Honeymoon Gang, as well as his abortive attempt to arrest Fernando Wood, in his memoir, titled *Recollections of a New York Chief of Police*.

2. Events during Wood's struggle with the state's Republican administration, and his split with William Marcy Tweed's Tammany faction, were of course covered by the New York press of the period.

3. Indicative of the thin line that frequently separated policeman and gangster in the early days, Headley described an incident in the July Fourth riots of 1857. A Metropolitan patrolman whose partner had been killed by Dead Rabbits during the early stages of the disturbance abandoned the police, joined a group of Bowery Boys, and fought through the balance of the rioting as one of their leaders.

CHAPTER 6. "THEY WILL AMOUNT TO NOTHING" (*pages* 44–48)

1. The so-called "conspiracy" to bring General McClellan to power was one of the many crackpot rumors of the time. But McClellan, unquestionably opposed to many of the Lincoln Administration's war policies, did become the Democratic candidate for the Presidency in 1864.

2. It appears strange that Greeley should have mentioned the mediation offer by Napoleon III, even obliquely. The Frenchman had indeed made such an offer some time earlier. But it was generally recognized as nothing more than a thinly veiled attempt to gain a foothold for France in Mexico. Horace Greeley himself was among those who had denounced it as such.

CHAPTER 7. "POOR JONES!" (*pages* 49–56)

1. The actual quotations used in the account of the proceedings at Number 677 Third Avenue are taken from the New York *Tribune* of Monday, July 13. The full description of the scene and of what went on, however, has been drawn from other local newspapers of the same date.

2. The confusion over the name of Masterson, or Cassidy, is typical of the dependence on oral reports by unnamed witnesses or alleged witnesses in most accounts of the riots from this point on. Journalists obviously had to rely on many such eyewitnesses, without being in any position to check their accuracy. No doubt, some were highly imaginative.

3. The locations of the Metropolitan District's thirty-two police precincts, and the captains in charge, were as follows: *First:* 20 Broad Street; Captain Jacob B. Warlow *Second:* 49 Beekman Street; Cap-

tain Squires *Third:* 160 Chambers Street; Captain Greer *Fourth:* 9
Oak Street; Captain Bryan *Fifth:* 49 Leonard Street; Captain Petty
Sixth: 9 Franklin Street; Captain John Jourdan *Seventh:* 247 Madison
Street; Captain Theron R. Bennett *Eighth:* 127 Wooster Street; Cap-
tain M. DeCamp *Ninth:* 94 Charles Street; Captain Jacob L. Sebring
Tenth: Essex Market; Captain T. C. Davis *Eleventh:* Union Market; Captain John Mount *Twelfth:* 126th Street near Third Avenue,
Harlem; Captain A. S. Relay *Thirteenth:* 178 Delancey Street; Cap-
tain Thomas Steers *Fourteenth:* 53 Spring Street; Captain J. J. Wil-
liamson *Fifteenth:* 221 Mercer Street; Captain C. W. Caffrey *Six-
teenth:* 156 West Twentieth Street; Captain H. Hedden *Seventeenth:*
First Avenue, corner of Fifth Street; Captain S. Brower *Eighteenth:*
163 East Twenty-second Street; Captain John Cameron *Nineteenth:* East Fifty-ninth Street near Third Avenue; Captain G. T.
Porter *Twentieth:* 352 West Thirty-fifth Street; Captain G. W.
Walling *Twenty-first:* 120 East Thirty-fifth Street; Captain A. M.
Palmer *Twenty-second:* Forty-seventh Street between Eighth and
Ninth avenues; Captain J. C. Slott *Twenty-third:* East Eighty-sixth
Street near Fifth Avenue; Captain Henry Hutchings *Twenty-fourth*,
the Harbor Police: Steamboat No. 1; Captain James Todd *Twenty-
fifth*, the Broadway Squad: 300 Mulberry Street; Captain Mills. Since
Mills was absent on leave, a Sergeant Burdick was acting captain at the
time of the riots. *Twenty-sixth:* City Hall; Captain Thomas W.
Thorne *Twenty-seventh:* 117 Cedar Street; Captain John Helm
Twenty-eighth: 550 Greenwich Street; Captain John F. Dickson
Twenty-ninth: East Twenty-ninth Street near Fourth Avenue; Captain
F. C. Speight *Thirtieth:* One Hundred and Thirty-first Street, Man-
hattanville; Captain J. Hart *Thirty-first:* Eighty-sixth Street, Bloom-
ingdale Road; Captain James Z. Bogart *Thirty-second:* Fort
Washington; Captain A. S. Wilson.

In addition, a small Sanitary Police division under Captain B. G.
Lord occupied two rooms of the headquarters building on Mulberry
Street.

4. John Andrews was not mentioned in the press until Tuesday, July
14. At that time the papers referred to him simply as "Andrews of
Virginia," without any further identification. The inference would
appear to be that he was already known to New York journalists, at
least by reputation.

CHAPTER 8. "NO DRAFT!" (*pages* 59–66)

1. At the time, and for some while afterward, an impression that the
mob was incited by the Knights of the Golden Circle appears to have
been quite prevalent. No doubt this was only natural, considering the
fierce partisan tempers of the day. But no responsible authority ever
charged the Knights with participation in the disorders, and no tangible evidence to link them with the rioters ever was produced.

2. Various estimates of the mob's size and strength appeared in the press next day.

3. It is not clear just when the first newspapermen arrived at 677 Third Avenue. But it probably was some time after the mob's arrival there. Then, no doubt, their information as to what had happened earlier was obtained from random witnesses, and later still from policemen of Captain Porter's detail. Reports of the presence of the Black Jokes may be ascribed to such witnesses. There can be little doubt that the Black Jokes were involved. To what extent, however, cannot be documented.

4. According to Charles Chapin, one of Porter's patrolmen was felled and badly injured before he could escape through the rear exit. He was saved, wrote Chapin, only through the timely intervention of a "Mrs. Eagen"—presumably the wife of the man who rescued Superintendent Kennedy a little later. The coincidence appears so striking that it must be open to question.

5. The paragraph describing the women in the mob is quoted from *The Bloody Week!*, a collection of anonymous eyewitness accounts published shortly after the events it describes. But other sources were virtually unanimous in remarking on the savagery of the mob's women.

6. The New York *Tribune* next day gave a vivid account of the murders of the two Invalid Corps troopers. Some other sources state that Lieutenant Reade was killed, as well. If so, the *Tribune* writer was apparently not aware of it.

CHAPTER 9. "YOU MUST ORGANIZE!" (*pages* 67–75)

1. All New York newspapers were in essential agreement on details of the early fighting in Third Avenue. Several of them described Sergeant McCredie's experience.

2. Like James Crowley, Mr. Chapin may well have been caught up in the rioting on his way to work that morning. The location of his home made it likely that he too would have taken the Third Avenue horse cars. So his description of the scene there was quite possibly based on personal observation, though he did not say so.

3. The statement on the makeup of the mob and the words ascribed to John Andrews are quotes from *The Bloody Week!*

4. The story of the journalist attacked by the mob as a "damned Abolitionist" appeared in the *Tribune*. Though he told it in the third person—a not-uncommon literary affectation in the nineteenth century—the reporter may himself have been the victim. The *Tribune* was well known and widely hated as an Abolitionist organ.

5. Various other incidents in this chapter—the one on Lexington Avenue, for example—were described in *The Bloody Week!*

6. The site of the Colored Orphan Asylum and its grounds is occupied today by the New York Public Library.

7. At some point in the rioting Chapin himself apparently had a narrow escape from a mob lynching "because of his known sympathy with the negroes saved by police." The information is contained in a note attached to his manuscript by his granddaughter, Mrs. Adelaide Chapin Haight Chapin. Since Chapin himself did not mention it, however, the circumstances are unknown.

CHAPTER 10. ". . . TAKE NO PRISONERS" (*pages* 76–86)

1. Thomas Acton's affiliation with the Union League was especially meaningful, since the League had been organized only the year before, specifically to combat the Knights of the Golden Circle and Copperhead sentiment in general. It also tends to back up the inference of his concern over possible Copperhead influences in the mob.
2. The alleged Five Points gangster killed at the armory was mentioned by several contemporary writers. None of them seemed to know his name or his actual gang connections. Neither, at any rate, ever was recorded.
3. The battle for the armory was covered in great detail by practically every contemporary observer.
4. By their very nature, the detectives' activities as undercover agents in the mobs were unlikely to have been reported in detail. And they were not. But David Barnes's version of the battle on Broadway, if true, indicates that they were not always successful in forecasting the mobs' movements.

CHAPTER 11. GENERALS FALL OUT (*pages* 87–92)

1. This account of General Brown's activities on Monday afternoon and evening—and particularly his personal contacts with generals Wool and Sandford—is drawn mainly from Brown's own story. He told it in a long and angry open letter to Wool, which was published in the New York *Herald* on July 30. Obviously, Brown's testimony cannot be called objective. But attached to his letter were others from several junior officers involved, including Wool's own adjutant. They agreed substantially with his own version of what took place. Commissioner Acton also backed Brown up in all essential details.
2. David Barnes's book *The Draft Riots in New York, July, 1863* was based on articles originally written for the New York *Times*. It leaves no doubt of his admiration for Seth Hawley, not only for Hawley's part in the Brown-Sandford controversy but also for his tact, good nature, and organizational ability in general.
3. It is not quite clear how Brown justified his denial that he had disobeyed any order, for Wool's directive appears simple and uncompromising. Possibly, however, Brown's claim was based on the fact that he received no orders from General Sandford *after* Wool issued it. Apparently he did not.

CHAPTER 12. "WE'LL HANG OLD GREELEY . . ." (*pages* 93–99)

1. Barnes's book includes a very concise and thorough summary of

mob atrocities and the measures taken by police to counter them, broken down according to the precincts in which they occurred. Throughout the rioting, however, the true sequence of events in relation to other events is frequently obscure.

2. Various accounts give different spellings for the name of "Windust's," or "Windhurst's," Restaurant. Apparently it was a popular eating place among newspapermen of the district.

3. Greeley's friend James Gilmore is the authority for the quotes ascribed to him.

4. According to Barnes, the police actually set a trap for the rioters in Printing House Square, with Carpenter's detachment waiting in ambush for the mob routed by Captain Warlow's force. In view of the confused situation at the time, however, coupled with the fact that the police undoubtedly had their hands full on several fronts at this point, such a prearranged plan appears unlikely.

5. The story of the old man clubbed down by mistake was also told by Barnes.

6. In later years there was a widespread impression that all New York newspapers were forced to suspend publication during the riots. This was untrue, as their files for the week of July 13 prove. There was a similar impression that *all* business in the city was brought to a standstill. This was not true, either. A great many businesses did close down, or their premises were destroyed. But many others remained in operation throughout the rioting.

7. Several accounts, Chapin's among them, state that Mayor Opdyke also requested military help from the governors of neighboring states. According to Chapin, these pleas were ignored. In any case, practically all of the surrounding states already had, like New York, sent all available troop units to Pennyslvania.

CHAPTER 13. ALARMS AND SUSPICIONS (*pages* 103–107)

1. Governor Seymour's eagerness to remove the Republican police commissioners apparently was well known. But Greeley's authority for the statement that he had "promised the mob" to do it on July 13 seems questionable. In the circumstances, it was a not-unlikely charge for the editor of an opposition paper to make.

2. Apparently the *World*'s and *Herald*'s versions of Greeley's behavior in Windust's Restaurant were widely accepted, at least by Greeley's many enemies. Some later writers, ignoring his denials or unaware of them, repeated the story as fact. As indeed it may have been—depending on which side one chooses to believe.

3. Secretary Welles's lugubrious remarks probably were an accurate reflection of the suspicions, frustration, and discouragement felt by a great many patriotic citizens during this period. All in all, the circumstances did suggest a far-reaching Confederate-Copperhead plot, or seemed to at the time. Even today a slight element of mystery surrounds the mission to Washington of Alexander H. Stephens, Vice-

President of the Confederate States. Beyond doubt it was concerned primarily with instigating some sort of peace negotiations; and had Lee's invasion of Pennsylvania not been turned back at Gettysburg, Stephens might have had a fair chance of success.

CHAPTER 14. RIOT INTO REBELLION (*pages* 108–115)

1. The most complete account of the damage to telegraph-bureau lines appeared in David Barnes's book. Barnes was also one of the few who wrote of Crowley's and Polhamus' heroic efforts to keep communications open. But even Barnes's information was all too brief and sketchy.

2. Greeley's words, again, were quoted by James Gilmore.

3. Barnes also told the story of James Costello's murder, in more detail than most other chroniclers. Costello's opponent, Maney, died of his wound some days later.

4. Most contemporary writers used the all-inclusive word "muskets" when referring to the firearms possessed by the mob. But, technically speaking, a musket was a smooth-bore weapon already obsolete, or nearly so, at the time of the War Between the States. The surmise that the mob must actually have looted a heterogeneous collection of firearms of various ages, calibers, and conditions seems logical. Scattered through the accounts of the rioting are frequent references to the mobs' apparent shortages of ammunition, especially as the fighting wore on.

5. So far as is known, Charles Chapin was the only man whose record of the riots accuses Colonel O'Brien of having been drunk during, or shortly after, his encounter with the mob. Yet Chapin appears unlikely to have been mistaken, and his character and background were not those of a man who would have listened to idle gossip. Nor did he have any known reason for wanting to blacken O'Brien's name. Because of the colonel's later fate, apparently, there was a disposition among contemporary writers to treat him as something of a hero-martyr. Possibly he did not altogether deserve it.

6. In retrospect, it seems strange that the mob holding the Union Steam Works chose to meet the police in the open and made little apparent use of their captured carbines. But none of those who reported the affair at the time offered any explanation of the blunder—if that was what it was.

7. Joel Tyler Headley, writing in 1872, had the most to say about the one-armed man and the mysterious youth. It was he who described the latter's incongruous undergarments and his aristocratic features. Who actually examined the bodies is uncertain; apparently it was policemen whose curiosity had been aroused during the fight.

CHAPTER 15. "MY FRIENDS . . ." (*pages* 116–123)

1. Press accounts of Seymour's arrival in the city were all quite brief

and somewhat colored by the political sympathies of the several newspapers. Allowing for that, the description given here seems a reasonably accurate summary of them all.
2. The governor's words were a matter of press record. The cries of
the crowd are quoted from the *Tribune* and from *The Bloody Week!*
3. Again, David Barnes gave the best overall picture of this day's scattered disorders.
4. The most complete account of the burning of the Weehawken
Ferry building, and especially of witnesses' identification of Andrews
as the mob's leader, appeared in *The Bloody Week!*
5. Colonel O'Brien's murder was covered in gruesome and almost in-
exhaustible detail by virtually every contemporary who wrote about
the riots, and by most later writers as well. The *Tribune*'s anonymous
informant was the only one who contradicted the stories of his tor-
ture.

CHAPTER 16. BARRICADES AND BROOKS BROTHERS (*pages* 124–130)
1. The incidents centered around Lamartine Place were well covered
in Barnes's book, in *The Bloody Week!*, and in most of the next day's
newspapers. None, however, identified the militia troop involved.
2. The battle at the Ninth Avenue barricades, one of the critical turning points in the rioting, was well covered by many sources. The
quotation referring to the "noble sons of Connecticut" is taken from
The Bloody Week!
3. As before, the reference to Horace Greeley originated with his
friend James Gilmore. The story is enlightening, also, as one more
indication that much of the city's business was carried on as usual, or
that the attempt was made.
4. The rumors referred to were reported by various contemporary
sources, though they were not always identified as rumors at the
time.
5. David's Island apparently bears a different name today. It has not
otherwise been identified.
6. Brooks Brothers, of course, remains in business in New York,
though the establishment was long since removed from its Catherine
Street address.

CHAPTER 17. "GIVE THEM GRAPE AND PLENTY OF IT" (*pages* 133–142)
1. David Barnes told of Crowley's and Polhamus' adventure with their
hack passengers. In doing so, he also referred, though somewhat
vaguely, to their earlier exploit in capturing a similar band of rioters.
2. The description of the elaborate defense measures taken at the Fifth
Avenue Hotel appeared in the *Tribune*.
3. The fullest account of the attempted burning of the *Dunderberg*
was probably the one in *The Bloody Week!* But the reference to the
Seventh Regiment, Old National Guard, points up a difficulty common
to research in many of the contemporary publications. The identifica-

tion of military units taking part in the various actions is frequently obscure and sometimes contradictory. National Guard and other volunteer reserve regiments, once mustered into active service, officially became U.S. Army regiments. Though they retained their state designations, such terms as National Guard, Old National Guard, Volunteers, and the like were no longer technically correct. They still were generally used by civilian writers, nevertheless. And many were prone to refer to them all, indiscriminately, as "militia." Hence, from the popular accounts of the time it is not always possible to say with certainty whether a given military unit had been ordered into action by General Brown or by General Sandford. It was not a matter of monumental importance, though it did bear on the truth or falsehood of some of the recriminations later exchanged between the two.

4. Details of the generals' relationship at this time are badly clouded by controversy. It appears that Brown had only indirect contact, at best, with either Sandford or Wool. Sometime afterward, Wool asserted (with approval) that Sandford had "countermanded" many of the orders issued by Brown. What he meant by that is not wholly clear. But such actions could have contributed to nothing save confusion—of which there obviously was plenty.

CHAPTER 18. "THE MOB AIN'T COMMENCED YET" (*pages* 143–152)

1. The incident at Alvord's printing company seems to have been overlooked by most reporters. The *Tribune* was the only newspaper to describe it at length or to see ominous implications in it.

2. Information on the composition of the column dispatched to First Avenue by General Sandford is sparse. Quite possibly, and even probably, it included men from a number of militia companies. At least one modern writer has described the troops as "veterans of Confederate attacks," possibly confusing them with the relief force which reached the scene sometime later. But there appears very little doubt that the two Zouave detachments made up the backbone of the militia column. Its conduct under fire indicates that there were few if any combat veterans in it.

3. Both Barnes and Headley, as well as several newspapers, told the story of Colonel Jardine's escape.

4. There is no record of any statement to the press by Commissioner Acton on Wednesday evening. Opdyke's proclamation appeared in most, though not all, of Thursday's papers.

CHAPTER 19. MR. CHAPIN'S VIGILANTES (*pages* 153–157)

1. Chapin's own story of his expedition to Yorkville was disappointingly brief—all the more so because no other contemporary has left us any account of the measures taken to deal with rioters in outlying districts, either. Citizens' vigilante groups may have been numerous. Chapin himself referred to one unnamed section in the northern part

of the city in which a Catholic priest and a Methodist minister—also nameless—collaborated in preaching restraint to a mob led by "a burly woman." Both clerics were highly respected, wrote Chapin, and "were able to some extent to maintain an influence over the crowd." But, again, details are lacking.

2. William Harlan Hale's biography of Horace Greeley includes a brief mention of the incident at the Greeley farm.

3. The incidents at Williams Bridge were described, though very briefly, in *The Bloody Week!* No reason was given for assuming the mob's representative to be "a Copperhead."

CHAPTER 20. THE LAST BATTLE (*pages* 158–164)

1. The fact that four men—a quarter of the total detective force—were assigned to arrest Andrews suggests that police officials considered him an important catch. In spite of a public impression, apparently quite general at the time, however, Andrews never was designated officially as a mob leader or formally accused. Presumably someone in authority questioned him after his arrest, but no information on that score ever was released to the public. On the other hand, the *Tribune's* account makes it evident that the reporter must have been given the opportunity for a lengthy and unrestricted interview. The ubiquitous David Barnes apparently was not at headquarters at the time; he has next to nothing to say about John Andrews.

2. It was Barnes who described the transfer of the refugees from the Colored Orphan Asylum to Blackwell's Island.

3. The incident of the gentleman attacked by the thug, and the latter's remark about three hundred dollars, was gleaned from *The Bloody Week!* No doubt it was but one of many individual experiences which never were reported.

4. The fact that Colonel Mott appears to have been under the orders first of General Brown and later of Wool and/or Sandford is probably one more instance of the confusion and conflict among military authorities.

CHAPTER 21. VICTORS AND VANQUISHED (*pages* 165–169)

1. As a matter of fact, New York was destined to see other riotous incidents before the end of the war, notably in May, 1864. At that time a large and unruly mob gathered on Wall Street and threatened a serious outbreak. It was put down without military assistance, however, as were other, lesser disturbances from time to time. But no subsequent ones approached those of 1863 in scope or savagery.

2. David Barnes summarized the activities of both the Colored Relief Committee and the one founded by Jerome. Both were referred to, as well, in items in various New York newspapers during the weeks following the riots.

3. Mr. Warburton's feelings about Irish responsibility for the Colored

Orphan Asylum were set forth in a long letter made public by the New York *Herald*.

EPILOGUE: AFTERMATH (*pages* 173–189)

1. The speech of Archbishop Hughes was carried verbatim in several newspapers. The remark as to its tardiness was made by Joel Tyler Headley.

2. Quotations describing the recovered loot are from the *Times*. It appears that much of this loot would have been difficult or impossible to identify. How the rightful owners established their claims was not explained.

3. A majority of the damage claims against the city were ultimately paid. As late as the 1870's, though, many still were being argued in the courts.

4. The story of the magistrate who dismissed all charges on the grounds that the draft law was unconstitutional appears in *The Gangs of New York*. Its origin is unknown. As usual in such cases, the political pressures exerted in behalf of accused rioters never were documented. Apparently there were no serious efforts to do so.

5. Contemporary newspaper coverage of the trials was, on the whole, disappointing to a researcher. Reading the various accounts, one is moved to suspect that they may have reflected a public weariness with the subject of riots and rioters, that the city was eager to forget the whole affair. And perhaps that was the case.

6. Lieutenant Headley's story was told, very briefly, in a book entitled *Confederate Operations in New York and Canada*, by John William Headley (apparently not a relative, and not to be confused with Joel T. Headley).

7. Lieutenant Headley's reference to a meeting with Governor Seymour's secretary would seem to be significant, in view of the accusations of Secessionist sympathies leveled at Seymour by his political opponents. Headley did not enlarge upon it, however, and gave no reason for the interview or any inkling of what was discussed.

8. Vallandigham's advice was quoted at considerable length in *A Rebel War Clerk's Diary*, kept throughout the war years by one J. B. Jones and first published in 1866.

Bibliography

BOOKS AND PUBLISHED ARTICLES

Asbury, Herbert. *The Gangs of New York*. Alfred A. Knopf, New York, 1928.

Bales, William Alan. *Tiger in the Streets*. Dodd, Mead and Company, New York, 1962.

Barnes, David M. *The Draft Riots in New York, July, 1863* (based on a series of articles originally written for the New York *Times*). Baker and Godwin, New York, 1863.

Beale, Howard K. (editor). *Diary of Gideon Welles, Vol. I, 1861–1864* (original ms. in the Library of Congress). W. W. Norton and Company, New York, 1960.

Berger, Meyer. *The Story of the New York Times, 1851–1951*. Simon and Schuster, New York, 1951.

Booth, Mary L. *History of the City of New York*. James Miller, New York, 1863.

Brace, Charles Loring. *The Dangerous Classes of New York*. Wynkoop and Hollenbeck, New York, 1872.

Costello, Augustine E. *Our Police Protectors; a History of the New York Police*. Privately printed, New York, 1885.

Dagget's New York City Street Directory. New York, 1863.

Davenport, John I. *The Election and Naturalization Frauds in New York City, 1860–1870*. New York, 1894.

Dickens, Charles. *American Notes for General Circulation*. Chapman and Hall, London, 1842.

Dunshee, Kenneth Holcomb. *As You Pass By*. Hastings House, New York, 1952.

Eye-Witness Reports. *The Bloody Week!* Coutant and Baker, New York, 1863.

Fry, James Barnet. *New York and the Conscription of '63*. G. P. Putnam's Sons, New York, 1885.

Gilmore, James R. *Personal Recollections of Abraham Lincoln and the Civil War.* Boston, 1898.

Hale, William Harlan. *Horace Greeley, Voice of the People.* Harper and Brothers, New York, 1950.

Harlow, Alvin F. *Old Bowery Days; the Chronicles of a Famous Street.* D. Appleton and Company, New York, 1931.

Headley, Joel Tyler. *The Great Riots of New York, 1712 to 1873.* E. B. Treat, New York, 1873.

Headley, John William. *Confederate Operations in New York and Canada.* Neale Publishing Company, New York, 1906.

Hyman, Harold M. "New Yorkers and the Civil War Draft." *New York History,* Cooperstown, N.Y., April, 1955.

Ingraham, Abijah. *A Biography of Fernando Wood, A History of the Forgeries, Perjuries, and Other Crimes of Our "Model" Mayor* (pamphlet, written anonymously). Privately published, New York, n.d.

Lee, Brother Basil Leo. *Discontent in New York City, 1861–65.* Catholic University of America Press, Washington, D.C., 1943.

Leonard, Ellen. "Three Days Reign of Terror." *Harpers Magazine,* New York, January, 1867.

Man, Albon P. "The Church and the New York Draft Riots of '63." *American Catholic Historical Society Records,* Philadelphia, March, 1951.

———. "Labor Competition and the New York Draft Riots of '63." *Journal of Negro History,* Washington, D.C., October, 1951.

Martin, Edward Winslow. *The Secrets of the Great City: A Work Descriptive of the Virtues and the Vices, the Mysteries, Miseries and Crimes of New York City.* Jones Brothers and Company, Philadelphia, 1868.

Miller's New York As It Is. New York, 1863.

Milton, George F. "Lincoln and the Fifth Column." *The Infantry Journal,* Washington, D.C., 1943.

Myers, Gustavus. *The History of Tammany Hall.* Boni and Liveright, New York, 1917.

Orth, Samuel P. *The Boss and the Machine, A Chronicle of the Politicians and Party Organization.* Yale University Press, New Haven, Conn., 1919.

Robinson, Solon. *Hot Corn: Life Scenes in New York Illustrated* (written anonymously). DeWitt and Davenport, New York, 1854.

Ross, Dr. Joel H. *What I Saw in New York; or, A Bird's Eye View of City Life.* Derby and Miller, Auburn, N.Y., 1851.

Stoddard, William O. *The Volcano Under the City.* Fords, Howard and Hulburt, New York, 1887.

The Strangers' Hand-Book for the City of New York; or, What to See and How to See It. C. S. Francis and Company, New York, 1845.

Swiggett, Howard (editor). *A Rebel War Clerk's Diary, by J. B. Jones.* New York, 1935.

Walling, George Washington. *Recollections of a New York Chief of Police.* Caxton Book Concern, Ltd., New York, 1887.

Werstein, Irving. *July, 1863.* Julian Messner, New York, 1957.

Wibberly, Leonard Patrick O'Connor. "The Coming of the Green." *American Heritage Magazine,* New York, August, 1958.

MANUSCRIPTS AND DOCUMENTS

Chapin, Charles Loring. *Personal Recollections of the Draft Riots of New York City, 1863.* Manuscript in the possession of the New-York Historical Society, New York.

United States War Department. *The War of the Rebellion: a Compilation of the Official Records of the Union and Confederate Armies, Vols. I, III.* The Archives, Library of Congress, Washington, D.C.

NEWSPAPERS, 1856–57; July–September, 1863

Boston *Globe*
Charleston, South Carolina, *Daily Courier*
Charleston *Mercury*
Chicago *Daily Tribune*
Chicago *Times*
New York *Daily News*
New York *Herald*
New York *Journal of Commerce*
New York *Sun*
New York *Times*
New York *Tribune*
New York *World*
Richmond, Virginia, *Daily Enquirer*
Washington, D.C., *Daily Morning Chronicler*
Washington *National Daily Intelligencer*

Index

Acton, Thomas C., 76-77, 78, 81, 82, 83, 89, 90, 91, 94, 99, 113, 125, 136, 141, 148, 150, 153-164, 168, 176, 178, 180, 196, 200
Alvord, A. C., 145-146, 159, 200
American Guards, 34
Andrew, John, 191
Andrews, John U., 55-56, 70-71, 72, 122, 145, 160-162, 164, 182, 184, 186-187, 194, 195, 199, 201
Arnold, Theodore, 185
Asbury, Herbert, 192

Barker, Isaac O., 38
Barnard, George G., 106, 107
Barnes, David, 83, 96, 179, 196, 197, 198, 199, 200, 201
Barnum, Philo F., 177
Barnum, Phineas T., 7, 20
Beecher, Henry Ward, 95
Bennett, James Gordon, 16, 54, 106, 183
Bennett, Theron R., 194
Bergen, John C., 76, 176
Biesel, Henry, 47-48
Bogart, James Z., 124, 194
Bowen, James, 76
Bowery Boys, 31-32, 37, 39, 41-42, 59, 114, 193
Boyd, Belle, 188
Boyle, Morris, 180, 184
Brennan, Comptroller, 177
Brower, S., 194
Brown, "Bull Run," 154

Brown, Harvey, 87, 89, 90, 91, 94, 99, 125, 139, 141, 146, 148, 149, 152, 175-176, 196, 200, 201
Brown, Mrs., 154
Bryan, Captain, 194
Buntline, Ned, 30
Burdick, Sergeant, 79, 80, 194
Burns, Kit, 24
Burnside, Ambrose, 3, 6, 143
Butler, Benjamin F., 144

Caffrey, C. W., 194
Calhoun, John C., 51
Cameron, John, 79, 194
Canby, E. R. S., 176
Carey, Dennis, 184
Carpenter, Charles H., 50
Carpenter, Daniel C., 83, 84, 85, 94, 96, 97, 109, 110, 111, 113, 129, 197
Cassidy, Thomas, 55, 63, 193
Chapin, Adelaide, 196
Chapin, Charles Loring, 52-54, 59, 62, 68, 69, 74, 75, 76, 77, 81, 82, 83, 84, 85, 91, 92, 108, 110, 113, 114, 122, 124, 126, 129, 133, 136, 138, 147, 153-157, 195, 196, 197, 198, 200-201
Chapin, Mrs. Charles, 154
Christiansen, C. T., 139, 140
Cody, Buffalo Bill, 30
Conover, Daniel, 40, 41
Conway, Joseph, 185
Cooper, James Fenimore, 15
Costello, James, 108, 179, 198

207

Crombie, Hugh, 177
Crowley, James, 53, 63-64, 67, 108, 133-135, 154, 195, 198, 199
Cull, Mother, 51
Curbin, William, 179, 185

Davis, Jefferson, 123, 145, 187
Davis, T. C., 194
Davis, William, 74
Dead Rabbits, 31, 32, 37, 38, 39, 41-42, 59, 114, 193
DeCamp, M., 194
Decker, John, 75
Derrickson, Ann, 135
Devlin, Charles, 40
Devoursney, Sergeant, 96
Dickens, Charles, 21, 192
Dickson, John F., 194
Dilks, George, 83, 114, 120-121
Dix, John A., 5, 176
Dolan, Peter, 74
Dougel, Dr., 127
Doyle, Michael, 185
Doyle, Patrolman, 84
Duffy, John, 175
Dunshee, Kenneth, 192
Dusenbury, Thomas, 55-56, 160
Duvall, John, 153

Eagen, John, xii, 68
Eagen, Mrs., 195
Eagleson, Lieutenant, 112
Ehrhardt, Joel B., 48
Elliot, H. H., 43
Eno, Amos, 14
Evans, Deputy, 179

Farley, Detective, 160
Folk, John, 83, 86
Fox, James, 18-19, 192
Franklin, Captain, 149
Frémont, John Charles, 186
Fry, James B., 50, 159, 175

Gay, Sidney, 95, 99, 126
Gibbons, Mr., 124, 128

Gilmore, James, 95, 109, 126, 197, 198, 199
Gorham, Richard O., 10-11
Grant, Ulysses S., 5, 169
Greeley, Gabrielle, 156
Greeley, Horace, 3, 7, 11, 44, 45, 46, 47, 95, 97, 104, 105, 106, 109, 119, 124, 126, 141, 156, 160, 169, 181, 183, 184, 186, 193, 197, 198, 199, 201
Greeley, Ida, 156
Greeley, Mary, 156
Greenhow, Rose, 188
Greer, Captain, 194

Haddon, Tommy, 25
Hale, William Harlan, 201
Hall, A. Oakey, 8, 184, 185, 186
Hart, J., 194
Hawley, Seth, 90, 91, 99, 109, 196
Headley, Joel Tyler, 192, 193, 198, 200, 202
Headley, John William, 202
Headley, Lieutenant, 188, 202
Hedden, H., 194
Helm, John, 194
Heuston, Peter, 93
Hoffman, Recorder, 184
Holt, Thomas, 152
Honeymoon Gang, 37-38, 193
Hooker, Fighting Joe, 3, 6
Howell, John H., 137, 159, 173-174
Hughes, Archbishop John, 128, 174, 202
Hughes, Bernard, 175
Hutchings, Henry, 194
Hyer, Tom, 32

Jardine, E. E., 148, 149, 200
Jenkins, Charles E., 49, 50, 51, 64
Jerome, Leonard, 15, 167, 201
Jones, J. B., 202
Jones, William, 50
Jones, William, 103-104, 108
Jourdan, John, 94, 194
Joyce, Councilman, 50-51
Judson, Edward Z., 30

Kelsey, Charles, 7
Kennedy, John A., xi-xii, 52, 56, 60, 65, 67, 68, 76, 77, 168, 191, 195
Kerrigan, Dan, 25
King, Governor, 39
Knights of the Golden Circle, 51-52, 183, 194, 196

Lee, Robert E., 12, 181, 182
Leonard, James, 83, 118, 135, 153
Lincoln, Abraham, 3, 4, 8, 12, 18, 45, 46, 50, 54, 144, 159, 186, 188, 193
Longstreet, General, 44
Lord, B. G., 194
Lucas, James, 153

McCabe, Francis, 178
McClellan, George B., 4, 6, 45, 98, 106, 107, 138, 188, 193
McCord, John, 56, 160
McCredie, Sergeant, 68-69, 79, 195
McCunn, John H., 180, 185
McDowell, Irvin, 90
McKay, Barney, 179
McKay, Donald, 138
Macready, Edwin, 118
Macready, William C., 35
Mag, Gallus, 24, 26
Maney, Mr., 108, 198
Manierre, B. F., 73
Marshall, Joseph, 185
Masterson, Pete, 55, 63, 193
Meade, George G., 3, 44, 45, 46
Mighty Mose, 193
Mills, Captain, 194
Monell, Charley, 24
Moran, Martin, 164, 184
Morgan, Edward, 77, 144, 165
Morse, Samuel F. B., 4, 53
Mott, Colonel, 136, 137, 163, 201
Mount, John, 194
Murphy, Henry C., 12

Napoleon III, 47, 193
Native Americans, 34, 38, 39, 42
Nicholas I, Czar of Russia, 53
Nugent, Robert, 46, 73, 108, 153

O'Brien, H. J., 111, 112, 113, 122-123, 174, 198, 199
O'Bryan, Mr., 121
O'Connell Guards, 34
O'Neil, James, 184
Opdyke, George, 43, 54, 73, 78, 79, 83, 85, 87, 91-92, 99, 106, 116, 117, 118, 128, 130, 139, 150-151, 159, 168, 197, 200

Palmer, A. M., 194
Paulding, Hiram, 88, 109
Pease, Lewis M., 26
Pendleton, George H., 10, 51
Petty, Captain, 194
Polhamus, Eldred, 53, 108, 133-135, 154, 198, 199
Poole, Bill (the Butcher), 32, 33
Pope, John, 3, 6
Porter, G. T., 62, 63, 64, 194, 195
Purple, Dr., 153
Putnam, Captain, 149, 164

Quinby, Edward, 156

Radford, Detective, 160
Raymond, Henry J., 105, 140, 141, 186
Reade, Abel, 65, 195
Relay, A. S., 194
Robinson, Solon, 192
Rynders, Isaiah, 30, 34, 35, 38, 41, 118

Sandford, Charles W., 87, 88, 89, 90, 91, 94, 99, 111, 125, 146, 147, 148, 152, 163, 176, 184, 196, 200, 201
Scott, Winfield, 90
Scuzack, Matthew, 179
Sebring, Jacob L., 194
Seymour, Horatio, 8-10, 45, 53-54, 77, 105, 116-118, 119, 120, 127, 139, 144, 145, 151, 168-169, 176, 186, 188, 192, 197, 198-199, 202
Seymour, Thomas H., 10
Silva, Mark J., 184

Slott, J. C., 125, 194
Southwick, George W., 50
Speight, F. C., 62, 67, 68, 73, 79, 194
Squires, Captain, 194
Stanton, Edwin M., 17, 18, 99, 130, 145, 151, 173
Steers, Thomas, 194
Stephens, Alexander H., 107, 197-198
Sue the Turtle, 94
Sullivan, Yankee, 32

Talmage, Frederick A., 39
Thompson, Patrolman, 84
Thorne, Thomas W., 194
Tighe, Bridget, 25
Tilden, Samuel J., 4, 165
Tilton, Theodore, 95
Todd, James, 99, 194
Tweed, William Marcy, 8, 31, 42-43, 107, 116-117, 118, 168, 185, 193

Umsted, Lillie Devereaux, 7

Vallandigham, Clement L., 10, 51, 188, 202
Van Orden, Sergeant, 52

Wadsworth, James S., 144
Wakeman, Abram, 97, 153
Walling, George Washington, 37-38, 40, 94, 120, 125, 128, 168, 180, 193, 194
Warburton, A. F., 167, 201
Warlow, Jacob, 94, 96, 97, 193, 197
Washington, George, 13, 23
Watson, William, 179, 185
Welles, Gideon, 12, 17, 43, 107, 119, 144, 165, 191, 192, 197
Wesson, Captain, 125
White, A. J., 121
Williams, Mr., 103, 108
Williamson, J. J., 194
Wilson, A. S., 194
Wilson, Josephine, 160
Winslow, Cleveland, 147, 148, 149
Wolfe, Sergeant, 68
Wood, Benjamin, 43, 47, 51, 71, 183
Wood, Fernando, 11, 38-39, 40, 41, 42, 43, 51, 183, 193
Wool, John E., 87, 88, 89, 90, 91, 109, 139, 140, 144, 146, 163, 176, 184, 196, 200, 201

Young, John, 55, 98

ABOUT THE AUTHOR

JAMES McCAGUE was born in Chicago, the son of a locomotive engineer. His first job, call boy at the New York Central Railroad roundhouse in Chicago during the heyday of the steam locomotive era, left him with an abiding interest in railroading, which has been reflected in much of his writing, most notably his 1964 book, *MOGULS AND IRON MEN*. Mr. McCague is also the author of five novels—including *THE BIG IVY, TO BE A HERO*, and *THE FORTUNE ROAD*— three juveniles, and several short stories published in various magazines. He was drawn to writing *THE SECOND REBELLION* because of the startling similarity he saw between conditions and events of today and those in New York in 1863. Married and the father of two sons, Mr. McCague now lives in Sarasota, Florida, where he writes full time.

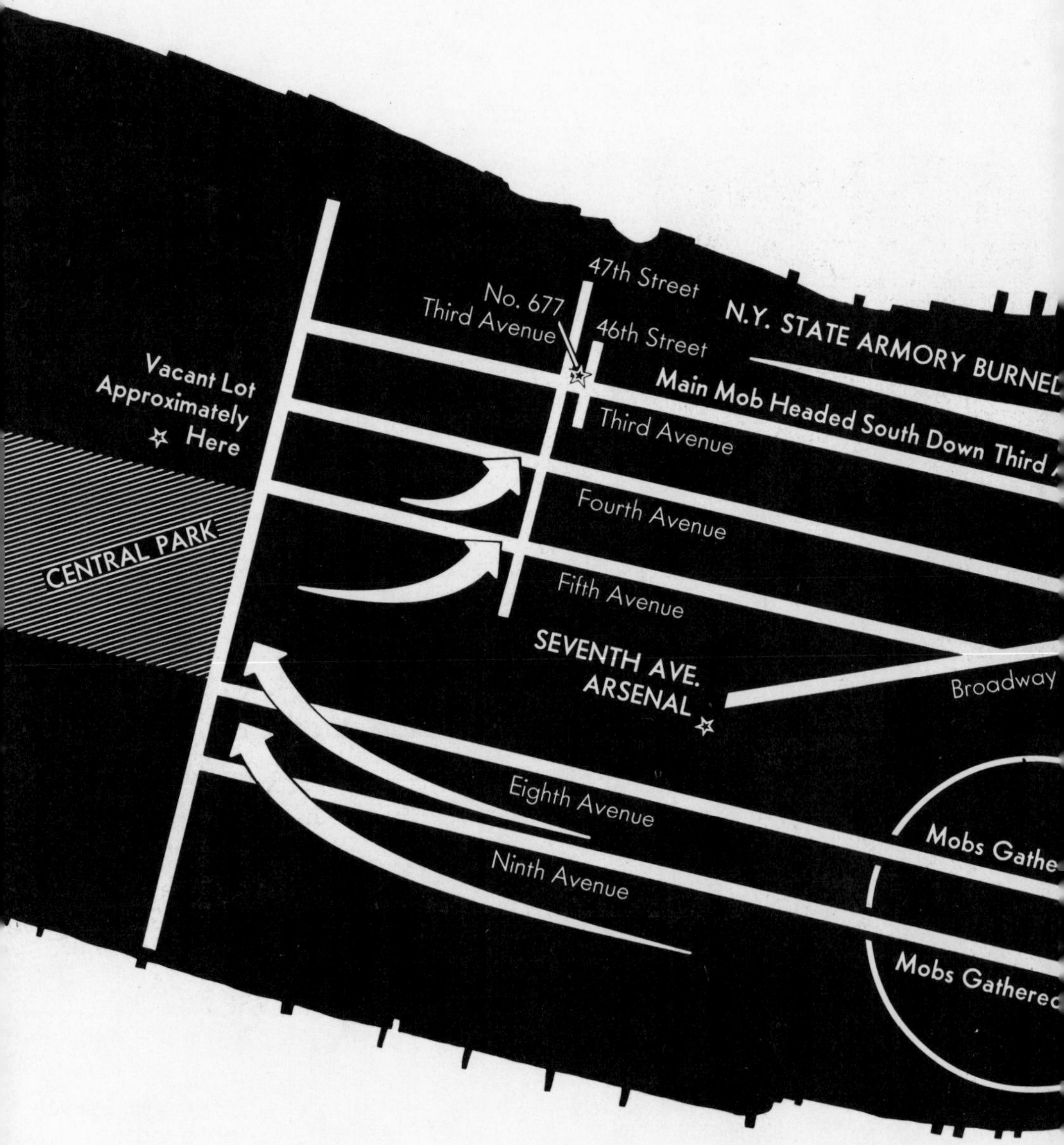
47th Street
No. 677
Third Avenue
46th Street
N.Y. STATE ARMORY BURNED
Main Mob Headed South Down Third
Vacant Lot
Approximately
Here
CENTRAL PARK
Third Avenue
Fourth Avenue
Fifth Avenue
SEVENTH AVE.
ARSENAL
Broadway
Eighth Avenue
Ninth Avenue
Mobs Gathe
Mobs Gathered